T5-AEX-444

TRANSACTIONS

of the

American Philosophical Society

Held at Philadelphia for Promoting Useful Knowledge

VOLUME 78, Part 1, 1988

A Bishop and his World before the Gregorian Reform: Hubert of Angers, 1006–1047

STEVEN FANNING

University of Illinois at Chicago

THE AMERICAN PHILOSOPHICAL SOCIETY

Independence Square, Philadelphia

1988

BX
4705
.H7678
F36
1988

Copyright © 1988 by The American Philosophical Society

Library of Congress Catalog
Card Number
International Standard Book Number 0-87169-781-5
US ISSN 0065-9746

CONTENTS

ACKNOWLEDGMENTS

I am grateful to the management and staff of the Bibliothèque nationale in Paris, the Archives départementales de Maine-et-Loire in Angers, and the Bibliothèque municipale d'Angers for their kindness and generosity in allowing me to use their archives of printed books and manuscripts that were essential in the preparation of this book. In addition, both the Bibliothèque nationale and the Archives départementales de Maine-et-Loire made available microfilm copies of a great many manuscript sources and rare books that were vital to my research. My research in France was made possible by grants from the French government, and I wish to thank the Centre Régionale des Oeuvres Universitaires et Scolaires in Paris for the assistance that it provided while I was there, and from the Graduate College of the University of Illinois at Chicago. I am also grateful to Professor Bernard S. Bachrach of the University of Minnesota for his continuing assistance and encouragement in my Angevin studies.

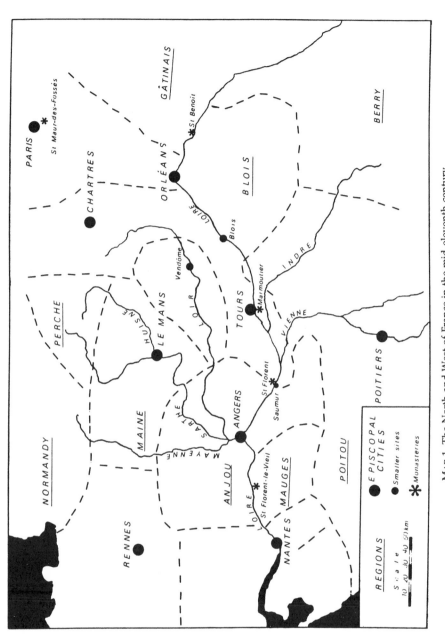

MAP 1. The North and West of France in the mid-eleventh century.

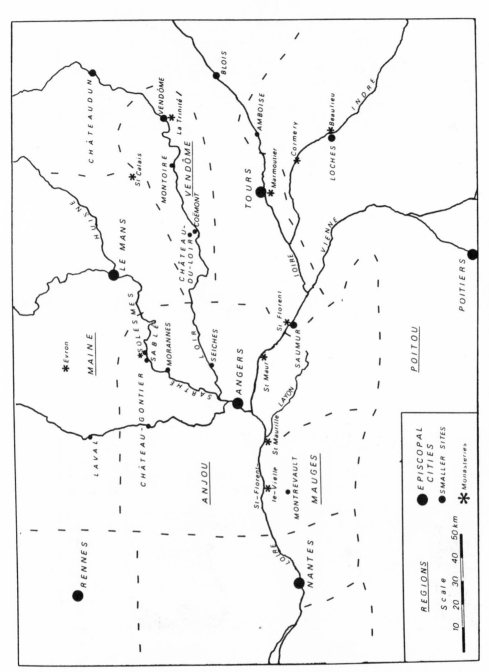

MAP 2. Anjou and its environs in the mid-eleventh century.

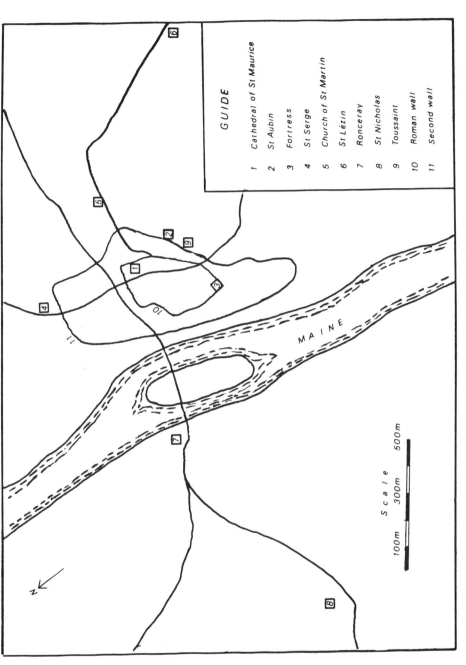

GUIDE

1 Cathedral of St Maurice
2 St Aubin
3 Fortress
4 St Serge
5 Church of St Martin
6 St Lézin
7 Ronceray
8 St Nicholas
9 Toussaint
10 Roman wall
11 Second wall

MAINE

Scale

100m   300m   500m

MAP 3. Angers at the time of Bishop Hubert.*

* After George H. H. Forsyth, Jr., *The Church of St. Martin at Angers*, figs. 179–181, and John McManners, *French Ecclesiastical Society under the Ancien Régime, A Study of Angers in the Eighteenth Century* (Manchester, 1960), end map.

A NOTE ON NAMES

One of the most vexing problems facing the medievalist is that of developing a consistent and rational system of nomenclature in the face of sources that present a bewildering variety of spellings for personal and place names, institutions, and officials. All of this is complicated by various conventional usages by historians and by current forms of names that may vary in different modern languages.

The forms found here are, frankly, inconsistent and idiosyncratic. In keeping with the most sensible thing to do, common English forms of many personal names are used here, as with Hubert, Stephen, Hugh, or Geoffrey. However, in some cases, after many years of working with this material in a secondary literature that is predominantly French, current French usage has become so familiar that Renaud, for example, has been firmly fixed as Bishop Hubert's episcopal predecessor, and to refer to him as Raginaldus, Rainaldus, Reginaldus, and especially as Reginald, would be almost to rob him and the other persons concerned of the identity that they have come to possess. On the other hand, some Latin forms have been used because their current English and French versions simply conjure up mental images that, perhaps based predominantly on personal impressions, seem inappropriate for these eleventh-century figures. Thus Ralph and Raoul have been forgone in favor of Radulfus. For the most part, the Latin forms of personal names (most of which are of germanic origin) have been retained here, with an effort to standardize spellings. To have dropped the Latin endings, to have Frotmund instead of Frotmundus, or to have Ingelbald instead of Ingelbaldus, would have unnecessarily and somewhat artificially germanized the world of Bishop Hubert.

ABBREVIATIONS

Arch. Maine-et-Loire	Archives départementales de Maine-et-Loire, Angers.
Bibl. d'Angers	Bibliothèque municipale d'Angers.
B. n.	Bibliothèque nationale, Paris.
B. n., D. H.	Bibliothèque nationale, Paris, Collection Touraine-Anjou (Dom Housseau).

PART ONE

I. THE BACKGROUND

In the obituary of the cathedral of Angers the canons listed those to be remembered in prayers and masses on the anniversary of their deaths. Most of the entries have simply the names, titles, and dates of death of those to be remembered, even for the bishops of the tenth and eleventh centuries. The canons obviously would have known those prelates well, if not necessarily with affection.

October 19, Aimo bishop of Angers died [by 966].

September 12, our bishop Nefingus died, in the year of the Lord 973.

June 12, Renaud [II], the illustrious, venerable, and generous bishop of Angers died, in the year of deliverance 1005, of his ordination thirty-one.

August 27, Lord Eusebius [Bruno, 1047–1081], bishop of Angers died, in the year of the Lord 1081; he ruled this church for thirty-five years, less three months.

October 9, Geoffrey [of Tours, 1082–1093], bishop of Angers, died, in the year of the Lord 1093.[1]

However, one episcopal entry during this period is extraordinary in its length and effusive praise. Of Hubert of Vendôme (1006–1047), the obituary states:

March 2, Lord Hubert, gentle bishop and most loving to the clergy, died. This man, in comparison with many of the bishops of this see who preceded him, was distinguished, illustrious, and noble. In a small restoration he was eager to raise the canons of our church from their low state that had miserably come about, in part due to the oppression of tyrants and in part due to the neglect of previous bishops. Because of the pious favors of his paternity and of his continuing merits, especially in comparison with other bishops, he is rightly always remembered by all the brothers of our chapter and even worthy of distinguished veneration. We think it necessary that we now and our successors in the future make a perpetual commemoration of him in our prayers and alms very honorably because of our debt to him, lest we be judged unworthy of the kindness that he showed to us and our place if we appear to be ungrateful.[2]

Who was this bishop who won far more praise and devotion from his own clergy than any other head of the diocese of Angers during this period, a prelate who was seen as having been far superior to his predeces-

---

[1] *L'obituaire de la cathédrale d'Angers,* ed. Ch. Urseau (Angers, 1930), pp. 23, 28, 33, 37, 38.

[2] Ibid., pp. 7–8.

sors? The existing studies, brief as they are, portray a figure unlikely to have been respected by his contemporary clerics or to have received such a lavish epitaph. He was a simoniac who was excommunicated for waging war against his own archbishop, or in the phrase that is repeated whenever Hubert's name is raised, he was "a cleric perhaps more expert in wielding a sword than in praying to God."[3] Nonetheless, the author of that phrase went on to note that Hubert was a rich and powerful seigneur in the region of Anjou.[4] However, the most recent examination of his career has produced a picture of Hubert as "more of a duped seigneur than a great prelate,"[5] who lost family lands and offices in the face of the machinations of his own count.[6] Thus, to modern eyes, Hubert has been scorned as a cleric for having been too secular, and then he has been ridiculed as an inept lord in the secular world. But in some way, Hubert must have awed his contemporaries as did no other bishop of Angers in one of the most important and crucial periods in the history of Anjou, and Hubert was bishop of Angers longer than any other man in the tenth, eleventh, and twelfth centuries.

Hubert's episcopacy began in the middle of Anjou's century-long rise to the domination of the region of the middle Loire under the Fulconian house. Under Charlemagne's grandson Charles the Bald (840–877), Anjou was in the block of counties given to the Robertian family to administer and defend during the crisis of the Viking raids. Subordinate to the Robertian *marchio*, in whose charge was most of Neustria, was a viscount in the chief city of each county.[7] The real founder of the Fulconian dynasty in the early tenth century was the viscount of Angers, Fulk I the Red. He was also lay abbot of St.-Aubin d'Angers as well as St.-Lézin d'Angers, and he was able to usurp the title of count of Anjou from his Robertian overlord. He succeeded in getting his son Guy named bishop of Soissons, while he was followed as count by another son, Fulk II the Good.[8]

This second Fulk expanded his interests beyond the frontiers of Anjou, marrying the widow of the count of Nantes and briefly making himself the master of the Nantais. Despite his eventual failure there, Fulk the Good did initiate the long Angevin ambition to control Nantes and he was able to pull the intervening county of the Mauges into Anjou's orbit. Fulk was also

[3] Louis Halphen, *Le comté d'Anjou au XIe siècle* (Paris, 1906), p. 115.

[4] Loc. cit.

[5] Olivier Guillot, *Le comte d'Anjou et son entourage au XIe siècle,* 2 vols. (Paris, 1972), 1: p. 224.

[6] Ibid., 1: pp. 234–236.

[7] Jan Dhondt, *Etude sur la naissance des principautés territoriales en France (IXe-Xe siècle)* (Bruges, 1948), pp. 22–24, 89–107; Jacques Boussard, "Les destinées de la Neustrie du IXe au XIe siècle," *Cahiers de civilisation médiévale* 11 (1968), pp. 15–24; Jacques Boussard, "L'origine des comtés de Tours, Blois et Chartres," *Actes du 103e Congrès national des sociétés savantes, 1977* (Paris, 1979), pp. 87–90; Jean Dunbabin, *France in the Making (843–1180)* (Oxford, 1985), pp. 66–68.

[8] Dhondt, *Principautés territoriales,* pp. 114, 143–145; Halphen, *Comté d'Anjou,* pp. 1–3.

active in royal politics, and thanks to the favor of King Lothair, his son Guy became bishop of Le Puy-en-Velay and his daughter Adelaide for a time was married to the future Louis V. Later she married Count William I of Arles and their daughter Constance was married to the second Capetian king of France, Robert II the Pious (996–1031), and beginning with their son Henry I (1031–1060), Fulconian blood was mixed with that of the Capetians.[9]

Fulk II was succeeded by his son Geoffrey Greymantle (ca. 960–987), who continued his father's policies as Anjou steadily rose in power and influence. Count Geoffrey dominated Nantes and repulsed the attempt of the count of Rennes to supplant him there. He was also close to King Lothair and participated in the king's campaign against Richard I of Normandy, as well as in the famous invasion of Lorraine in 978 and in the equally famous defense of Paris against Otto II's counter-invasion. Geoffrey's royal alliance permitted him to begin to meddle in the county of Maine by securing the appointment of Segenfridus, an opponent of the count of Maine, to the bishopric of Le Mans. At the same time, Geoffrey was still in good favor with the Robertians who were by rights his lords for the county of Anjou. He was active in the election of Duke Hugh Capet to succeed Louis V in 987 and he died helping to stamp out resistance to Hugh's ascendancy, on 21 July 987.

Geoffrey also began an Angevin penetration of the south and northeast. From William Iron-Arm of Aquitaine he gained several fortresses as well as the town of Loudun. He allied with Bouchard the Venerable, count of Vendôme, which resulted in the marriage of Geoffrey's son Fulk Nerra and Bouchard's daughter Elizabeth. Since Bouchard's only son was also the bishop of Paris, the county of Vendôme was very likely to move into Angevin hands.[10]

Fulk III Nerra was about seventeen when his father died in 987, and soon he won a reputation for military ability as well as guile and ruthlessness. With these traits he made Anjou into the leading power of the middle Loire as the eleventh century began. Fulk continued to dominate Nantes to the west and steadily expanded to the east by thrusting more deeply into the lands of the count of Tours, Blois, and Chartres. For a brief time he even held the city of Tours.

Fulk controlled the county of Vendôme through his daughter Adele and her family, held a preponderant influence over the county of Maine through alliance when possible or by treachery when necessary, and finally incorporated the county of the Mauges into the Angevin heartland. He pursued his father's advance to the south, by thoroughly dominating

---

[9] Halphen, *Comté d'Anjou*, pp. 4–6.

[10] Ibid., pp. 6–9; Guillot, *Comte d'Anjou*, 1: pp. 2–15; Bernard S. Bachrach, "Geoffrey Greymantle, Count of the Angevins, 960–987: A Study in French Politics," *Studies in Medieval and Renaissance History* 17 (1985), pp. 3–67.

William the Great of Aquitaine, establishing his hegemony over most of northern Poitou, and even gaining the important city of Saintes in the southwest. Fulk was also active in royal affairs, and King Robert II was married to his first cousin Constance.[11]

In 1040 Fulk died and his son Geoffrey II Martel consolidated and expanded Fulk's work during his twenty-year rule. He had already married Agnes, widow of Duke William the Fat of Aquitaine, and through her Geoffrey was one of the leading figures of Aquitaine until her sons came into power in their own right in the 1040s, and when her daughter Agnes married Emperor Henry III, he was active in international politics. Geoffrey continued his father's domination of Vendôme by the intermediary of his subordinate nephew Count Fulk l'Oison, and he fought a series of wars that left him in total mastery of Maine. Angevin expansion to the east was unrelenting, and in 1044 he seized the city of Tours. Soon the Touraine was added to the territories under the direct authority of the count of Anjou. However, this conquest upset the semblance of a balance of power in the middle Loire, greatly alarming King Henry I. The king then opposed Geoffrey Martel, but the even more menacing growth of Normandy under Duke William the Bastard led to a renewal of the old Angevin-Capetian alliance in the 1050s. Geoffrey Martel was one of a handful of dominant princes who were determining the character and shape of France in the High Middle Ages. His power ran from the Saintonge to Maine, from the Mauges to the Touraine.[12]

---

[11] Halphen, *Comté d'Anjou*, pp. 13–132; Guillot, *Comte d'Anjou*, 1: pp. 15–55; Dunbabin, *France in the Making*, pp. 184–182. Currently Bernard S. Bachrach is significantly revising previous views of the history of Anjou and the surrounding regions during the reign of Count Fulk Nerra. In addition to the work cited in note 10 above, see his "Early Medieval Fortifications in the 'West' of France: A Revised Technical Vocabulary," *Technology and Culture* 16 (1975), pp. 531–569; "A Study in Feudal Politics: Relations Between Fulk Nerra and William the Great, 995–1030," *Viator* 7 (1976), pp. 111–121; "The Idea of the Angevin Empire," *Albion* 10 (1978), pp. 293–299; "Robert of Blois, Abbot of Saint-Florent de Saumur and Saint-Mesmin de Micy (985–1011): A Study in Small Power Politics," *Revue bénédictine* 88 (1978), pp. 123–146; "Fulk Nerra and His Accession as Count of Anjou," in *Saints and Heroes, Studies in Medieval Culture in Honour of Charles W. Jones*, ed. Margot H. King and Wesley M. Stevens (Collegeville, Minn., 1979), pp. 331–342; "Fortifications and Military Tactics: Fulk Nerra's Strongholds circa 1000," *Technology and Culture* 20 (1979), pp. 531–549; "Toward a Reappraisal of William the Great, duke of Aquitaine," *Journal of Medieval History* 5 (1979), pp. 11–21; "The Family of Viscount Fulcoius of Angers: Some Methodological Observations at the Nexus of Prosopography and Diplomatics," *Medieval Prosopography* 4:1 (1983), pp. 1–8; "The Angevin Strategy of Castle Building in the Reign of Fulk Nerra, 987–1040," *American Historical Review* 88 (1983), pp. 533–560; "Henry II and the Angevin Tradition of Family Hostility," *Albion* 16 (1984), pp. 111–130; "Enforcement of the *Forma Fidelitatis*: The Techniques Used by Fulk Nerra, Count of the Angevins (987–1040)," *Speculum* 59 (1984), pp. 796–819; "Pope Sergius IV and the Foundation of the Monastery at Beaulieu-lès-Loches," *Revue bénédictine* 95 (1985), pp. 240–265; "The Pilgrimages of Fulk Nerra, Count of the Angevins, 987–1040," in *Religion, Culture, and Society in the Early Middle Ages, Studies in Honor of Richard E. Sullivan*, ed. Thomas F. X. Noble and John J. Contreni (Kalamazoo, Mich., 1987), pp. 205–217.

[12] Halphen, *Comté d'Anjou*, pp. 13–132; Guillot, *Comte d'Anjou*, 1: pp. 56–101; Dunbabin, *France in the Making*, pp. 187–188.

In less than a century, counts of Anjou, descendants of Geoffrey Greymantle and Fulk Nerra, would sit on the thrones of the kingdoms of
Jerusalem and of England and be lords of half of France. From the mid-
tenth century onwards, Anjou was one of the most important of the "territorial principalities" that emerged out of the breakup of the Carolingian
Empire. The first great age of Angevin expansion had occurred under
Geoffrey Greymantle, Fulk Nerra, and Geoffrey Martel, from 960 to 1060,
and for forty of those years, 1006 to 1047, Hubert of Vendôme presided
over the diocese of Angers.

This phenomenal political ascendancy was accompanied by the trans-
formation of the religious life of Anjou during the first half of the eleventh
century. Breton attacks and Viking raids had greatly disrupted the
churches and monasteries of the county, but the Vikings were the greater
hazard from the 840s through the 870s. By the beginning of the tenth
century, the monastery of St. Aubin had taken shelter behind the walls of
Angers, while that of St.-Maur de Glanfeuil had been abandoned by its
monks for the distant St.-Maur-des-Fossés near Paris. The small cell of St.
Maurille at Chalonnes was in ruins, and the monastery of St.-Serge
d'Angers had fallen into decay as the monks had been replaced by canons.
Even at St. Aubin, canons had supplanted monks. It was common for
laymen to hold church offices.[13]

Under Count Geoffrey Greymantle, the religious foundations of Anjou
began to improve with the return of monks to St. Aubin in 966.[14] Bishop
Renaud II (973–1005) began the restoration of St. Serge and the enhance-
ment of the depleted domains of the cathedral of Angers. But in doing so,
he clashed with Count Fulk Nerra and his episcopacy ended in failure
while he was in virtual exile.[15] When Hubert became bishop in 1006 he
found a diocese that in most ways was no better off than it had been forty
years earlier. In addition to the longstanding problems, Bishop Renaud's
gifts to St. Serge and the cathedral had been stripped away, and
the cathedral was still in ruins after a disastrous fire in Angers in the
year 1000.[16]

But the eleventh century inaugurated a new age for the church of Anjou.
Hubert rebuilt the cathedral of Angers and founded a school there, en-
trusting it to educated masters. New monasteries were founded (Beaulieu,
St.-Nicolas d'Angers, Ronceray), others were rebuilt (St.-Maur-sur-Loire
and St.-Florent de Saumur), others were restored (St. Maurille and St.-
Serge d'Angers), and new churches were built (St.-Martin d'Angers and

---

[13] Halphen, *Comté d'Anjou*, pp. 81–83; Jean-Marc Bienvenue, "Des origines à l'an mil," and
"Renouveau de l'Eglise angevine (an mil-1148)," in *Angers*, Histoire des diocèses de France,
vol. 13, ed. François Lebrun (Paris, 1981), pp. 15–18; Pierre Riché, "Conséquence des invasions normandes sur la culture monastique dans l'occident franc," *Settimane di studio del
Centro Italiano di Studi sull'Alto Medioevo* 16 (Spoleto, 1969), pp. 705–721, esp. 716–720.

[14] Guillot, *Comté d'Anjou*, 1: pp. 138–151.

[15] See below, chap. 3, nn. 20–23.

[16] See below, chap. 4, n. 4.

Baracé). Hubert recovered churches from laymen and replaced laymen with clerics in ecclesiastical offices.[17] The religious life of Anjou flourished in a climate of recovery, reform, and renewal under Bishop Hubert and the counts of Anjou, even before Leo IX launched the church reform movement in Rome in 1049.

This great age of Angevin political and religious expansion was fueled by the economic recovery from the decline of the Carolingian Empire and the devastation of the Viking assaults. The first signs of this revival were evident in Europe as a whole in the late tenth and early eleventh centuries. Population growth and increased food supplies proceeded apace. The region of Anjou and Maine experienced an "agricultural resurrection" during this time, as fallow land was put to the plow and the vast wooded areas were cut back to make room for more farmland and the many *burgi* that seemed to sprout up everywhere. In the towns the increasing population left its traces in an expanding religious structure of new churches, oratories, monasteries, and parishes.[18]

The revived economy is most clearly evident in the remarkable building program that required a tremendous outlay of wealth and dedication by the people of Anjou. On the one hand there was the religious renewal that produced the new cathedral and its school, the foundation of new monastic houses for men and women, and the endowment of their landed wealth (including Geoffrey Martel's establishment of La Trinité in nearby Vendôme), and the rebuilding and restoration of monasteries and churches. On the other hand, Anjou was also supporting the ambitious military enterprises that established it as one of the major powers of France under Geoffrey Greymantle, Fulk Nerra, and Geoffrey Martel. Angevin arms were carried in all directions, and Count Fulk Nerra built about thirty fortresses, many of them in stone, at a tremendous expenditure of labor and resources, to secure newly won lands and to serve as points of attack for future acquisitions.[19] The flourishing Angevin economy made it possible to raise up new fortresses that announced Anjou's victories over its opponents on all sides, as well as to found new churches and monasteries that proclaimed the higher aspirations of its warriors, townsmen, and peasants.

Hubert of Vendôme won his outstanding reputation at a time when Anjou was rising to heights of power and influence in France. The diocese of Angers was being revitalized after more than a century of decadence

---

[17] See below, chap. 4, n. 45.

[18] Georges Duby, *Rural Economy and Country Life in the Medieval West,* tr. Cynthia Postan (Columbia, S.C., 1968), pp. 63–67; idem., *The Early Growth of the European Economy: Warriors and Peasants From the Seventh to the Twelfth Century,* tr. Howard B. Clarke (Ithaca, N.Y., 1974), pp. 159–162. On the region of Anjou, Maine, and Normandy, see Robert Latouche, *The Birth of the Western Economy,* tr. E. M. Wilkinson (New York, 1966), pp. 273–279; David Bates, *Normandy Before 1066* (London and New York, 1982), pp. 96–98.

[19] Bachrach, "Early Medieval Fortifications in the 'West' of France," "Fortifications and Military Tactics," and "The Angevin Idea of Castle Building."

and neglect. Both the people and the land were prospering. Whoever Bishop Hubert really was and whatever he accomplished, the times were extraordinary, and his actions must have impressed his contemporaries during a period of so many extraordinary events. As head of the Angevin church, with its lands, resources, and soldiers, as one of the most powerful secular lords of the region and a member of a large and powerful family network, and as a trusted follower of the count of Anjou, Hubert was one of the most powerful men in the lands of Anjou at one of the most important and decisive periods in the history of the county. He played a major role in politics and warfare under Fulk Nerra and Geoffrey Martel for more than forty years, and he supervised the greatest religious renewal that Anjou and its region had ever seen. Bishop Hubert was a powerful man in a dominant principality at a turning point in Angevin history.

An exploration of Hubert's career sheds revealing light on the interplay of religious and secular forces in the "First Feudal Age" and how they cooperated to play a role in Anjou's rise to prominence. It also illustrates the means by which Anjou and similar regions brought about a significant reform of their religious life at a time when the papacy was mired in the politics of Rome and Italy and its influence beyond the Alps was negligible. This local reform was accomplished by what is usually seen as a "feudalized church" dominated by secular lords and worldly prelates. Hubert's actions also show how an aristocratic family promoted its own interests, gained new lands and offices, and survived the tumultuous and erratic political storms buffeting the west of France as principalities rose and fell under the swords of strong and able leaders such as Fulk of Anjou and William of Normandy. It can also be learned why Hubert was the most impressive bishop of Angers to his own contemporaries during the course of the tenth and eleventh centuries—that is, what made a successful bishop in the period before the Gregorian Reform movement imposed new standards on the behavior of clergy and laity alike.

Bishops of the tenth and eleventh centuries, such as Hubert, were the heirs of two different traditions. They were the descendants of the powerful episcopacy created by the early Carolingians intent on centralizing authority without a clear boundary between things spiritual and things secular. At the same time the Carolingian decline had removed the royal supervision that had maintained order and discipline in the church.[20]

The civil wars of the Carolingian family led to the collapse of even the appearance of unity of the *Imperium Christianum* created by Charlemagne

---

[20] F.-L. Ganshof, "The Church and the Royal Power in the Frankish Monarchy under Pippin III and Charlemagne," *The Carolingians and the Frankish Monarchy, Studies in Carolingian History*, tr. Janet Sondheimer (Ithaca, N.Y., 1971), pp. 205–239; Karl Frederick Morrison, *The Two Kingdoms: Ecclesiology in Carolingian Political Thought* (Princeton, N.J., 1969), pp. 136–164; Rosamund McKitterick, *The Frankish Church and the Carolingian Reforms, 789–895* (London, 1977), pp. 45–79; J. M. Wallace-Hadrill, *The Frankish Church* (Oxford, 1983), pp. 278–292.

and nurtured with such effort by Louis the Pious, and the invasions of Vikings, Saracens, and Magyars confronted those in power with a crisis of public order. The depletion of the royal treasury and fisc forced public institutions to meet increasing demands for defense with diminishing supplies of economic resources and political authority. Combined with this challenge was a revival of the particularisms of submerged nationalities in the West that not even the efforts of Pepin the Short and Charlemagne had succeeded in eliminating during the height of their powers. In France, the result was the growth of the territorial principalities, in which the king usually acted only through the intermediary of the marquis, duke, or count of the region.[21] These were the men who actually exercised power in their areas and often usurped the rights that kings had been accustomed to hold.

The bishops of France retained their power and influence during this time of change. Carolingian bishops had been used as key members of the administration of the realm and often as royal counsellors. The kings had strengthened the position and prestige of the bishops by enhancing their authority within the church. Royal officials were ordered to protect the church and the kings made extensive grants of judicial and economic immunities to churches and especially to cathedrals. Royal donations of landed property to the churches and efforts taken to safeguard the integrity of episcopal estates provided the revenues for the bishops to carry on their burdensome schedule of secular functions. Thus while royal authority declined, the bishops of the Carolingian lands were deeply involved in the affairs of the world. They possessed extensive governmental authority and material wealth.[22]

In the latter ninth and tenth centuries, the bishops were forced to adapt to the new political structures that emerged. A great many bishoprics fell under the control of territorial princes and local magnates who possessed public authority and military strength. Some bishops even came to hold the remnants of public authority and formed ecclesiastical lordships, such as at Reims and Langres.[23]

In some cases, the kings retained their right to name bishops to their sees, but in other areas the duke, count, or even viscount had assumed that power. The extent of civil authority exercised by the bishop also varied from diocese to diocese.[24] In some regions the secular authority was so weak and the resulting disorders so threatening to public order that the

---

[21] Dhondt, *Principautés territoriales.*

[22] Friedrich Kampf, "The Church and the Western Kingdoms from 900 to 1046," *The Church in the Age of Feudalism*, tr. Anselm Biggs, vol. 3 of Handbook of Church History, ed. Hubert Jedin and John Dolan (New York, 1969), pp. 194–196.

[23] Marc Bloch, *Feudal Society*, tr. L. A. Manyon, 2 vols. (Chicago, 1970), 2: pp. 348–352, 401–407.

[24] P. Imbart de la Tour, *Les élections épiscopales dans l'église de France du IXe au XIIe siècle (Etude sur la décadence du principe électif (814–1150)* (Paris, 1891).

bishops took the lead in establishing the Peace and Truce of God movements to protect noncombatants and to curb warfare.[25]

By their control of a complex of economic, political, and spiritual powers and authority, the bishops continued to be men of great importance in their society. But that very power made it essential that the lay princes control the bishops. These secular magnates often judged the fitness of a bishop for his office by standards that differed from those laid down in the laws of the church. The bishops frequently came from the same class of magnates as their secular lords or their principal supporters. Once in office, the prelates often found it difficult to cease being merely lay lords who now wore the miter and ring. Some continued to take up arms in the service of their lords and administered their diocese in the service of political and familial ends.

In the age of the "dislocation of the *pagus*" when the former Carolingian administrative boundaries were being rearranged into new political structures,[26] the diocese was no longer coterminous with secular boundaries, but began to take on new shapes as political and episcopal fortunes fluctuated. Some bishops retained their ecclesiastical authority and their control of their dioceses, while others saw their position erode. Many churches no longer returned revenues to their bishop, and some monasteries escaped from the bishop's jurisdiction.[27] The system of proprietary churches and monasteries threatened the authority of the bishop within his diocese.[28]

The decline of centralization in both church and state was accompanied by the growth of uncanonical practices. Simony had not been eradicated by the unity and power of the Carolingian church, and now it became widespread. Likewise, a common sight was the married cleric, providing for his family from the goods of the church or the offices entrusted to his care. In many cases, church offices became virtual hereditary positions passing from one generation to the next.[29]

The domination of the church by secular lords and the flouting of existing canon law were resisted by some reformers within the church. By the mid-eleventh century, secular control of the episcopacy was abhorred by a

---

[25] H. E. J. Cowdry, "The Peace and the Truce of God in the Eleventh Century," *Past and Present* 46 (1971), pp. 42–67; Daniel Callahan, "Adémar de Chabannes et la Paix de Dieu," *Annales du Midi* 89 (1977), pp. 21–43.

[26] Jean-François Lemarignier, "La dislocation du 'pagus' et le problème des 'consuetudines' (Xe–XIe siècles)," *Mélanges d'histoire du moyen âge dediés à la mémoire de Louis Halphen* (Paris, 1951), pp. 401–410.

[27] Jean-François Lemarignier, "Political and Monastic Structures in France at the End of the Tenth and the Beginning of the Eleventh Century," *Lordship and Community in Medieval Europe*, ed. and tr. Frederic L. Cheyette (New York, 1967), pp. 111–121; H. E. J. Cowdry, *The Cluniacs and the Gregorian Reform* (Oxford, 1970), pp. xvii–xxvii.

[28] See below, chap. 4, nn. 5, 159–165.

[29] A. Dumas, "Les vices du clergé et les aspirations à une réforme de l'église seculière," *L'église au pouvoir des laïques (888–1057)*, vol. 7 in *Histoire de l'église depuis les origines jusqu'à nos jours*, ed. Augustin Fliche and Victor Martin (Paris, 1948), pp. 465–482.

growing number of such reformers at Rome. Their program, the Gregorian Reform movement, at first attacked simony and clerical marriage, but soon the system of proprietary churches and monasteries fell under their condemnation. At last secular control of the episcopate was added to the list of practices to be opposed.[30]

Some ninth-century popes had advocated clerical control of the church, and there were attacks on simony and clerical marriage in the early eleventh century. But it was only with Pope Leo IX that the reform program, led by an invigorated papacy, became a significant movement in Europe. Leo brought reformers from various parts of western Europe to Rome and he held synods in the West to combat the worst abuses. Most importantly for France, in October of 1049 he held a council at Reims which attacked bishops who had gained their offices by simony. This was a fundamental challenge to secular control of the episcopacy.[31]

The French episcopate from 950 to 1050 had adapted to the new post-Carolingian realities and retained many of the civil, economic, and social powers of its Carolingian predecessor. However, the Gregorian Reform movement presented a serious challenge to its authority, status, and behavior, for the previous Cluniac reform program had not been aimed at the episcopate.[32] Thus the rise of the reformed papacy marks the close of two-phased era in the history of the French church—the Carolingian creation of a strong episcopate with centralized authority within the spiritual worlds as well as extensive powers in the secular world, and the evolution of this system into regional or local churches as the Carolingian Empire declined and the French monarchy was challenged by the nascent territorial principalities. The career of Bishop Hubert of Angers follows these general lines in the post-Carolingian period. It was set in a territorial principality firmly in the hands of a powerful count who had replaced the king as the preponderant authority over the bishop, and the church of Anjou knew virtually all the evils that the reformers were denouncing.

To understand the nature of the church, politics, and society of France in the post-Carolingian age, one must focus on the bishops, who played such an important role in the religious, political, governmental, judicial, administrative, military, and economic life of their times. But it is very difficult to develop a cogent view of the French episcopate in the Carolingian and post-Carolingian periods because there have been few modern scholarly

---

[30] Friedrich Kampf, "The Gregorian Reform," *Handbook of Church History*, 3: pp. 351–358; Walter Ullmann, *The Growth of Papal Government in the Middle Ages*, third ed. (London, 1970), pp. 262–309; J. P. Whitney, *Hildebrandine Essays* (Cambridge, 1932); Gerd Tellenbach, *Church, State and Christian Society at the Time of the Investiture Contest*, tr. R. F. Bennett (Oxford, 1959).

[31] Walter Ullmann, *A Short History of the Papacy in the Middle Ages* (London, 1972), pp. 128–134; E. Amann, "Papes impériaux et papes romains," *L'église au pouvoir des laïques*, pp. 98–102.

[32] A. Dumas, "La réforme monastique," *L'église au pouvoir des laïques*, pp. 320–332.

studies of the careers of individual bishops or even of groups of bishops for this crucial time. Occasional articles have appeared, but they are usually based on a narrow selection of published documents. Systematic studies utilizing modern historical standards and investigating all the available primary sources are generally lacking.[33] By contrast, the bishops of Germany and Lorraine have enjoyed this detailed attention, due to the important role that they played in royal and imperial government. They have been presented as administrators rather than as prelates with religious and familial policies.[34]

For France, the few bishops who have been studied are the exceptional ones such as Adalbero of Laon,[35] who had a decisive role in secular and ecclesiastical politics at the highest levels, or Fulbert of Chartres, who was notable for his literary production and influence on education.[36] Thus more is learned of a politician or educator than of a bishop. For a balanced view of the bishops of France in the pre-Reform period in the many spheres of their activities and in their role in society as a whole, it is best to turn to less prominent figures who are more representative of the typical bishops of this age. The background, politics, and policies of the French episcopate in general cannot be learned from studies of such unusual prelates, with their emphasis on activities that were not shared by the ordinary bishops of France.

There are discussions of the episcopate in the many excellent regional studies concerned with this period. David Bates devoted nine pages to the ten bishoprics of Normandy in the century and a half before the conquest

[33] For example, Auguste Dumas in his section on bishoprics and secular churches in *L'église au pouvoir des laïques*, pp. 177–290, could cite no monograph on an individual bishop of France who was not a literary figure. When David Douglas studied the Norman episcopate from 1035 to 1066 ("The Norman Episcopate Before the Norman Conquest," *Cambridge Historical Journal* 13 [1957], pp. 101–115), he was able to use only two secondary studies of bishops. Jean-François Lemarignier's brief synthesis, "Une église de premier âge féodal," *Institutions ecclésiastiques*, vol. 3 of *Histoire des institutions françaises au moyen âge*, ed. Ferdinand Lot and Robert Fawtier (Paris, 1962), pp. 49–77, contains references to only two works on the episcopate by modern historians, and one of those was Douglas's study of Normandy cited above. And when Jacques Boussard turned his attention to the bishops of Neustria during this period ("Les évêques en Neustrie avant la réforme grégorienne [950–1050 environ]," *Journal des savants*, 1970, pp. 161–196), he could find only two secondary works on bishops of the sees of Angers, Tours, Orléans, Chartres, and Le Mans, and one of those concerned the educational activities of Fulbert of Chartres (L. C. MacKinney, *Bishop Fulbert and Education at the School of Chartres* [Notre Dame, Ind., 1957]).

[34] For Lotharingia, see the many works cited by E. de Moreau in the bibliography of his *La formation de l'église médiévale en Belgique du premier quart du XIIe siècle*, vol. 2 of *Histoire de l'église en Belgique des origines aux débuts du XIIe siècle* (Brussels, 1940), pp. 340–350. For Germany, see Edgar Nathaniel Johnson, *The Secular Activities of the German Episcopate 919–1024*, University Studies, vols. 30–31 (1930–1931) (Lincoln, 1930–1931), and his bibliography, pp. 259–265; and the bibliography to Georg Jenal, *Erzbischof Anno II. von Köln (1056–75) und sein politische Werken*, 2 vols., Monographien zur Geschichte des Mittelalters, vol. 8 (Stuttgart, 1974), 1: pp. xix–xxviii.

[35] Robert T. Coolidge, "Adalbero, Bishop of Laon," *Studies in Medieval and Renaissance History* 2 (1965), pp. 1–114.

[36] MacKinney, *Fulbert and Education*.

of England.[37] Oliver Guillot has a chapter dealing with the bishopric of Angers from 973 to 1109,[38] and Michel Bur studies the four bishoprics of Reims, Châlons-sur-Marne, Meaux, and Troyes up to the mid-eleventh century in a single chapter in his work on Champagne.[39] Guy Devailly specifically discusses the archbishops of Bourges in the tenth and eleventh centuries for eleven pages of his chapter on the church in Berry.[40] André Chédeville looks at the bishopric of Chartres over a period of three centuries for seven pages.[41] Georges Duby, however, does not deal directly with the church or its bishops in his work on the Mâconnais in the eleventh and twelfth centuries.[42]

The difficulty in relying on the results of these efforts is that often a number of bishoprics are studied over periods of one, two, or even three centuries, and thus an even greater number of individual bishops must be reckoned with over these long periods. Even when only one bishopric is investigated, as for example with Angers or Bourges, again the diocese is looked at over a relatively long period that covers the careers of many different bishops.[43] In all these works, which are usually lengthy studies, very little attention is given to the church or its bishops. For the most part, the bishops receive only brief glances. Most importantly, none of these regional studies can cite a single full-length study of the episcopates that they were concerned with or of the career of a single bishop whom they discussed. Thus even their brief surveys of the episcopates are founded on almost no detailed research that is based on a thorough investigation of all the available information. These works are essentially efforts at synthesis concerning the episcopate, yet there is virtually no body of research to synthesize.[44]

Most research has centered on the rising political units of the post-Carolingian period. Counties and duchies have been studied, as well as states as a whole. With a fascination for the rise of the French principalities, it is natural that attention has been drawn to them, and other aspects of society are examined to determine their relationship with the dominant secular powers. The bishops have been studied as ancillary figures who react to the world about them. They are seen to react to secular powers, to great trends in the life of the church, or to important social and economic move-

---

[37] *Normandy Before 1066*, pp. 209–218.

[38] *Le comte d'Anjou*, 1: ch. 3.

[39] *La formation du comté de Champagne, v. 950–v. 1150* (Nancy, 1977), ch. 2, pt. II.

[40] *Le Berry du Xe siècle au milieu du XIIIe siècle* (Paris–La Haye, 1973), pp. 138–148.

[41] *Chartres et ses campagnes, XIe-XIIIe siècles* (Paris, 1973), pp. 261–268.

[42] *La société aux XIe et XIIe siècles dans la région mâconnaise* (Paris, 1971).

[43] See above, nn. 37–42, and see R. A. Fletcher, *The Episcopate in the Kingdom of León in the Twelfth Century* (Oxford, 1978) and Paul H. Freedman, *The Diocese of Vic: Tradition and Regeneration in Medieval Catalonia* (New Brunswick, N.J., 1983); see also Constance Brittain Bouchard, *Spirituality and Administration: The Role of the Bishop in Twelfth-Century Auxerre* (Cambridge, Mass., 1979).

[44] For a review of the literature, see Steven Fanning, "Family and Episcopal Election, 900–1050, and the Case of Hubert, Bishop of Angers, 1006–1047," *Medieval Prosopography* 7:1 (1986), pp. 39–42.

ments, but they are not seen as possessing independent policies of their own. No effort has been made to discover their own careers, to discern their own policies and motivations. It is little wonder that our view of the post-Carolingian church is one of an institution dominated by secular authorities. The "feudalized church" is what scholars have assumed and what they have looked for, and it is no surprise that they have found it, but its nuances and limitations have scarcely been considered.

The limitations thus imposed on understanding the French episcopate in this period can be seen in Jacques Boussard's investigation of the bishops of Neustria (the dioceses of Angers, Tours, Orléans, Le Mans, and Chartres) from 950 to 1050.[45] This excellent short study surveys the individual bishops of these sees and draws a general picture of the backgrounds and careers of the prelates. They were usually great seigneurs and they often bore arms in battle, and many of them were married and had children. But Boussard found that the Neustrian episcopate had not declined as seriously as it had previously been believed or to the degree seen in other regions. Again, however, this attempt at synthesis could not be based on even a single full-length study of an individual bishop or group of bishops. Only the surface characteristics of those bishops could be observed, and no policies or programs that they followed could be discerned, and no evaluations of their careers could be made. Even in the important area of church reform, only monastic reform could be discussed.

The problems in the existing studies are evident when their presentation of one particular bishop is reviewed, that of Hubert of Angers. In his study of the bishops of Neustria, Boussard devoted more attention to Bishop Hubert than to any of the other prelates, and he undertook some original research in primary sources for that work. Yet as will be seen clearly after an intensive study of Hubert's career, major errors and misunderstandings resulted. Boussard was able to name many of the immediate members of Hubert's family, but he misread a key document and wrongly believed that Hubert had a brother named Radulfus who must have succeeded their father as viscount of Vendôme. Moreover, he uncritically accepted a much earlier opinion of the identity of Bishop Hubert's brother-in-law, which then led him to suggest that Hubert was related to several previous bishops of Angers. This in turn resulted in the hypothesis that the bishopric of Angers was a kind of family see that had pertained to this family for a century and a half, and thus it was typical of the many family-dominated bishoprics of the region in that time. This fact then implied that the count of Anjou could not exercise complete freedom of choice in naming the bishop of Angers, that the claims of this family to the bishopric had to be respected by the counts.[46]

However, there is no evidence of the supposed identity of the brother-in-law and no reason to believe that Hubert was related to those previous

---

[45] "Les évêques en Neustrie."
[46] Ibid., pp. 166–171; Fanning, "Family and Episcopal Election," pp. 42–44.

bishops. In fact, all the information points to an entirely different identification of the family background of Bishop Hubert. So even on such basic points as the family origins of Bishop Hubert, who his immediate relatives were and what offices they held, and the relationship of successive bishops of Angers and the implications that this has for the very nature of the Angevin diocese and the power of the count of Anjou, this view of Hubert has serious limitations and at times it is unreliable and misleading. Since Boussard briefly examined the bishops of five dioceses over the course of a century, it is clear that our understanding of the post-Carolingian episcopate even in the region of Neustria is very limited.

While Boussard spent only four pages on Bishop Hubert, Olivier Guillot gave twenty-five pages to his study of Hubert's episcopate.[47] This is the most extensive work to date on Hubert's career and involves new research often based on primary sources. However, this examination is only one section of a chapter on the church that is part of a two-volume work concerned with the count of Anjou and his power structure in the eleventh century. Hubert's career was not studied in its own right, and its dynamics were lost in the focus on the dominant actions of Fulk Nerra and Geoffrey Martel.

Through his more detailed and painstaking research, Guillot was able to dismiss Hubert's nonexistent brother Radulfus, and he was not distracted by the erroneous connection between Hubert and previous bishops of Angers. But he could not know Hubert's career in detail, and he was led into errors as serious as Boussard's. Guillot found evidence of another brother for Bishop Hubert, this time named William. To explain the silence of the sources about him, Guillot constructed a theory in which the counts of Anjou would induce vicontiel families to seek the bishopric of Angers for their sons so that the count of Anjou could then take over the viscountship when its incumbent died without heirs. Guillot then harshly judged Bishop Hubert as a secular seigneur on the basis of this inexplicable and even self-destructive decision.[48]

However, more research proves that there was no such disappearing brother William and indeed the viscountship of Vendôme remained in Hubert's family through the remainder of the eleventh century. Thus one must reevaluate Hubert's career as well as the motives and actions of the count of Anjou when he named the bishop of Angers. Guillot also misdates the warfare between Bishop Hubert and Archbishop Hugh of Tours and errs in his suggestion of a rift between Bishop Hubert and Count Fulk in the latter 1020s, which has important implications for the general relationship between bishop and count.[49] An understanding of the whole career of Hubert permits one to correct these major interpretative and factual errors.

---

[47] Guillot, *Comte d'Anjou,* 1: pp. 224–249.
[48] See above, nn. 5, 6; and Fanning, "Family and Episcopal Election," pp. 43–45.
[49] Guillot, *Comte d'Anjou,* 1: p. 242; but see Steven Fanning, "La lutte entre Hubert de Vendôme, Evêque d'Angers, et l'Archevêque de Tours en 1016: Un épisode dans l'histoire de

The second problem with Guillot's presentation is simply that he is concerned with the count of Anjou and not with the bishop of Angers. Hubert is seen primarily as a weak figure reacting to comital policies and pressures. There is no appreciation of his own actions as bishop, seigneur, warrior, or family member in such a study. One cannot understand the career of a bishop such as Hubert on the basis of any existing research. Until there are many detailed investigations of Hubert and his episcopal colleagues, we shall know very little of the bishops of France in the post-Carolingian period. Only with many such studies shall we gain an understanding of its bishops and the church and society to which they belonged.

These bishops, often seen as being simoniacal, worldly, and warlike, were thus necessarily closely connected to their own society. The boundary between the world and the church was not clearly defined. In many ways, the bishops of the period before the triumph of the Gregorian Reform movement could have had a great influence on the world around them. They were active in all spheres of life.

Hubert's career spanned most of the first half of the eleventh century, and it was confined to Anjou and its immediately neighboring counties. There is no indication that he operated on a wider stage of secular or ecclesiastiacal life. In every sense, he was a local and regional figure. His life was bound up in the affairs of the middle Loire, in the age of the territorial principalities.

He was consecrated bishop of Angers on 13 June 1006,[50] no doubt in a ceremony in the church of the monastery of St. Aubin. The cathedral of St. Maurice in Angers was still in ruins after the great fire that had swept the city six years earlier, but also Count Geoffrey Greymantle had confirmed to St. Aubin its right as the place of consecration for new bishops when he reformed the monastery in 966.[51] Precisely a year had passed since the death of Bishop Renaud II, on 12 July 1005,[52] and Count Fulk Nerra would have used the episcopal vacancy to enjoy the revenues of the diocese and to continue his revocation of the grants made to the cathedral and the monastery of St. Serge by Bishop Renaud.

The right to name the bishop of Angers clearly belonged to the count of Anjou,[53] and it was one of the most important appointments that the count could make. The bishop of Angers was in charge of the diocese, with its lands and revenues that made it an economic power in the county second only perhaps to the count himself. The diocesan estates also made it possible for the bishop to maintain numbers of soldiers who would be of use in supporting the unceasing expansionism of the counts in the tenth and eleventh centuries. This military force would also make the bishop one of

---

l'Eglise des principautés territoriales," *Bulletin de la Société archéologique, scientifique et littéraire du Vendômois* (1980), pp. 31–33.

[50] Halphen, *Comté d'Anjou*, p. 115, n. 1.

[51] Guillot, *Comte d'Anjou*, 1: p. 198.

[52] See above, n. 1.

[53] Guillot, *Comte d'Anjou*, 1: p. 201.

the most important political figures in the county. The bishop could be a helpful ally or a troublesome opponent for the count.[54] The many ecclesiastical offices that were the responsibility of the bishop to fill allowed him to assist the count, who needed to reward his followers with a variety of lands and positions. At the same time, the bishop could satisfy the demands of his own circle of friends, family, and supporters for a share in the wealth and power that were attached to many of these posts.

It was rare for the count to name a bishop more than once in his lifetime (Geoffrey Greymantle, Fulk Nerra, and Geoffrey Martel each had but one such opportunity),[55] so the decision was made very carefully. There would have been many families eager to place one of their members on the episcopal chair of Angers, in command of the complex of revenues, offices, and powers that were associated with it, and they would have been ready to pay the count a high price for his favor. The counts did demand a substantial payment when they made this weighty decision.

In the previous episcopal appointment, Count Geoffrey Greymantle believed that Viscount Renaud of Angers had promised that his extensive family lands in the county of the Mauges, located to the southwest of Angers on the left bank of the Loire, would be handed over to the count in return for the naming of the viscount's son, also named Renaud, to the bishopric. The transferral would not occur until after the death of the newly appointed bishop.[56] Since the Renauds were descendants of ninth- and tenth-century counts of Herbauge, dukes of Nantes, viscounts, abbots, and previous bishops of Angers,[57] their patrimony in the Mauges would have been extensive and well worth the long wait before the count could actually take over the inheritance. The price may have been unusually high, but the younger Renaud was designated bishop even while his predecessor Nefingus was still alive.[58] Renaud gained the appointment prematurely and Count Geoffrey deprived himself of the income from a vacancy when Nefingus did die.

When Fulk Nerra named Hubert bishop in 1005 or 1006, he was in great need of the support of Hubert's family in the Vendômois as well as of the cooperation of a loyal bishop,[59] so the cost to Hubert's family may not have been as great as that paid by the Renauds. All that is known with certainty is that one estate and its church were given by Viscount Hubert of Vendôme to Count Fulk for the appointment of the younger Hubert as bishop.[60] It is doubtful that this was the only transaction for such an important appointment, for this was actually a return rather than a gain of

---

[54] See below, chap. 3, nn. 19–24.
[55] Geoffrey Greymantle named only Renaud II, Fulk Nerra chose only Hubert, and Geoffrey Martel picked only Eusebius Bruno for the see of Angers.
[56] Guillot, *Comte d'Anjou*, 1: pp. 215–223.
[57] Richard Hogan, "The *Rainaldi* of Angers: 'New Men' or Descendants of Carolingian *Nobiles?*," *Medieval Prosopography* 2:1 (1981), pp. 35–62.
[58] Guillot, *Comte d'Anjou*, 1: p. 201.
[59] See below, chap. 3, nn. 1–10, 19–24.
[60] See below, Part II, No. 1.

new property by the count. He had previously given the estate and church to Viscount Hubert. It seems certain that Fulk would have demanded a much greater price for the bishopric of Angers, but Hubert's family retained its lands and position as well as the viscountship of Vendôme, so it did not suffer greatly in the negotiations that preceded the consecration in 1006.

Was Hubert then a simoniac? While Fulk did exact a price for his favor, that alone did not constitute simony as it was then understood. The Carolingian church had forbidden payments only if they resulted in the appointment of those who otherwise would not have gained an office or favor.[61] Unfortunately, not enough is known of Hubert's life before 1006 to judge his fitness for the office of bishop.

Hubert's age at consecration is not certain. Twenty years later, he was referred to as a *juvenis* by the master of his cathedral school.[62] This is not a precise word, for in the twelfth century, a *juvenis* was an adult and could be used to describe a soldier until he was married and sometimes even beyond. In the thirteenth century, it could refer to the time of a man's life between the ages of twenty and forty.[63] Its usage in the eleventh century is not known so well, but it could be consistent with the later evidence. Hubert's contemporary Bishop Fulbert of Chartres wrote that he himself was a *juvenis* when he was consecrated, and he must have been at least in his mid-thirties at that time.[64] So Hubert might have been born ca. 980–985 to have been described as a *juvenis* forty years later. He could have been twenty or twenty-five at the time of his consecration.

The scanty evidence suggests that he was probably not very much younger in 1006. He appeared in extant charter evidence by 1012,[65] and in 1016 he led troops into battle.[66] Both of his parents were dead by 1025,[67] and he lived until 1047,[68] almost forty-one years after his consecration. He had been in ill health for some time before his death.[69] The one surviving document that Hubert subscribed carries the cross that he traced on the parchment just one year before he died. It is drawn with a very shaky line

---

[61] Joseph H. Lynch, *Simoniacal Entry into Religious Life from 1000 to 1260: a Social, Economic and Legal Study* (Columbus, Ohio, 1976), pp. 61–63; N. A. Weber, *A History of Simony in the Christian Church From the Beginning to the Death of Charlemagne (814)* (Baltimore, 1909), pp. 219–220.

[62] *Liber Miraculorum Sancte Fidis*, ed. A. Bouillet, Collection de textes pour servir à l'étude et à l'enseignement de l'histoire, fasc. 21 (Paris, 1897), p. 2.

[63] Georges Duby, "Etudes dans la France du Nord-Ouest au XIIe siècle: les 'jeunes' dans la société aristocratique," *Annales, Economies, Sociétés, Civilisations* 19 (1964), p. 836; Philippe de Navarre, *Les quatre âges de l'homme, traité moral de Philippe de Navarre*, ed. Marcel de Frévalle, Société des anciens textes français 26 (Paris, 1888), V. 195, p. 104.

[64] *The Letters and Poems of Fulbert of Chartres*, ed. and tr. Frederick Behrends (Oxford, 1976), p. xvi and no. 133.

[65] When he discovered the remains of St. Lupus; see George H. Forsyth, Jr., *The Church of St. Martin at Angers* (Princeton, N.J., 1953), p. 45 n. 80, p. 108, and see below, chap. 4, nn. 150–151.

[66] See below, chap. 3, nn. 48–51.

[67] See below, chap. 2, n. 22.

[68] See below, n. 72.

[69] See below, n. 73.

that contrasts with the firm lines drawn next to it by Count Geoffrey Martel, who was then thirty-nine.[70] While illness may have been responsible for Hubert's unsteady hand in 1046, it may also have been due to his advanced years. Thus his being called a *juvenis* ca. 1020–1025, the death of his parents by 1025, and the circumstances in the last year of his life all point to his birth around 980 to 985, his consecration in 1006 at age twenty to twenty-five, and his death in 1047 at age sixty to sixty-five.

Hubert was probably reared in the county of Vendôme and as the son of the viscount of Vendôme who might well have succeeded to that office himself, he may have received the training typical of a secular lord in his age, with an emphasis on soldierly abilities. His cousin Vulgrinus was a *miles* before entering his own clerical career,[71] so this could well have been true for Hubert as well. Certainly his only documented military campaign was very successful. It has been asserted that he was a monk before he became a bishop, but there is no evidence in support of this claim. It is certain that he was not also the abbot of St.-Aubin d'Angers as some have believed, for the necrology of the convent of Ronceray records the death of Abbot Hubert on 29 July, while Bishop Hubert died on 2 March.[72]

At the end of his life, Hubert was probably in his sixties and suffering from a variety of infirmities. In a charter issued sometime within the last year of his life, he stated that his body was acting as a whip in forcing him to consider the health of his soul. His death was probably anticipated, for there was a *medicus* with him when he died,[73] and he was buried in a grand ceremony on 3 March 1047, just one day after his death. His funeral was supervised by Bishop Gervais of Le Mans, Abbot Frederick of St. Florent, and his own cousin Abbot Vulgrinus of St.-Serge d'Angers, along with the other abbots of Anjou, a large crowd of laymen and clerics, and "with deserved public mourning." Hubert's body was taken to his special monastery of St. Serge, where it was interred.[74]

In their obituary notice, the cathedral canons made known the very great esteem that they had for Bishop Hubert, and the description of his funeral makes it clear that this feeling was shared by the abbots and the diocese as a whole. At the end of Hubert's life, his career was judged a success by those who knew him and who were determined to honor his memory so that subsequent generations could likewise appreciate his merits and give their thanks. A study of Hubert's role in his own family, the use that he made of his considerable political and military powers, and his activities as the head of the diocese of Angers indicates the reasons why he was the most revered bishop of his diocese in the First Feudal Age.

---

[70] See below, Part II, No. 53, ms. A.

[71] *Actus Pontificum Cenomannis in Urbe Degentium,* ed. G. Busson and A. Ledru (Le Mans, 1902), pp. 373–374. On the career of Vulgrinus, see below, chap. 2, nn. 98–107.

[72] Bibl. municipale d'Angers, ms. 849 (761), fol. 49 v, fol. 18 v; on the death of Bishop Hubert, also see above, n. 2.

[73] Part II, No. 79; note also that two of Bishop Hubert's men had to manage that transaction for him.

[74] Part II, No. 81.

II. THE WORLD OF THE FAMILY

The importance of the family in the early medieval world has long been emphasized. In germanic society, the family provided a person's identity and security, and wergelds, compensations, and bloodfeuds were common practices indicating the strength and vitality of the family; they were carried over into the states that emerged after the decline of the Western Roman Empire.[1] But it has been argued that in the Carolingian period the position and importance of the family began to be challenged. In this view, the rise of feudalism substituted the relationship between lord and vassal for the family as the framework of society. Kinship was no longer a decisive factor in understanding the behavior of the people who dominated the political, economic, social, and ecclesiastical structures of the Carolingian and post-Carolingian periods. To Marc Bloch, feudal institutions and strong kinship groups were incompatible.[2] To many, every facet of medieval society is explicable by the all pervasive system of feudalism.[3]

Recent studies have challenged this view of the weakness of the family, especially for the ninth, tenth, and eleventh centuries. A number of German, Austrian, and French scholars argue that there was basic continuity between the aristocracy of Carolingian Europe and that of the tenth and early eleventh centuries.[4] They demonstrate that the Carolingian aristoc-

---

[1] On these points, see Steven Fanning, "From *Miles* to *Episcopus:* The Influence of the Family on the Career of Vulgrinus of Vendôme (ca. 1000–1065)," *Medieval Prosopography* 4:1 (1983), p. 9 and n. 5.

[2] Ibid., n. 6. Marc Bloch, *Feudal Society,* 1: pp. 142, 224–227.

[3] For a criticism of this overemphasis on feudalism by historians of the Middle Ages, see Elizabeth A. R. Brown, "The Tyranny of a Construct: Feudalism and Historians of Medieval Europe," *American Historical Review* 79 (1974), pp. 1063–1088.

[4] See Gerd Tellenbach, *Königtum und Stämme in der Werdezeit des deutschen Reiches* (Weimar, 1939), "Zur Bedeutung der Personenforschung für die Erkenntnis des früheren Mittelalters," *Freiburger Universitätsreden* (Freiburg, 1957), and "Der Grossfränkische Adel und die Regierung Italiens in der Blütezeit des Karolingerreiches," in his *Studien und Vorarbeiten zur Geschichte des grossfränkischen und frühdeutschen Adels. Forschungen zur Oberrheinischen Landesgeschichte* (Freiburg, 1957); Michael Mitterauer, *Karolingische Markgrafen im Südosten,* Archiv für österreichische Geschichte, vol. 123 (Vienna, 1963); Joseph Fleckenstein, "Fulrad von Saint-Denis und der fränkische Ausgriff in den süddeutschen Raum," *Studien und Vorarbeiten,* ed. Gerd Tellenbach, "Über die Herkunft der Welfen und ihre Anfänge in Süddeutschland," *Studien und Vorarbeiten,* ed. Tellenbach; Karl Schmid, "Königtum, Adel und Klöster zwischen Bodensee und Schwarzwald," *Studien und Vorarbeiten,* ed. Tellenbach; Karl Ferdinand Werner, "Untersuchungen zur Frühzeit des französischen Fürstentums (9.–10. Jahrhundert)," *Die Welt als Geschichte* 17 (1958), pp. 256–289, 19 (1959), pp. 146–193, and 20 (1960), pp. 87–119, and "Bedeutende Adelsfamilien im Reich Karls des Grossen," in *Karl der*

racy retained its position into the post-Carolingian age. For the tenth and early eleventh centuries, lands, offices, and power came to those whose families had already held them. This continuity of family status has also been seen for the seigneurial families of the lower nobility in the middle Loire in the early eleventh century.[5]

Research on the family has thus aimed at examining the question of the survival of early medieval family structures, the importance of family ties and identity, and the role that feudal relationships played in medieval society. It has looked at the question of continuity or change in the composition of the nobility.

Naturally this interest leads to the subject of the family background of the bishops who were of such importance in medieval society. Effort has been made to determine their social class and their geographical origins in order to evaluate the significance of their episcopal appointments. Were the bishops from established aristocratic and noble families who were already of the ruling elite, or were they new men who had risen to prominence by intelligence and ability? Were they local figures who had strong power bases in the region of their diocese, or were they outsiders who might be in opposition to entrenched local interests? Was the king, duke, or count free to name whomever he wished to the bishopric, or did certain families traditionally provide bishops for certain sees, making them a virtual part of their patrimonies?[6] Studies of episcopal family origins are important in understanding the nature of the episcopate as well as the nature of the family in the Middle Ages. Moreover, they are necessary in order to gain a clearer picture of the process by which a man was chosen to be bishop—what considerations were important in the election of a bishop and how much freedom of choice was there for those who had the right to make that choice.

Most of this recent research has focused on the period after the mid-eleventh century, when there is a relative abundance of information.[7] Unfortunately, this is also the period that was most influenced by the Gregorian Reform movement, which began to alter the criteria for judging the qualifications for a potential bishop and the standards for episcopal behavior, and it challenged the right of the traditional powers to control such elections.[8] These studies are not very informative for the pre-Reform

Grosse—Lebenswerk und Nachleben, vol. 1, *Persönlichkeit und Geschichte,* ed. Helmut Beumann (Düsseldorf, 1965), pp. 83–142; L. Genicot, "La noblesse au Moyen Age dans l'ancienne 'Francie,'" *Annales, Economies, Sociétés, Civilisations* 17 (1962), pp. 282–292; J. Wollasch, "Königtum, Adel und Kloster im Berry während des 10en Jahrhunderts," *Neue Forschungen über Cluny und die Cluniacenser,* ed. Gerd Tellenbach (Freiburg, 1959), pp. 17–165; and see also Hogan, "The *Rainaldi* of Angers."

[5] Jacques Boussard, "L'origine des familles seigneuriales dans la région de la Loire moyenne," *Cahiers de civilisation médiévale* 5 (1962), pp. 303–322.

[6] On these points, see Fanning, "Family and Episcopal Election," pp. 39–41.

[7] Ibid.

[8] See above, chap. 1, nn. 30–32.

episcopate. There have been a few works concerned with the tenth and eleventh centuries, but they are for the most part efforts at synthesis dealing with numbers of bishops or dioceses over relatively long periods of time. As has been seen earlier, there are virtually no full-length studies to serve as the foundation for these works.[9] As a result, only the immediate family members of the bishops can be known, and even here there are sometimes serious errors.[10] Rarely can the bishops' wider family connections be discerned.

Due to these limitations, while we often know from what social class a bishop was drawn, and while we know with varying levels of assurance the closest members of his family, we are unable to see a bishop in his general family setting. Current research is concerned with the survival of a social class or with the general nature of the episcopate or of a diocese, which are important considerations. But it does not focus on the family as a living and active force in the life of the bishops of this time.

We cannot see the bishop's kinship group in action or ascertain to what degree family considerations affected his whole career. Out of our ignorance of all but the closest relatives of important figures such as bishops, it is almost inevitable that what is well known receives the emphasis in attempts to interpret this period. And what is known is the rise of the territorial princes and the existence of feudal practices. Of the functioning of the family we know very little. Thus we have the First Feudal Age virtually out of default, due to lack of information to compete with what seems obvious to modern scholars. Currently it is almost impossible to assess the relative importance of these features of society because of the imbalance of our present knowledge. We are almost certain to see the preponderance of feudal relationships over those of the family when we know so little of family networks in this period and how they actually operated. A more thorough understanding of the family network of a bishop and of its importance in his career will greatly assist our efforts to interpret the vital and meaningful forces of the society that dominated the life of France in the tenth and eleventh centuries. But the problem has long been the difficulty in being able to trace the family members of all but a few individuals in this period.

The developing methodology of prosopography has provided the means of expanding our knowledge of the family origins of the ruling elite of the poorly documented tenth and eleventh centuries.[11] The techniques used by Gerd Tellenbach and his "school,"[12] and more recently by Karl Ferdi-

---

[9] See above, chap. 1, nn. 33–45.

[10] See above, chap. 1, nn. 46, 47.

[11] See George Beech, "Prosopography," in *Medieval Studies: an Introduction,* ed. James M. Powell (Syracuse, N. Y., 1976), pp. 156–171; and Neithard Bulst, "Zum Gegenstand und zur Methode von Prosopographie," in *Medieval Lives and the Historian: Studies in Medieval Prosopography,* ed. Neithard Bulst and Jean-Philippe Genet (Kalamazoo, Mich., 1986), pp. 1–16.

[12] On this "school," see D. A. Bullough, "Europae Pater: Charlemagne and his achievement in the light of recent scholarship," *English Historical Review* 84 (1970), p. 74; Beech,

nand Werner,[13] have proven very useful in exploring family relationships when there are few sources that explicitly give this information. Although easily misunderstood and misapplied, these methods are an invaluable aid in the study of families.[14]

One must not only note the names that are prominent in families, the *Leitnamen,* but also all the names that are known to have been used within a family—its *Namengut,* or Name Bank—as clues to possible ties of kinship. Then the nature of offices, such as viscount or bishop, that tend to be held hereditarily must be observed, as well as any continuous possession of the same property, common attachments to particular monastic houses, and shared persistent political loyalties. Thus the more that two individuals share common family names, lands, patterns of donations to monasteries, and political traditions, the greater is the likelihood of their being related to each other. Likewise, the lack of these congruencies is a negative indicator of possible family relationships.[15]

When used with care and restraint, these methods can make it clear when two individuals are not related to each other, and they can point to specific families that must be related, even if it is impossible to determine the precise ties of kinship between them. Armed with this new information, it is then possible to uncover a much wider kinship group than was previously known and to see previously hidden facets of the role that family considerations played in the lives of the men who held power in the tenth and eleventh centuries.

These techniques are of special usefulness in studying the family of Bishop Hubert, for the extant documents are informative only of the identity of his parents, his sister and her family, and a cousin. We know that Bishop Hubert's mother was named Emma, or sometimes the hypocoristic form Emelina is found.[16] His father was Viscount Hubert of Vendôme,[17] who was active in that office by July 1005 at the latest.[18] He was a supporter of both Bouchard the Venerable, count of Vendôme, and Count Fulk Nerra of Anjou.[19] Thus he was involved in the Angevin-Vendômois political connection that went back to Geoffrey Greymantle of Anjou and Count Bouchard. Since Bouchard was also count of Corbeil, of Melun, and of Paris,[20] he was in the county of Vendôme only infrequently, and Vis-

---

"Prosopography," p. 156; and Jane Martindale, "The French Aristocracy in the Early Middle Ages: a Reappraisal," *Past and Present* 25 (1977), p. 10 and n. 20.

[13] See above, n. 4.

[14] For an overly skeptical appraisal of this methodology, which is presented in simplistic terms, see Dunbabin, *France in the Making,* p. 107.

[15] For a general discussion of these techniques, see Beech, "Prosopography," pp. 156–171.

[16] See below, Part II, Nos. 10, 52.

[17] See below, Part II, Nos. 1, 10, 52.

[18] *Chartes de Saint-Julien de Tours (1002–1227),* ed. L.-J. Denis (Le Mans, 1912), no. 5; see Guillot, *Comte d'Anjou,* 2: no. 24.

[19] He already held lands from Count Fulk before his son's nomination as bishop of Angers; see below, Part II, No. 1.

[20] On Bouchard, see Charles Bourel de la Roncière, introduction to *Vie de Bouchard le Vénérable* (Paris, 1892), pp. vi–xx.

count Hubert would have been the most powerful figure resident in the Vendômois. He was capable of exercising an independent policy towards his neighbors. A century earlier, virtually autonomous viscounts had been able to usurp the title of count and establish powerful dynasties in territories such as Anjou and Tours. But apparently Hubert's loyalty and the growing dominance of Geoffrey Greymantle and Fulk Nerra kept Vendôme a secondary county in the middle Loire.

When Bishop Hubert dedicated his newly rebuilt cathedral in Angers on 16 August 1025,[21] he acknowledged the assistance that his parents had given him in the great undertaking, and it is clear that neither of them was still alive.[22] Since Emma died on an April 20,[23] she might have lived into 1025. Viscount Hubert died on an October 28,[24] so he could not have lived beyond 1024. He may have been dead by December 1022, for he was not present at the large gathering of his family at Vendôme, along with Count Fulk, at that time.[25]

It is known that Bishop Hubert had a sister named Hadeburga,[26] whose date of death was 27 May.[27] She was married to a man named Stephen,[28] by whom she had one known child, a daughter named Emma (or Emelina),[29] for her maternal grandmother. It was this younger Emma who became the heiress of her uncle Bishop Hubert, and much more concerning her will be discussed later. It has been claimed that Stephen was the seigneur of Montrevault[30] and even that he was the brother of Renaud II,[31] Bishop Hubert's predecessor in the see of Angers, but there is no evidence for either suggestion. All that is known of him is the identity of his wife and daughter, and that he and Hadeburga were dead by 1058 and were buried at the monastery of St.-Serge d'Angers, where Bishop Hubert was also buried and where their daughter would also be interred.[32] (See Chart A.)

The published reconstruction of the obituary of the cathedral of St.-Maurice d'Angers records October 28 as the day of the death of Viscount William, the brother of Bishop Hubert.[33] But the manuscript in the Bibliothèque nationale in Paris gives that day for the death of Viscount Hubert, the father of Bishop Hubert,[34] and there is no mention of any brother

---

[21] See below, Part II, No. 10.

[22] Ibid., "quos [Viscount Hubert and Emma] sane voluntas divina ante de mundanae vitae incolatu assumptos ad hujus diei gaudia mecum in carne pertingere non permisit . . ."

[23] *Obituaire de la cathédrale d'Angers*, p. 16.

[24] See below, nn. 33, 34.

[25] See below, Part II, No. 7.

[26] See below, Part II, No. 81.

[27] *Obituaire de la cathédrale d'Angers*, p. 21.

[28] See below, Part II, No. 81.

[29] Ibid.

[30] Halphen, *Comté d'Anjou*, p. 159.

[31] Célestin Port, *Dictionnaire historique, géographique et biographique de Maine-et-Loire* (Paris, 1876), 2: p. 728.

[32] See below, Part II, No. 81.

[33] *Obituaire de la cathédrale d'Angers*, p. 39.

[34] B. n., coll. Baluze, vol. 39, fol. 32 v.

GENEALOGICAL CHART A: THE FAMILY OF BISHOP HUBERT OF ANGERS

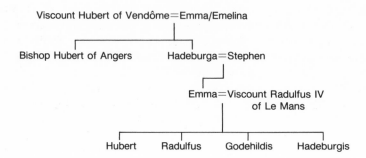

named William. In fact, there is no documentary evidence to suggest that there ever was such a Viscount William, and he can be dismissed from a consideration of Bishop Hubert's family.

The only other uncontestably known relative of Bishop Hubert was his cousin Vulgrinus. From a career as a *miles* in Vendôme, Vulgrinus entered the religious life at the famed abbey of Marmoutier at Tours. He rose to the position of prior of that monastery, was then named as the abbot of St.-Serge d'Angers by Bishop Hubert, and finally was chosen to be bishop of Le Mans by Count Geoffrey Martel of Anjou.[35]

Thus Bishop Hubert's known family has been limited to a very small circle, including a cousin whose own immediate family has been suspected, but never firmly established. Not even any of Viscount Hubert's predecessors in that office at Vendôme have been known. It has been impossible to do more than to establish Bishop Hubert's social class and geographical origin in attempting to examine his family,[36] and no effort could be made actually to study the role of the family in his career. But the Tellenbach–Werner prosopographical techniques have been used to uncover Hubert's wider kinship network and then to apply this knowledge to his career.[37]

Bishop Hubert's father was preceded at Vendôme by Viscount Fulcradus, who in 985 was the *fidelis* of both Count Geoffrey Greymantle and Count Bouchard the Venerable of Vendôme.[38] The only site for a convergence of both counts' power and influence was the county of Vendôme, and in this same year of 985 negotiations were underway for the marriage

---

[35] *Actus Pontificum Cenomannis*, pp. 373–374. On the family and career of Vulgrinus, see Steven Fanning, "Les origines familiales de Vulgrin, Abbé de Saint-Serge d'Angers (1046–1056) et Evêque du Mans (1056–1065), petit-fils du vicomte Fulcrade de Vendôme," *La Province du Maine* 82 (1980), pp. 243–255, and Steven Fanning, "From *Miles* to *Episcopus*," pp. 9–30.

[36] Boussard, "Les évêques en Neustrie," pp. 166–171.

[37] This has been studied in detail in Fanning, "Origines familiales de Vulgrin," which should be consulted for a more extensive presentation of this information.

[38] *Livre des serfs de Marmoutier*, ed. André Salmon (Tours, 1864), no. 1; Bachrach, "Geoffrey Greymantle," pp. 27–28.

of Geoffrey's son Fulk to Bouchard's daughter Elizabeth. This same twin
loyalty is found with Viscount Hubert, who was not only loyal to Count
Bouchard, but also held lands from Count Fulk Nerra.[39] Since it was
customary for viscountships in the west of France to be transmitted hereditarily, Viscount Hubert was probably related to Viscount Fulcradus.
Certainly the meager information permits the suggestion that Fulcradus,
who is known only in 985, was succeeded by Hubert, who is not known
before 1005.

These clues appear more certain when one turns to a study of Hubert's
cousin Vulgrinus. Along with Bishop Hubert, Vulgrinus came from the
highest stratum of Vendômois society; he was from the *castrum* of
Vendôme, and it was known that he had a *nepos* named Fulcherius.[40]
These pieces of information point to the family of Fulcherius the Rich of
Vendôme, one of the most prominent families of that county throughout
the eleventh century. Fulcherius the Rich was married to Hildegardis, also
called Aldeardis. Their family has been reconstructed to reveal six known
children. Their two sons, Vulgrinus and Fulcherius, are not well known.
Their daughter Hildegardis (Domitilla) was married to Ingelbaldus Brito
and had six known children, Vulgrinus, Fulcherius, Geoffrey Paganus,
Hugh, Hildegardis, and Lucia. Another daughter was Hersendis, the wife
of Gradulfus Albus of Montigny, whose children were Fulcherius, Peter,
Guy, and Hadensis (Adhuisa). A third daughter was Adela. By her first
marriage to Roger (son or brother to Robert of Montcontour) she had
Agnes and Fulcherius de Turre, and she was later married to the *miles*
Hugh. A fourth daughter was Emelina, married to Joscelin the Bastard, and
mother of Fulcherius, Fulcradus, and Geoffrey (see Genealogical Chart B
for a sketch of the family of Fulcherius the Rich).[41]

Thus, it can be seen that Vulgrinus the son of Fulcherius the Rich and
Hildegardis matches the known information on Hubert's cousin Vulgrinus.
He was from Vendôme, he had a *nepos* named Vulgrinus (the son of
Hildegardis and Ingelbaldus Brito), and his disappearance from the
Vendômois is explained by his entry into the monastic life. This suspicion
is made certain by evidence from the charters. Members of the family of
Fulcherius the Rich and Bishop Hubert held lands at Bezay and Nourray in
the Vendômois.[42] And when the family of Hubert's niece Emma gave their
authorization for a sale of lands at Bezay, three members of the family of
Fulcherius the Rich were present as witnesses.[43] The two families often
appear together in acts for Marmoutier and Trinité de Vendôme. Half of
Bishop Hubert's appearances in charters for the Vendômois concern

---

[39] See above, n. 19. On all of these points, see Fanning, "Origines familiales de Vulgrin."
[40] *Recueil des actes des ducs de Normandie (911–1066)*, ed. Marie Fauroux (Caen, 1961), no. 165.
[41] Fanning, "Origines familiales de Vulgrin," pp. 244–247.
[42] *Cartulaire de Marmoutier pour le Vendômois*, ed. Trémault (Vendôme, 1893), nos. 30, 34, 59, 94; see also below, Part II, No. 9.
[43] *Cart. Marmoutier pour le Vendômois*, no. 90; among the witnesses were Ingelbaldus Brito and his son Vulgrinus, and Fulcradus the son of Joscelin the Bastard.

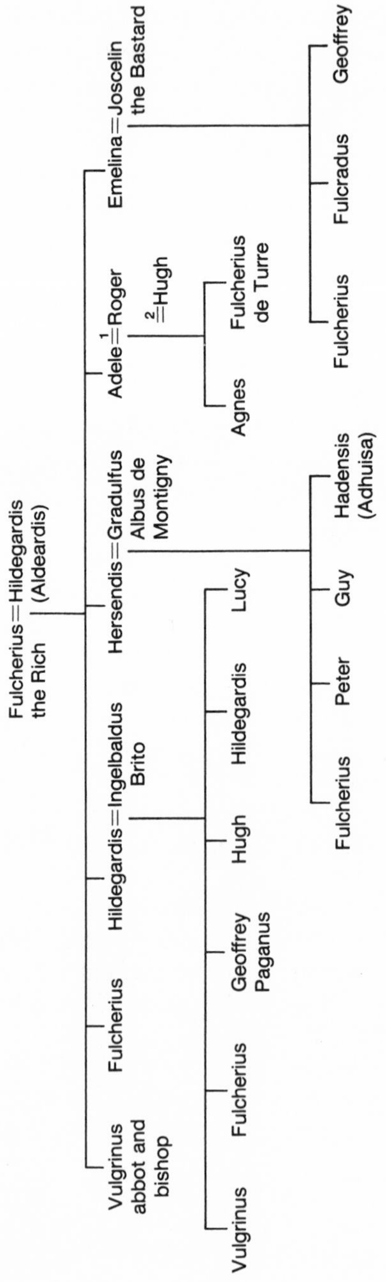

GENEALOGICAL CHART B: THE FAMILY OF FULCHERIUS THE RICH OF VENDÔME

Fulcherius = Hildegardis
the Rich   (Aldeardis)

Vulgrinus abbot and bishop

Fulcherius

Hildegardis = Ingelbaldus Brito

Hersendis = Gradulfus Albus de Montigny

Adele =[1] Roger
      =[2] Hugh

Emelina = Joscelin the Bastard

Vulgrinus

Fulcherius

Geoffrey Paganus

Hugh

Hildegardis

Lucy

Agnes

Fulcherius de Turre

Fulcherius

Fulcradus

Geoffrey

Fulcherius

Peter

Guy

Hadensis (Adhuisa)

GENEALOGICAL CHART C: THE FAMILY OF VISCOUNT FULCRADUS OF VENDÔME

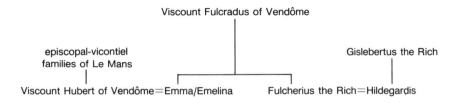

members of the family of Fulcherius the Rich.[44] Thus it is obvious that Hubert was related to that family, and it must be through Vulgrinus, his known cousin from Vendôme.

Since Hubert and Vulgrinus were cousins, either Viscount Hubert or his wife Emma was the brother or sister of Fulcherius the Rich or his wife Hildegardis. The evidence indicates that Hubert's mother Emma was the sister of Fulcherius the Rich. The name Emma appears in the family of Fulcherius, carried by his daughter in its hypocoristic form Emelina. The name Hubert is not carried by any of the many known members of the family of Fulcherius. Thus Bishop Hubert was related to this family through his mother, and the evidence suggests that Fulcherius's wife Hildegardis was from a different family. She had a brother named Gislebertus, whose sons were Arnulf and Nihard, and none of these three ever appears with Bishop Hubert or members of his family.[45] Hildegardis's father appears to have been Gislebertus the Rich of Vendôme.[46] (See Chart C.)

The names Fulcradus and Fulcherius are forms of the same name,[47] so the Viscount Fulcradus of Vendôme who was Viscount Hubert's predecessor appears to have been the father of Emma and Fulcherius the Rich. Thus Fulcradus was succeeded in the viscountship by his son-in-law Hubert and not by his son Fulcherius. Fulcherius may have been considerably younger than his sister Emma, perhaps having been born after the marriage of Hubert and his sister Emma when the viscountship could have been promised to Fulcradus's new son-in-law. Bishop Hubert's side of the family seems to have died much sooner than those of the same generation of the children of Fulcherius the Rich. Bishop Hubert died in 1047 and his sister Hadeburga was dead by 1058.[48] But Vulgrinus did not die until

---

[44] See below, Part II, Nos. 7, 71, 73; the acts not concerning his family members are Part II, Nos. 21, 74, 75.

[45] *Cart. Marmoutier pour le Vendômois,* nos. 30, 173; *Cartulaire de l'abbaye de la Trinité de Vendôme,* ed. Ch. Métais (Vendôme, 1892), 1: no. 136; see Fanning, "Origines familiales de Vulgrin," n. 75.

[46] Fanning, "Origines familiales de Vulgrin," n. 75.

[47] Ibid., p. 252.

[48] See below, Part II, No. 81.

1065[49] and his sister Hildegardis was still alive in 1096,[50] fifty years after Hubert's death. Hubert and Hadeburga were probably much older than Vulgrinus and Hildegardis, which indicates that Fulcherius the Rich was much younger than Emma and Viscount Hubert.

But other information provides another possible explanation for the transmission of the viscountship of Vendôme from Fulcradus to his son-in-law Hubert. A search for the origins of Viscount Hubert, using the prosopographical criteria of family names, offices, lands, and political alliances leads to the county of Maine, where the name Hubert is prominent in the vicontiel and episcopal families going back to the early tenth century.

There was a bishop of Le Mans named Hubert ca. 913–ca. 951.[51] His successor Mainardus (ca. 951–ca. 971) was the brother of the viscount of Le Mans, and the name Hubert appears in the vicontiel family as well.[52] The bishopric was a see that tended to be a hereditary office, for it is known that ca. 971, ca. 997, and ca. 1036, nephew succeeded uncle at Le Mans, from Segenfredus to Avesgaudus to Gervais.[53] Therefore it is very likely that they were related to their earlier tenth-century predecessors Hubert and Mainardus, and thus that they were also related to the viscounts of Le Mans.

Throughout the tenth century, the bishops of Le Mans maintained a common policy of loyalty to the Robertian family of Neustrian marquises and hostility to the family of counts who had succeeded in usurping the county of Maine by 929.[54] This alliance with the Robertians, family relationship between the bishops and viscounts of Le Mans, and prominence of the name Hubert among them suggest that the Viscount Hubert who appeared with Count Robert of Neustria ca. 888–890[55] was a relative, perhaps father or uncle, of Bishop Hubert of Le Mans and was an ancestor of Viscount Radulfus, whose son was named Hubert. It is clear that the bishops and viscounts continued to be closely related at least to the end of the tenth century.

The episcopal–vicontiel clan of Le Mans was supported in its struggle

---

[49] *Actus Pontificum Cenomannis*, p. 373.

[50] *Cart. de la Trinité de Vendôme*, (Vendôme, 1894), 2: no. 354.

[51] *Actus Pontificum Cenomannis*, pp. 348–349.

[52] Ibid., p. 350; and see the original charter, Arch. Maine-et-Loire, H 2106, no. 1 (eleventh-century copy, B. n., ms. lat. nouv. acq. 1930, fol. 130 r-v), published in Paul Marchegay, "Chartes mancelles de l'abbaye de Saint-Florent près Saumur, 848–1209," *Revue historique et archéologique du Maine* 3 (1876), no. 3.

[53] Boussard, "Les évêques en Neustrie," pp. 181–183.

[54] Dhondt, *Principautés territoriales*, p. 101; Boussard, "Les destinées de la Neustrie," pp. 20–22; Latouche, *Histoire du comté du Maine pendant le Xe et le XIe siècle*, Bibliothèque de l'Ecole des hautes études, fasc. 183 (Paris, 1910), pp. 14–16; Werner, "Untersuchungen," 1958, pp. 279–283.

[55] *Cartulaire noir de la cathédrale d'Angers*, ed. Ch. Urseau (Angers, 1908), no. 15. For the dating of this charter, see K. F. Werner, "Zur Arbeitsweise des Regino von Prüm," *Die Welt als Geschichte* 19 (1959), p. 107, n. 30.

against the counts of Maine by its fellow Robertian stalwarts, the counts of Anjou and of Vendôme. Count Geoffrey Greymantle made an alliance with Segenfredus to obtain the bishopric of Le Mans for him around 971.[56] Later, when the bishop clashed with Count Hugh of Maine around 987, he was forced to leave Le Mans. But he found refuge with Count Bouchard of Vendôme and the two allied against Count Hugh.[57]

So far it is evident that Bishop Hubert's family shares a common *Leitname* with the episcopal–vicontiel clan of Le Mans, both hold the offices of viscount and bishop, they share a Robertian (Capetian) alliance, and they are similarly connected to the Anjou–Vendôme political axis. They also have a record of a common landholding. Land at Coëmont in the county of Maine was held by the widow Aremburgis from Bishop Hubert.[58] She was succeeded at Coëmont by her son-in-law Matthew of Montoire, and when he later gave the customs that he held there to the convent of Ronceray, he did so "by the concession of Gervais of Château-du-Loir," the nephew of Bishop Gervais of Le Mans.[59] And when a dispute over that land arose, it was settled in the presence of Bishop Gervais.[60] Therefore both Bishop Hubert and the family of Bishop Gervais of Le Mans held authority over lands at Coëmont in Maine. This confirms the family connection between the two, for it is otherwise difficult to account for such a joint dominion, especially when other evidence already clearly points to such a relationship. The conclusion then is that Viscount Hubert of Vendôme was an outsider to the Vendômois, and actually was a member of the family of the viscounts of Le Mans, which was also very closely related to the bishops of Le Mans.

The most likely time for a matrimonial alliance between the vicontiel families of Le Mans and Vendôme was when Bishop Segenfredus of Le Mans joined with Count Bouchard against the count of Maine, and when the count of Anjou was also a supporter of Segenfredus. Since Bouchard was rarely personally in the county of Vendôme, it must have fallen to the

---

[56] *Actus Pontificum Cenomannis*, p. 353. The text actually gives the name of the count of Anjou who helped Segenfredus as Fulk, but since the former became bishop in 971 (ibid., p. 352) and Count Fulk the Good was succeeded by his son Geoffrey Greymantle ca. 960 (Halphen, *Comté d'Anjou*, p. 6), it must have been Geoffrey who provided the aid to Segenfredus. See also Bachrach, "Geoffrey Greymantle," pp. 25–26, esp. n. 106.

[57] *Actus Pontificum Cenomannis*, pp. 353–354. The date seems reasonable because Anjou was the dominant partner in the alliance with Vendôme. For example, Segenfredus had gone to the count of Anjou for help in gaining the bishopric (see note 56 above). Had Geoffrey Greymantle been able to aid the bishop again, he probably would have returned to him for support. That he did not is most easily explained by the death of Count Geoffrey and the accession of his young and untested son Fulk after 21 July 987 (Halphen, *Comté d'Anjou*, p. 8).

[58] See below, Part II, Nos. 19, 20.

[59] *Cartulaire de l'abbaye du Ronceray d'Angers*, ed. Paul Marchegay (Paris, 1900), no. 392. This Gervais was the son of Robert of Château-du-Loir (*Cartulaire de Château-du-Loir*, ed. Eugène Vallée [Le Mans, 1905], no. 27), who was the brother of Bishop Gervais (*Cartulaire de l'abbaye de Saint-Aubin d'Angers*, ed. Bertrand de Broussillon, 3 vols. [Paris, 1903], no. 402, and *Actus Pontificum Cenomannis*, p. 362).

[60] *Cart. Ronceray*, no. 393.

viscount of Vendôme to assist the count of Anjou in nurturing this alliance. Marriages between families in Maine and the Vendômois are known to have taken place in this period,[61] and it is reasonable that the political union between Bishop Segenfredus and Count Bouchard was accompanied by a marriage between one of Segenfredus's close relatives and a member of the family of Bouchard's assistant and chief supporter in Vendôme, Viscount Fulcradus. And Fulcradus was already connected to the count of Anjou, who was likewise allied with Segenfredus.

The alliance between Segenfredus and Count Geoffrey Greymantle was accomplished by ca. 971, and between Segenfredus and Count Bouchard by ca. 985, so such a marital connection between Le Mans and Vendôme would have occurred in that same period. Bishop Hubert's birth around 980–985 is consistent with this information. The picture that emerges is one that illuminates the nature of the politics of the middle Loire in the latter tenth century, as well as the dynastic policies of the great families of that region.

As Angevin expansion turned to the north, Count Geoffrey Greymantle exploited the antagonism between the counts of Maine and the family of the bishops and viscounts of Le Mans, which also supported the Robertians of Paris. Count Geoffrey used his connections with King Lothair to assist Segenfredus in obtaining his appointment to the see of Le Mans. Count Bouchard of Vendôme cooperated fully with Anjou in hostility towards the count of Maine and allied with Segenfredus. Count Hugh of Maine now faced an Angevin threat from the south and a Vendômois threat from the east. As the resident power in Vendôme, Viscount Fulcradus was Segenfredus's steady friend in Vendôme. Sometime in the 970s or early 980s, the two sealed their alliance by a marriage between Fulcradus's daughter Emma and Hubert, a close relative of Segenfredus, perhaps a younger brother, nephew, or cousin. Hubert was promised the viscountship after Fulcradus's death, perhaps because this union was of such great importance to Fulcradus, Bouchard, or Geoffrey Greymantle. Or it may have been that Fulcherius the Rich had not yet been born, and when he was, his father's office had already been promised or transmitted to his brother-in-law Hubert.

When Count Fulk designated the younger Hubert as bishop of Angers in 1005 or 1006, he was able to nurture two relationships at once. In the Vendômois, he rewarded Viscount Hubert for his fidelity and also the family of Fulcherius the Rich at a time when, as will be seen, the Angevin hold on Vendôme was in great danger of slipping away. The importance of these two families can be seen from the Customs of Count Bouchard,[62]

---

[61] For example, Odelina the daughter of Viscount Radulfus of Le Mans married Hugh of Lavardin (*Gesta Ambaziensium dominorum* in *Chroniques des comtes d'Anjou*, ed. Louis Halphen and René Poupardin [Paris, 1913], p. 76).

[62] *Cart. Trinité de Vendôme*, no. 2.

which names the seven men who had the duty of guarding the *castrum* of Vendôme, and who were thus the most powerful men in the county. Of these seven, four appear to belong to this family group—Viscount Hubert and Fulcherius the Rich, and Gislebertus the Rich (father of Fulcherius's wife Hildegardis) and Gundacrius (another of her relatives). Additionally, Viscount Hubert and Gundacrius are among the nine magnates of the Vendômois to whom Bishop Fulbert of Chartres addressed a letter attempting to establish his authority over the county.[63]

Hubert's nomination to the Angevin see also brought his relatives in the county of Maine even more closely into Count Fulk's network of alliances. The known members of his family formed three of the most powerful groups in Maine. The family of the viscounts of Le Mans from which Viscount Hubert originated can be traced back with certainty to the mid-tenth century, about the time that he would have been born. As mentioned earlier, the Viscount Hubert of the late 880s and Bishop Hubert of Le Mans of the first half of the tenth century were probably earlier representatives of the family.

This Bishop Hubert was succeeded by Mainardus, whose brother was the viscount of Le Mans. In 967 and 969 the viscount was named Radulfus,[64] and it is certain that Mainardus was still bishop in 969,[65] so this Radulfus was probably his brother. By ca. 971, Mainardus had been succeeded by Segenfredus, but the next information on the viscount comes from just after the year 1000, when the viscount is again named Radulfus, his wife is Widenoris, and their sons are Ivo (or Ivelinus) the cleric who was also the first-born son, Geoffrey, Radulfus, Hubert, and Odo.[66] Ivelinus became an archdeacon of the cathedral of Le Mans, while Hubert became its treasurer.[67] This provides further evidence of the kinship between the vicontiel family and the bishop of Le Mans, in this case Avesgaudus, the nephew and successor of Segenfredus. The brother Geoffrey was the apparent founder of the house of Sablé, important in the affairs of Maine throughout the eleventh century.[68] This second Radulfus was followed at

---

[63] *Letters and Poems of Fulbert of Chartres*, no. 10; and see below, chap. 3, n. 17.

[64] Ch. de Grandmaison, "Fragments de chartes du Xe siècle provenant de Saint-Julien de Tours," *Bibliothèque de l'Ecole des chartes* 47 (1886), nos. 21, 23. On the viscounts of Le Mans, see J. Depoin, "Recherche sur la chronologie des vicomtes du Maine," *Bulletin historique et philologique du Comité des travaux historiques et scientifiques* (1909), pp. 125–146; Latouche, *Comté du Maine*, app. 5, "Les premiers vicomtes du Maine," pp. 127–131; Abbé Angot, "Les vicomtes du Maine," *Bulletin de la commission historique et archéologique de la Mayenne* 30 (1914), pp. 180–232, 320–342, 404–424.

[65] *Chartularium Insignis Ecclesiae Cenomannis Quod Dicitur Liber Albus* (Le Mans, 1869), no. 108.

[66] See above, n. 52, and see below, Part II, Nos. 3, 4.

[67] *Cartulaire des abbayes de Saint-Pierre de la Couture et de Saint-Pierre de Solesmes*, ed. Bénédictines de Solesmes (Le Mans, 1881), no. 4 (for the dating of this act, see Latouche, *Comté du Maine*, catalogue des actes no. 16, p. 141); *Cartulaire de Saint-Vincent du Mans*, ed. S. Menjot d'Elbenne (Le Mans, 1888–1913), no. 186 (see also Latouche, *Comté du Maine*, catalogue des actes, no. 19).

[68] See below, Part II, Nos. 3, 4.

Le Mans by his younger son Radulfus (also called Roscelinus, the hypocoristic form of Radulfus), who appears as viscount by around 1015 and is
still seen in the 1030s. His wife's name was Godehelt, and their sons were
a fourth Radulfus, who became viscount of Le Mans, and Geoffrey, who
succeeded his father-in-law Hugh as lord of Braitel.[69]

Radulfus IV married Emma, the niece of Bishop Hubert of Angers by his
sister Hadeberga.[70] The marriage probably took place not long after 1022,
for it was in that year that a Viscount Radulfus and another Radulfus
appear in Vendôme with Bishop Hubert, many members of his family, and
Count Fulk.[71] This has the appearance of a meeting to arrange the marriage
between Radulfus IV and Emma. As will be seen, Emma and Radulfus
emerge as Bishop Hubert's heirs and greatly prosper under his tutelage.

Since Bishop Hubert's father seems to have come from this family, how
was he related to it? Bishop Hubert's birth in the early 980s, Viscount
Hubert's death by 1024, his functioning as viscount of Vendôme between
987 and 1005, all point to his own birth in the 950s or 960s. His marriage to
the daughter of the viscount of Vendôme and his succession to that office,
and this marriage's being part of an Angevin–Vendômois alliance against
the count of Maine indicate that he was very closely related to Bishop
Mainardus and his brother Viscount Radulfus I of Le Mans, both of whom
were active from ca. 950 to ca. 970. Viscount Hubert's birth in the 950s or
960s gives the appearance that he was of the next generation, that is
probably the son of Bishop Mainardus, of Viscount Radulfus I, or of an
otherwise unknown brother or son to them (see Genealogical Chart D).

The origins of the bishops of Le Mans after Mainardus are also poorly
known before the year 1000. Segenfredus succeeded Mainardus, and he in
turn was followed by his nephew Avesgaudus.[72] This nephew was the son
of Ivo of Bellême and Godehildis. His brother William succeeded their
father Ivo as lord of Bellême, his sister Hildeburgis married Haimo of
Château-du-Loir, while his sister Godehildis was the mother of Abbot
Albert of Micy and grandmother of Archbishop Arnulf of Tours. Avesgaudus was succeeded as bishop of Le Mans by his nephew Gervais of
Château-du-Loir, the son of his sister Hildeburgis.[73] Thus this family had
two important and powerful branches that were leading figures in the
county of Maine, that of Bellême and that of Château-du-Loir. (See
Chart E.)

---

[69] *Cartulaire de Saint-Victeur au Mans*, ed. Paul de Farcy (Paris, 1895), no. 1, 4; Viscount
Radulfus III witnessed a charter issued under Bishop Gervais of Le Mans, who was ordained
19 December 1038 at the latest (see the dating of Part II, No. 38, below), *Cartulaire de
Saint-Vincent du Mans*, no. 363; for his son Geoffrey, see *Cart. St.-Vincent*, nos. 590, 624, and
on the lords of Braitel, see S. Menjot d'Elbenne, "Les sires de Braitel au Maine du XIe au XIIIe
siècle," *Revue historique et archéologique du Maine* 1 (1876), pp. 192–213, 234–239.

[70] See below, Part II, No. 81.

[71] See below, Part II, No. 7.

[72] See above, n. 53.

[73] Jacques Boussard, "La seigneurie de Bellême aux Xe et XIe siècles," *Mélanges . . . de Louis
Halphen*, pp. 44–47.

GENEALOGICAL CHART D: THE FAMILY OF THE VISCOUNTS OF LE MANS

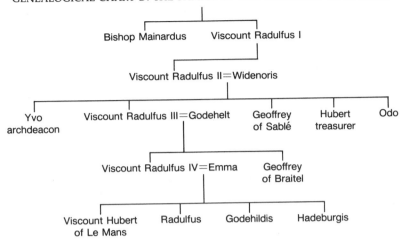

It is not known if Segenfredus was the brother of Ivo of Bellême or of Godehildis, but the latter is the more attractive hypothesis. Segenfredus passed the bishopric on to his nephew Avesgaudus, and when a see was transmitted from uncle to nephew in this period, it was usually from

GENEALOGICAL CHART E: THE HOUSES OF BELLEME AND CHATEAU-DU-LOIR*

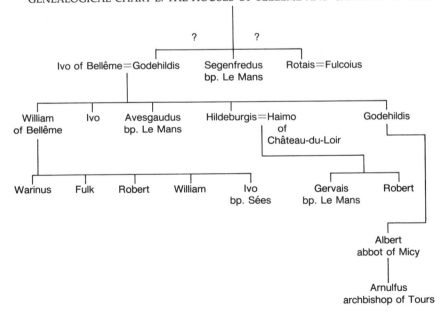

* After Boussard, "La seigneurie de Bellême aux Xe et XIe siècles," p. 47.

mother's brother to sister's son.[74] As has been seen, Segenfredus was probably related to his episcopal predecessor Mainardus. The connection between the viscounts of Le Mans and Segenfredus and Avesgaudus is reinforced by two of the children of Viscount Radulfus II, Ivo and Hubert, gaining the important cathedral offices of archdeacon and treasurer under Avesgaudus. Noting that Gervais and Avesgaudus were nephew and uncle matrilineally suggest the same relationship for Avesgaudus and Segenfredus, and also for Segenfredus and Mainardus. Of course this cannot be known with certainty, but it is a strong possibility that a sister to Bishop Mainardus and Viscount Radulfus I was the mother of Bishop Segenfredus. It would also explain how Bishop Hubert of Angers, as a second generation descendant of the siblings Mainardus, Radulfus I, or their sister, and Bishop Gervais of Le Mans, as a third generation descendant of that same group, came to have the common land holding at Coëmont in Maine.

Whatever the precise nature of these family ties, it is clear that Hubert was related to the families of the viscounts Radulfi as well as to the houses of Bellême and Château-du-Loir in the county of Maine. When Fulk named Hubert bishop of Angers, he chose a scion of the most powerful families of both Maine and Vendôme, and both branches of the family were to be of great use in Fulk's maneuvers to the north and northeast.

Bishop Hubert is not known to have had any children of his own, and after he was in office, he devoted special attention to two of his relatives, his niece Emma and his cousin Vulgrinus. Emma was the only known child of Hubert's sister Hadeberga and her husband Stephen.[75] As has been seen, she married Viscount Radulfus IV of Le Mans. The marriage may have been arranged by the end of 1022, but it must have been concluded by 1026, for two years later Emma and Radulfus appear with at least two children in a charter along with Bishop Hubert.[76]

Since Emma was the only grandchild of Viscount Hubert of Vendôme and Emma, she and her husband Radulfus stood as the heirs to all the lands and to the viscountship of Vendôme.[77] Bishop Hubert clearly saw Emma, Radulfus, and their children as his heirs, for they repeatedly appear in charters with him when he disposed of family lands, so that they could also give their authorizations for his donations.[78] Hubert's preponderant influence on the family can be seen by Emma's burial at the monastery of St. Serge, Bishop Hubert's own episcopal abbey, where he and both of Emma's parents were also buried.[79] Also, the elder son of Emma and Radulfus was named Hubert, and he succeeded his father as viscount of Le

---

[74] For example, Archbishop Hugh of Tours was succeeded in 1023 by his sister's son Arnulf (Boussard, "Les évêques en Neustrie," p. 176).

[75] See below, Part II, No. 81.

[76] See below, Part II, No. 20.

[77] The next known viscount of Vendôme after Bishop Hubert's father is Radulfus; see below, Part II, No. 73.

[78] See below, Part II, Nos. 20, 52, 81.

[79] See below, Part II, No. 81.

Mans.[80] For four generations, viscounts of Le Mans had been named Radulfus, but there is this one Hubert (named when Bishop Hubert was exerting such an influence on the family), and then the succession of Radulfi resumes for several more generations. While the name Hubert was not unknown to the family of the viscounts of Le Mans, the fact that it was given to the heir to the viscountship was unusual. And since the younger son of Emma and Radulfus IV was named Radulfus but succeeded to the maternal inheritance, it is clear that Bishop Hubert was being honored by Emma and Radulfus when the son who received the paternal inheritance was given his name.

Emma, Radulfus IV, and their younger son Radulfus Paganus did inherit the family position in Vendôme, obviously with the approval of the counts of Anjou who were the real masters of the county. Radulfus IV and Bishop Hubert were associated together as seigneurs in the Vendômois,[81] Radulfus IV and his two sons maintained the family interests at Bezay and elsewhere in the region,[82] and Radulfus IV succeeded his wife's grandfather Hubert as viscount of Vendôme.[83] His son Radulfus Paganus followed him as viscount, and was seen at such old family lands as Bezay and Mazé. He married Agatha, daughter of Count Fulk l'Oison of Vendôme,[84] so the family position at the center of power in the county was secured through the end of the eleventh century.

Bishop Hubert was important to Emma and Radulfus IV in more ways than simply in favoring them as they inherited lands and offices in Vendôme. They also benefited from Hubert's position as bishop of Angers, at whose disposal were the church lands of the diocese and ecclesiastical offices in the cathedral and monasteries of Anjou. Bishop Hubert was an important conduit to the favor of the counts of Anjou, who of course granted lands and offices to their *fideles*. With the great expansion of Angevin domination under Fulk Nerra and his son Geoffrey Martel, such a connection could be very beneficial.

Hubert's role in advancing his niece and her husband can be seen in the affair of the Mauges, an extensive territory to the southwest of Angers, touching both the Loire and Loyon rivers on the north. As will be seen, the Mauges patrimony of Bishop Renaud II, Hubert's predecessor, became the focus of a dispute between that bishop and Count Fulk Nerra after Renaud made a number of donations from his lands to the cathedral of Angers and the monastery of St.-Serge d'Angers. Immediately before Renaud's death in 1005 or just after it, Fulk nullified the bishop's donations and distributed

---

[80] *Cartulaire du prieuré de Saint-Hippolyte de Vivoin et ses annexes,* ed. L.-J. Denis (Paris, 1894), p. 217, no. 1.

[81] See below, Part II, No. 73.

[82] See above, n. 42.

[83] See above, n. 77.

[84] See above, n. 42; *Cart. Marmoutier pour le Vendômois,* no. 94; *Cart. Trinité de Vendôme,* no. 271.

the lands to his own *milites*. He also built the fortress of Montrevault in the center of the Mauges to guard Angers on the southwest.[85]

When Hubert became bishop of Angers, he continued his family's policy of loyalty to the counts of Anjou, supporting Fulk's actions in the Mauges even though they meant a loss to the cathedral and monastery.[86] In his turn, the count came to entrust the territory to Hubert, who later gained Fulk's permission to repurchase some of the disputed lands. Part of these lands he returned to St. Serge, but others he gave to his niece Emma.[87] She, her husband Radulfus IV, and their son Radulfus Paganus soon formed the principal family in the Mauges.[88] Radulfus Paganus gained his family's maternal inheritance, so he not only stepped into the family position in Vendôme, but also in the Mauges. He maintained his family's preponderant position in the Mauges, and he also possessed the fortress of Montrevault. He was viscount of Montrevault,[89] and he was succeeded in that office by his son and grandson.[90] Thus Bishop Hubert was instrumental, along with the agreement of the counts of Anjou, in making his family the dominating force in the Mauges.

Probably due to the favor of Count Fulk and the consistent family loyalty, Radulfus IV was also viscount of Lude.[91] Thus from his marriage to Emma and the resulting beneficence of her uncle Bishop Hubert and that of the counts of Anjou, Radulfus IV, already viscount of Le Mans and a major power in Maine, came to inherit his wife's extensive lands in the Vendômois and the viscountship of Vendôme, to receive many lands in the Mauges and perhaps the *castrum* and viscountship of Montrevault (since his son certainly held them later), and the viscountship of Lude. Indeed, he must have been one of the most important men in the entire region. It is small wonder that his elder son and heir was named Hubert.

Hubert's heirs through Emma and Radulfus IV held their powerful position through the end of the century. As has been seen, Radulfus

---

[85] See below, chap. 3, n. 24.

[86] Ibid.

[87] See below, Part II, No. 81.

[88] See below, chap. 3, nn. 35–38.

[89] Paul Marchegay, "Chartes angevines des onzième et douzième siècles," *Bibliothèque de l'Ecole des chartes* 36 (1875), no. 16; for his possession of the *castrum*, see the second cartulary of St. Serge, Musée départementale Dobrée, Nantes, ms. 3, fol. 153, no. 351.

[90] He was succeeded as viscount by his son Fulk (*Cart. noir de la cathédrale d'Angers*, nos. 63, 66), who was succeeded by his son Roscelinus (B. n., ms. lat. 5446, p. 314).

[91] After Radulfus and his son Hubert authorized and witnessed the sale of lands at Bezay to Marmoutier (*Cart. Marmoutier pour le Vendômois*, no. 90), in 1071, Radulfus the son of Viscount Radulfus of Lude made a calumny against that sale and against land at Nourray because he had not given his authorization to them (ibid., no. 94). Between 1056 and 1058, Viscount Radulfus and Emma gave part and sold part of the church of Luché to St. Aubin (*Cart. St.-Aubin*, no. 355), and later a calumny against that church was given up by Hubert, the son of Viscount Radulfus of Lude (ibid., no. 356). Moreover, the wife of Radulfus's son Hubert was called the viscountess of Lude (*Cart. St.-Aubin*, no. 370). Therefore it is clear that Viscount Radulfus of Le Mans was also the viscount of Lude. See also below, Part II, No. 81, for an association of Viscount Radulfus with Lude.

Paganus was a leading magnate in the Vendômois and the Mauges, was viscount of Vendôme and Montrevault, and married a daughter of the count of Vendôme. His older brother Hubert succeeded their father Radulfus IV (who died ca. 1065–70)[92] and was viscount of Le Mans and of Lude. He held the fortresses of Beaumont (from which his family later took its name), Fresnay, and Ste.-Suzanne.[93] It was as the celebrated Viscount Hubert of Ste.-Suzanne that he resisted the efforts of Duke William of Normandy to conquer the county of Maine. Finally Duke William had to come to terms with him.[94] Hubert married well, to the daughter of Count William of Nevers.[95] The memory of the family's association with the bishopric of Angers lingered on to the turn of the thirteenth century, when this Hubert's descendants Radulfus of Beaumont (1177–1197) and William of Beaumont (1202–1240) also sat on the Angevin episcopal chair that their distant kinsman had previously occupied.[96]

Emma and Radulfus had two daughters, named Godehildis and Hadeburgis. The former married William, lord of Bellême and the grandson of Ivo of Bellême (the founder of the house and brother-in-law to Bishop Segenfredus).[97] Thus the vicontiel and episcopal houses of Le Mans were again briefly connected. Godehildis was the daughter of Radulfus IV while William was brother to Bishop Yvo of Sens, cousin to Bishop Gervais of Le Mans, nephew to Bishop Avesgaudus, and great-nephew to Bishop Segenfredus.

The other relative of Bishop Hubert who benefited significantly from his high office and political connections was his cousin Vulgrinus, son of Fulcherius the Rich. After a military career, he entered his family's favorite monastery, Marmoutier at Tours.[98] Under Abbot Albert, his fellow man of the Vendômois and possibly one of his relatives,[99] Vulgrinus rose to be prior to the abbey. Then, in 1046, as his cousin Bishop Hubert was com-

---

[92] He was still alive in 1065 (*Cart. Marmoutier pour le Vendômois*, no. 90), but he had been succeeded at Le Mans by his son Hubert by 1069–1070 (*Recueil des actes de Philippe Ier, Roi de France [1059–1108]*, ed. M. Prou [Paris, 1908], no. 50, pp. 134–137).

[93] *Cart. St.-Vincent*, no. 626.

[94] Ibid., no. 492; *The Ecclesiastical History of Orderic Vitalis*, ed. and tr. Marjory Chibnall (Oxford, 1973), 4: VII. 10.

[95] *Recueil Philippe Ier*, no. 50.

[96] See Angot, "Les vicomtes du Maine," pp. 202–207.

[97] Boussard, "Seigneurie de Bellême," pp. 46–47.

[98] See above, n. 35.

[99] On Albert's origins, see Guillot, *Comte d'Anjou*, 1: p. 245; A. Clerval, "Albert," *Dictionnaire d'histoire et de géographie ecclésiastiques*, vol. 1, ed. Alfred Baudrillart, Albert Vogt, and Urbain Rouziés (Paris, 1912), cols. 1432–1435. Albert's brother was Hubert of la Ferté (see Dom Claude Chantelou, *Cartulaire tourangeau et sceaux des abbés*, ed. Paul Nobilleau [Tours, 1879], p. 27). Therefore the Hubert of la Ferté who had the duty of guarding the *castellum* of Vendôme during November (*Cart. Trinité de Vendôme*, no. 2) was probably the father of Abbot Albert and Hubert of la Ferté. The sons of the younger Hubert of la Ferté were Sanzo, Hubert, Hugh, Baldwin, and Sulpicius (Clerval, "Albert," col. 1432), so Hubert was a *Leitname* of this family, just as it was in Bishop Hubert's family. Hence a tie of kinship may have united Abbot Albert, Bishop Hubert, and Vulgrinus. On the closeness between Bishop Hubert and Abbot Albert, see Guillot, *Comte d'Anjou*, 1: pp. 245–247.

pleting his restoration of the monastery of St.-Serge d'Angers, Hubert
"asked" Abbot Albert to nominate one of his monks as a suitable abbot for
St. Serge. It could have been no surprise that to Albert the most suitable
candidate was Vulgrinus, who by now was frequently seen in the company
of Bishop Hubert. Vulgrinus was installed as abbot on 1 March 1046,[100]
and now was close to Count Geoffrey Martel and the associate of powerful
abbots and bishops of the region.

Vulgrinus had an even brighter church career ahead of him. In 1056
Count Geoffrey Martel used the right given him earlier by King Henry to
name the bishop of Le Mans.[101] This was a critical nomination for Geoffrey. For a decade he had been struggling with Bishop Gervais of Le Mans
for control of the county of Maine. Geoffrey had lost the first round of the
warfare, but he was successful in the second. He captured Gervais in 1048,
and by 1051 he was the master of Maine. He then freed Gervais, who
found refuge at the court of Duke William of Normandy, whose ambitious
eyes now fell on Maine. Gervais, who could not return to Le Mans, was an
embarrassment to the church. At last King Henry, also alarmed at Normandy's rise under William, found a solution to the dilemma by translat-
ing Gervais to the archiepiscopal see of Reims and allowing Count Geoffrey to name his own man as the new bishop of Le Mans.[102]

Obviously this was a crucial time for Geoffrey. He was at last in possession of Le Mans after twenty years of difficulties with its bishop. Duke
William was ever more menacing to the north, having captured some
fortifications on the Norman–Maine frontier (1051–1052), and defeated
Count Geoffrey and King Henry at Mortemer-sur-Eaune (1054), and established Norman control over strategic Ambrières.[103] It was essential for
Geoffrey to have a cooperative bishop in Le Mans to help keep the county
in Angevin hands.

The choice of Vulgrinus for Le Mans in 1056 has been seen in simplistic
terms. Vulgrinus has been described as an Angevin and as Geoffrey's
protégé,[104] and it has been implied that Vulgrinus was chosen after Geoffrey consulted with the people of Le Mans.[105] Yet the real clue to Vulgrinus's selection in 1056 was undoubtedly his family connections. He was

---

[100] See below, Part II, No. 53.

[101] Guillot, Comte d'Anjou, 1: pp. 58–94, esp. 92–94. The date when the king transferred
this right to Count Geoffrey and the circumstances surrounding it are not clear. For differing
accounts of these events, see Guillot, loc. cit.; Bates, Normandy Before 1066, p. 78; Halphen,
Comté d'Anjou, pp. 76, 79, and n. 1, 80, 125 n. 5; Latouche, Comté du Maine, pp. 27–30, 79; Jan
Dhondt, "Henri Ier, l'Empire et l'Anjou (1043–1056)," Revue belge de philologie et d'histoire 25
(1946–47), p. 87 n. 1.

[102] Latouche, Comté du Maine, pp. 26–33; Halphen, Comté d'Anjou, pp. 66–80; David C.
Douglas, William the Conqueror: The Norman Impact upon England (Berkeley, 1967), pp. 57–72;
Guillot, Comte d'Anjou, 1: pp. 63–96; Bates, Normandy Before 1066, pp. 76–78; Fanning,
"Origines familiales de Vulgrin," n. 7.

[103] Ibid.

[104] Halphen, Comté d'Anjou, p. 80; Bates, Normandy Before 1066, p. 78.

[105] Latouche, Comté du Maine, p. 83.

first cousin to Bishop Hubert, whose father was of the episcopal and vicontiel families of Le Mans. He was Hubert's protégé, and Hubert's heirs were Radulfus IV and Emma, the viscount and viscountess of Le Mans, who were strongly attached to Count Fulk and Count Geoffrey, and they held vital fortresses in the county of Maine. Radulfus IV may have been strongly anti-Norman, for certainly his son Hubert of Ste.-Suzanne was a constant source of irritation for Duke William. Thus in naming Vulgrinus to the see of Le Mans, Geoffrey was adding to his strength there.[106] Viscountess Emma and Vulgrinus were cousins, she and her husband had appeared together with Vulgrinus and Bishop Hubert, and from 1046 on they were frequently seen with Vulgrinus.[107] The record indicates close and friendly ties among them.

Geoffrey Martel named worthy men who met the "modern" standards to his bishoprics,[108] but Vulgrinus's appointment shows that while he was a good monk who made a good bishop, he was also the man who could best promote Angevin interests in Le Mans in the face of Duke William's threats. Now the bishop and viscount of Le Mans were united behind Count Geoffrey and closely tied by kinship. They both had prospered under the aegis of Bishop Hubert and it was he who first brought them all together in the 1040s. The key to understanding why Count Geoffrey named this particular man to be bishop of this particular see at this particular time is provided by Bishop Hubert.

While there is no clear evidence that Bishop Hubert favored any other relatives as he did Emma, Radulfus, and Vulgrinus, it is probable that Vulgrinus's predecessor as abbot of St.-Serge d'Angers was also his kinsman, for he was also named Hubert.[109] This was an episcopal abbey, and it is likely that Bishop Renaud II had named one of his relatives to its abbotship earlier.[110] It would be unusual if Abbot Hubert were not a relative of Bishop Hubert, but since so little is known of him, it cannot be a certainty.[111]

---

[106] Fanning, "Origines familiales de Vulgrin," and "From *Miles* to *Episcopus.*"

[107] See below, Part II, No. 52.

[108] As in his selection of Eusebius Bruno as bishop of Angers in 1047; Guillot, *Comte d'Anjou,* 1: pp. 249–252, 263–268.

[109] See below, Part II, No. 10.

[110] Under Bishop Renaud, the abbot of St. Serge was also named Renaud; B. n., ms. lat. 1930, Livre noir de Saint-Florent, fol. 23v–24v.

[111] It is also possible that Bishop Hubert used his cathedral's archidiaconate to reward his relatives (this was common, as in the case of Archbishop Anno of Cologne [Karl Leyser, "Maternal Kin in Early Germany: A Reply," *Past and Present* 49 (1970), p. 134], and Bishop Gervais of Le Mans served as the treasurer of the cathedral of Le Mans under his uncle Avesgaudus before he succeeded to the see [*Cart. St.-Pierre de la Couture,* no. 7]). The archdeacons Burchard and Guy (below, Part II, no. 10; and see below, chap. 4, n. 33) may have been related. Burchard also had a son named Guy (*Cart. St.-Aubin,* no. 399). The names Burchard and Guy were common in the Vendômois (*Cart. Trinité de Vendôme,* nos. 34, 70, 78; and see below, Part II, No. 13), and one of Hubert's own relatives was named Guy (see above, n. 41, and below, n. 113). Moreover, Archdeacon Guy's wife was named Emma (below, Part II, No. 13; *Cart. Ronceray,* no. 40), one of the prominent names in Bishop Hubert's family. One

Towards the end of Hubert's life, another relative from Vendôme may have been moving into Hubert's entourage. In the last year of Hubert's life, Guy the son of Gradulfus twice appeared as a witness to donations made to St. Serge and Marmoutier by Bishop Hubert.[112] This appears to be Guy, the son of Hersendis (daughter of Fulcherius the Rich) and Gradulfus Albus of Montigny.[113] Guy, his brothers Peter and Fulcherius, their parents, and Bishop Hubert had also cooperated to sell half of a church to Geoffrey Martel's wife Agnes, who in turn gave it to the monastery of Trinité de Vendôme.[114]

This examination of Bishop Hubert's family has revealed that he was indeed a "typical" bishop in the region of the middle Loire in the period 950–1050. He was of the upper nobility and he was from the region of his see. But by being able to trace his ancestors back to the mid-tenth century, by following his family members into the later eleventh century, and by being aware of his family considerations, we can move beyond classifying Hubert as a certain type of bishop. We can begin to assess the importance of the family to a great figure like Hubert and we can judge the role of the family in the noble society as represented by Hubert and his kin.

First, it is clear that there was more to becoming a bishop than having the proper social and geographical background. In 1005, there must have been dozens of men who were from comital, vicontiel, and episcopal families in the region of the middle Loire. But the son of the viscount of Vendôme was chosen by Count Fulk for a variety of reasons. As will be seen in the next chapter, Fulk's hold on the county of Vendôme was in great jeopardy, and by naming young Hubert, he thus brought many of the most powerful families of that county into a closer association with him, which greatly secured his power there. Also, Fulk was intent on making further inroads into the county of Maine, and Hubert's kinship with the bishops and viscounts of Le Mans would have been of great usefulness in this effort.[115]

But it is also clear that his family's tradition of loyalty to the counts of Anjou must have been a primary consideration that went far in recommending Hubert to Count Fulk. His appointment can be seen as a reward

---

of the sons of Guy and Emma was Albericus (below, Part II, No. 13), and Bishop Hubert may have had a *nepos* named Albericus (below, Part II, No. 77). Albericus is present in the episcopal–vicontiel family of Le Mans, to which Bishop Hubert was related (*Actus Pontificum Cenomannis*, p. 354; *Gesta Ambaziensium Dominorum*, p. 76). Another indication of a Vendômois origin for Archdeacon Burchard is that when he gave the church at Briollay to St. Serge (below, Part II, No. 44), witnesses from Vendôme were present (Nihard of Lavardin, Renaud the son of Drogo, who was probably the son of Drogo of Vendôme [*Cart. Marmoutier pour le Vendômois*, no. 95]). This information is not conclusive, but it does indicate the strong possibility that archdeacons Burchard and Guy were related to each other, that they were from Vendôme, and that they were related to Bishop Hubert.

[112] See below, Part II, Nos. 77, 79.
[113] See above, n. 41.
[114] See below, Part II, No. 71.
[115] Fanning, "Family and Episcopal Election," pp. 42, 46–50.

for past faithfulness, but there was also the promise of future loyalty. After his recent conflict with Bishop Renaud II, Fulk must have been anxious to have a faithful supporter at the head of the Angevin see, especially since he was probably already at work despoiling Renaud's donations of lands in the Mauges to the ecclesiastical establishments. He would have wanted a cooperative bishop who would cause no trouble for him in the Mauges and who would support him in his other enterprises as well.[116] Therefore it was to a family of proven loyalty that Fulk turned in 1005/1006 to find his bishop. The life-long support for the count of Anjou that Bishop Hubert demonstrated, and the backing of Angevin policies in Vendôme, Maine, and the Mauges given by his family over several generations are evidence of the wisdom of Fulk's selection in 1005/1006. This choice was not just a judgment of the candidate himself. It was also a consideration of his family's position with the count of Anjou.

Second, the importance of the family to a great magnate such as Hubert can be seen. Once in office, Hubert stayed firmly attached to his relatives. He continued to be an important seigneur in the Vendômois and he can be seen taking care of his family lands there, acting in a family setting. He was prominent as a *paterfamilias* after the death of his father Viscount Hubert. He took his niece Emma and her husband Radulfus IV under his protection as his heirs and helped secure Radulfus's succession to the viscountship of Vendôme, with the support of the count of Anjou.

Moreover, Hubert was bishop of Angers in a family setting as well. His mother and father assisted him in his rebuilding of the cathedral of Angers. He appointed one kinsman, Hubert, as abbot of St.-Serge d'Angers, and after him he brought in his cousin Vulgrinus to head the same house, thus introducing him to the very heart of the Angevin power network. This in turn led to Vulgrinus's rise to the bishopric of Le Mans, an appointment that was vitally dependent upon his family connections through Bishop Hubert and the same tradition of family loyalty to the Angevin counts. Just as Hubert succeeded the troublesome Renaud II at Angers, Vulgrinus succeeded the vexatious Gervais at Le Mans. When it was vital that the counts have a loyal bishop, they turned to the same family. Bishop Hubert also used church resources as well as his personal wealth and his good offices with the counts of Anjou to establish Emma and Radulfus IV as the dominant family in the Mauges. Thanks in great part to Hubert, they came to hold a vast complex of fortresses and vicontiel offices in Maine, Vendôme, and the Mauges. When Hubert became bishop, his whole family prospered along with him.

Third, it is clear that Hubert had a family policy of his own that was independent of the larger politics that swirled around him. He remained a seigneur of the Vendômois after his episcopal appointment. He was there frequently with members of his family and he saw to it that his niece and

---

[116] See below, chap. 3, nn. 19–32.

her family succeeded to the hereditary lands and offices there. He also used his position as bishop of Angers to promote his family. His niece and her husband gained church lands that made them powerful in the Mauges, while his cousin Vulgrinus, and probably other relatives as well, were given church offices. In addition, these kinsmen were brought into a close relationship with the counts of Anjou, which brought them additional favors, lands, and promotions. Bishop Hubert was not a dupe who spinelessly followed the aggressive policies of Angevin counts. He was busy throughout his episcopacy looking after his patrimony and his relatives, and he used every means available to him to advance their resources and interests. His rise to the bishopric of Angers in 1006 was only the beginning of his personal program of taking care of his kinsmen. Whatever the cost to his family in obtaining Count Fulk's nomination of Hubert, it was well worth the price. It was merely an investment that could lead to even greater returns in the future.

It is evident that the family was still seen in a wide context in the first half of the eleventh century. Hubert's concern extended at least to his niece, his first cousin, and his first cousins once-removed. There does not seem to have been a concentration on patrilineal descent in Bishop Hubert's family and in its associated branches. His father obtained the viscountship of Vendôme from his father-in-law, Hubert himself devoted his attention to his sister's daughter, and Viscount Radulfus IV named his elder son and heir for his wife's uncle. It is also apparent that primogeniture was not a major factor in determining family policy. Bishop Hubert seems to have been the only son born to his parents, yet he became a bishop, which resulted in the end of the male line of his family. It should be recalled that the eldest of the five sons of Viscount Radulfus II of Le Mans was a cleric, while a younger brother succeeded to the viscountship.[117]

In this age in the area of the middle Loire, first-born sons or even only sons could be destined for an ecclesiastical career. The explanation seems to be that the family was conceived of in wide terms, and not narrowly from father to eldest son. There was a large family with which one identified. Bishop Hubert's career illustrates this point. His father may not have been succeeded by a son or by a descendant in the male line, but it must not have mattered very greatly to him. In gaining a bishopric for his son, the family had far greater resources available to it. Not only were the family lands and offices retained at least through the end of the century, but also new lands and offices came to it as a result of young Hubert's episcopacy.

One can also observe how Hubert's family maintained and augmented its position over the period of a century and a half. They made marriages with families of equal or greater social and economic standing than their

---

[117] See above, n. 66.

own. They were consistently loyal to the counts of Anjou, which ensured for them a flow of lands, offices, and goodwill with the success of Angevin enterprises throughout the region. They also actively supported and promoted each other when they had such opportunities. They had a family consciousness and a family policy. Hubert's episcopacy was a vital part of his family's prosperity, which is why they sought it eagerly and were willing to pay Count Fulk for Hubert's nomination. In the career of Bishop Hubert, there is no sign of a declining family giving way to feudalism.

As will be seen in the following chapters, Hubert's political and ecclesiastical policies will be discussed, but they can never be isolated from his family concerns. It is clear that for prelates like Hubert, life was not simply a choice between secularization, or politicization, and clericalization. The church could also be an important aspect of one's family identity. As bishop of Angers, Hubert never separated from his family, but he devoted much of his effort and resources to it as he followed an independent course of using all his powers to promote its members. One can observe a great family in pursuit of its own interests. To understand Hubert the bishop, one must comprehend his career in its family setting.

III. THE POLITICAL WORLD

When Bishop Renaud II died in 1005, Count Fulk faced threats to his position from different directions. Renaud had been uncomfortably close to Fulk's archenemy Count Odo I of Blois–Tours–Chartres and his family and allies,[1] and for several years Fulk had been locked in a bitter dispute with the bishop over the latter's patrimony in the Mauges.[2] The growing menace of the count of Nantes made Angevin control over that strategic intervening county essential.[3] Thus Fulk needed a loyal supporter to be his new bishop. At the same time, Fulk's attention was drawn to his northeastern frontier. In 985 he had married Elizabeth, the daughter of Count Bouchard the Venerable of Vendôme. Bouchard's son Renaud was the bishop of Paris, so the county would come to Fulk through her, and then to any of their children.[4] Vendôme was important to Angevin plans. It bordered Maine on its west, and it had long been part of an Angevin–Vendômois threat to the counts of Maine. At the same time, it was a buffer between Anjou and the counties of Chartres, Blois, and Tours, which were all held by Count Odo I and then his son Odo II, who were the most consistent opponents of Angevin expansion in the late tenth and early eleventh centuries.

But in the year 1000, Fulk's hold on Vendôme was shaken. His wife Elizabeth died by fire just before a conflagration swept the city of Angers.[5] The nature of these events is not clear, and Fulk may even have had a hand in her death,[6] but his direct control of Vendôme was not secure. The county would pass from Bouchard the Venerable to his son Bishop Renaud of Paris, and then to Adele, Fulk's daughter by Elizabeth, and to whomever she should marry.[7] Fulk would not be able to exercise the countship directly on behalf of his wife, although he naturally would continue to exert a great personal influence over his daughter and her future husband. He also had his network of allies in Vendôme who would act on his behalf. But clearly he needed to nurture his Vendômois connections at a time when his rivals at Tours–Blois–Chartres were active against him. This was

---

[1] Bachrach, "Robert of Blois," pp. 126–130, 138.
[2] See below, nn. 20–24.
[3] Halphen, *Comté d'Anjou*, pp. 25, 51–52.
[4] Bachrach, "Geoffrey Greymantle," p. 27.
[5] Halphen, *Comté d'Anjou*, p. 62; Bachrach, "Pilgrimages of Fulk Nerra," p. 212.
[6] Halphen, op. cit., p. 62 n. 3, p. 130; Bachrach, loc. cit.
[7] Ibid., pp. 62–63.

especially a menace when King Robert II was infatuated with Bertha, the widow of Count Odo I and mother of Counts Theobald and Odo II.[8]

Thus when Viscount Hubert of Vendôme approached Count Fulk in 1005 suggesting that his son Hubert be the next bishop of Angers, he knew that his overture would be well received. This viscount's family in Maine had been allied with the Angevin counts for at least thirty years, while his father-in-law Viscount Fulcradus of Vendôme had been in the Angevin camp two decades earlier. Viscount Hubert himself was already one of Fulk's supporters and held at least one *fevum* from him.[9] So the demonstrated fidelity of the family would have recommended young Hubert to Fulk as a reliable bishop who would cooperate with the count's plans for the Mauges and elsewhere, and who would help shore up the weakened Angevin position in Vendôme as well.

Not only would Viscount Hubert be much more closely attached to the fortunes of the count of Anjou, but also would his family. That would include the viscount and bishop of Le Mans, who were Hubert's close relatives, as well as the Vendômois kinsmen of his wife Emma—Fulcherius the Rich and his wife's father and brother, Gislebertus the Rich and Gundacrius. Together these were four of the seven men who had control of the strategic *castellum* of Vendôme.[10]

Fulk knew that this might be his one opportunity to name a bishop of Angers,[11] and he must have weighed his decision very carefully. With the great collection of lands and offices that were under the control of the bishop, this was one of the most important appointments that Fulk would ever make. When he announced that young Hubert was indeed to be bishop of Angers, it was recognition of the past loyalty of his family, anticipation of its future adherence to the Angevin cause, and acknowledgment that keeping control of the Vendômois was one of Fulk's principal concerns for the future. Young Hubert was not the only candidate for the see of Angers, but he was obviously the one who best suited Fulk's needs at that time. Fulk would have counted on the active support of Hubert and his kin, while they would have looked forward to the benefits of having one of their own presiding over the power and wealth of the Angevin diocese. Power and politics had led to Hubert's appointment, and those same factors were to help shape his career. As a bishop, as a seigneur, as a member of a noble family, he could not have remained apart from the struggle for dominance of the middle Loire in the first half of the eleventh century.

Fulk's nurturing of his Vendômois frontier paid almost immediate dividends. Only a few month after Hubert's ordination, in September or Oc-

---

[8] Ibid., pp. 30, 232–233; Bachrach, "Robert of Blois," pp. 131–132; Jean Dhondt, "Sept femmes et un trio de rois (Robert le Pieux, Henri Ier et Philippe Ier)," *Contributions à l'histoire économique et sociale* 3 (1964–65), pp. 41–46.

[9] See below, Part II, No. 1.

[10] See above, chap. 2, n. 62.

[11] See above, chap. 1, n. 55.

tober of 1006, the diocese of Chartres received its new bishop, the re-
nowned Fulbert.[12] The Chartrain was part of the collection of counties
under Count Odo II of Tours, and Fulbert was one of Odo's supporters.[13]
The newly ordained bishop of Chartres tried to take advantage of the
recent retirement of Count Bouchard the Venerable of Vendôme to the
monastery of St.-Maur des Fossés near Paris[14] to withdraw Vendôme from
the Angevin orbit and to establish himself, with his Blésois affiliations, as
the overlord of the county.[15] He wrote to Bishop Renaud of Paris, Bouchard's son and successor, demanding that old Chartrain claims to the
county be recognized. Fulbert wanted control of the fortress of Vendôme
as well as Bishop Renaud's *auxilium* against all men, saving only his fidelity to King Robert II. Fulbert also demanded the commendation of Renaud's *milites* who possessed benefices from Fulbert's *casamentum*.[16]

Fulbert then attempted to establish direct contacts with the magnates of
the Vendômois. He wrote to nine of them, including Viscount Hubert and
his kinsman Gundacrius, who possessed holdings from the church of
Notre-Dame of Chartres by a grant from Bishop Renaud. He ordered them
to come before him and do service, or else prove that they did not possess
those *casamenta* from him. If this were not done, Fulbert threatened them
with excommunication, warned them of an interdict against hearing the
divine service, receiving communion, or being buried, and he menaced
Vendôme with the threat of an interdict on the entire region. He closed by
stating that he would give their *casamenta* to others and not make peace
with them. Then he prayed that God would "convert" them.[17]

It is not known what direct response Fulbert received from Viscount
Hubert and the others, but it is certain that his attempt to pull Vendôme
away from Anjou and into the Blésois camp was a failure.[18] The powerful
men of the county remained unmoved by his claims and were steadfast in
their adherence to the Anjou–Vendôme axis. Bishop Fulbert remained an
outsider to Vendôme and without real influence or power there. Count
Fulk was still the dominant force there and his hold on the county was
unbroken. Bishop Fulbert may have continued to nurse his theoretical

---

[12] Christian Pfister, *De Fulberti Carnotensis Episcopi Vita et Operibus* (Nancy, 1885), pp.
47–48.

[13] Chédeville, *Chartres et ses campagnes,* pp. 32, 39.

[14] Bourel de la Roncière, *Vie de Bouchard,* p. xviii.

[15] Guillot, *Comte d'Anjou,* 1: pp. 28–33, and the authorities cited by him (ibid., p. 29 n. 149);
also see R. de Saint-Venant, "Commentaires sur deux chartes vendômoises du XIe siècle,"
Bulletin de la Société archéologique, scientifique et littéraire du Vendômois 44 (1906), pp.
146–164.

[16] *Letters and Poems of Fulbert of Chartres,* no. 9.

[17] Ibid., no. 10.

[18] J.-F. Lemarignier, "Political and Monastic Structures in France," pp. 109–110, felt that
Bishop Fulbert was successful in this effort. But the complete political exclusion of the bishop
of Chartres from Vendôme speaks more eloquently of Fulbert's failure. See Chédeville,
Chartres et ses campagnes, p. 264, and R. de Saint-Venant, "Commentaires sur deux chartes
vendômoises," p. 162.

claims to the overlordship of Vendôme, but they were without effect. Fulk had already taken care to keep the support of Viscount Hubert and the other Vendômois magnates in naming young Hubert to the Angevin see.

The personal loyalty of the new bishop was immediately tested by his reaction to the Mauges affair, which had been a major conflict between Count Fulk and Hubert's predecessor Bishop Renaud II. From his accession as count of Anjou in 987, Fulk had many difficulties keeping the support of Bishop Renaud, and by the mid-990s the bishop had drawn close to Fulk's sometime opponent Abbot Robert of St. Florent and to his constant rival, the House of Blois.[19] Hostility between Fulk and Renaud blazed into the open between 1001 and 1005 over the bishop's disposition of his inheritance, especially that in the county of the Mauges.

Count Fulk and his half brother Maurice claimed that the bishop's father, Viscount Renaud of Angers, had promised part of his lands to their father, Count Geoffrey Greymantle, in order to obtain the bishopric for Renaud II. But instead, they said, after his father's death, the bishop had given the promised lands to the cathedral of Angers. Bishop Renaud had evidently been concerned that his grants to the cathedral be safeguarded by the power of a higher authority, for he had obtained Pope John XVIII's confirmation of those grants (1003–1005).

Bishop Renaud also gave some parts of the disputed inheritance to the abbey of St.-Serge d'Angers, which included at least the half-church of St.-Rémy-en-Mauges and two *quartae* of land belonging to Juigné-la-Prée, and also many returns to that monastery, including the land of Champigné-sur-Sarthe. These gifts as well the bishop had confirmed, this time by King Robert II. Perhaps the donations from Renaud's inheritance had first been made to the cathedral, for the *census* was retained by its canons.[20]

Strategic considerations justified Fulk's great concern over the disposition of the Mauges lands. Viscount Renaud had held the strong points of Champtoceaux and Châtelliers,[21] along the left bank of the Loire between Angers and Nantes, and the Mauges stood between Anjou, the Nantais, and Poitou. Fulk had secured his position in the west by his victory over Conan of Nantes at Conquéreuil in 992. He then forced the recognition of Count Hoël I's bastard son Judicaël as the count of Nantes. The young count was placed under the supervision of Fulk's supporter Viscount Aimery of Thouars. In 994, Fulk established Judicaël in full possession of Nantes. However, Viscount Aimery then began dealing with Abbot Robert of St. Florent and Count William Iron-Arm of Poitou. Judicaël was then killed in a surprise attack by Count Geoffrey-Berenger of Rennes around 1004, and Fulk's western position was in jeopardy.[22]

---

[19] Bachrach, "Robert of Blois," pp. 126–130, 135–138.
[20] Guillot, *Comte d'Anjou,* 1: pp. 213–224, and in general pp. 226–233.
[21] Ibid., 1: pp. 202–205.
[22] Ibid., 1: pp. 41–43; Halphen, *Comté d'Anjou,* pp. 25, 51–52.

Thus at the very time that Bishop Renaud was consorting with Fulk's enemies, when Renaud appeared to be reneging on his father's promise to give his Mauges patrimony to the count of Anjou, Fulk's control of Nantes had been wrested from him. He now needed the Mauges more than ever and probably was not in a mood to listen to Bishop Renaud's protest that the patrimony had never been promised to the count in the first place. Fulk returned from the first of his pilgrimages to Jerusalem in early 1005, and Bishop Renaud then himself departed Anjou bound for the Holy City. While Renaud's exit from Angers may have been a genuine pilgrimage, it also may well have been an exile either forced on him by Fulk or voluntarily undertaken for his own good. But Renaud did not reach his destination. He died in Provence on 12 June 1005.[23]

Count Fulk no doubt took advantage of Renaud's absence from Anjou and the subsequent year-long vacancy in the see to revoke Renaud's donations to the cathedral and to the monastery. When he built the fortress of Montrevault, located in the center of the Mauges, he distributed the lands to his *milites* in benefice. Thus Fulk constructed a strong point in the heart of the strategic *pagus* and rewarded his fighting men by plundering Renaud's gifts.[24]

This was the situation faced by Hubert upon his ordination in June of 1006. Being loyal to Fulk, Hubert had no thought of attempting to overturn the count's resolution of the Mauges controversy. Rather, he accepted the sacking of Bishop Renaud's grants even though they had been fortified by royal and papal confirmations. It does not seem likely that Hubert himself actually carried out these depredations. Fulk would not have waited for over a year with no bishop to oppose him before settling the controversy to his own liking. Hubert would have been presented with a *fait accompli*.

For his own part, Hubert immediately set out to incorporate the Mauges, previously in the diocese of Poitiers and then in that of Nantes, into his own Angevin diocese.[25] Two inauthentic acts produced at St. Florent shed

---

[23] Guillot, *Comte d'Anjou*, 1: pp. 223–224; Halphen, *Comté d'Anjou*, p. 114 and n. 2, pp. 213–214; Bachrach, "Robert of Blois," p. 137.

[24] See below, Part II, No. 81.

[25] See J.-F. Lemarignier, *Etude sur les privilèges d'exemption et de juridiction ecclésiastique des abbayes normandes depuis les origines jusqu'en 1140* (Paris, 1937), p. 93. On the incorporation of the Mauges into the diocese of Angers, see Auguste Longnon, *Pouillés de la province de Tours*, Recueil des historiens de la France, Académie des inscriptions et belles-lettres, Pouillés, vol. 3 (Paris, 1903), and his *Atlas historique de la France depuis César jusqu'à nos jours*, Texte explicatif des planches, part one (Paris, 1907); and F. Uzureau, "Angers," *Dictionnaire d'histoire et de géographie ecclésiastiques*, vol. 3, ed. Alfred Baudrillart, R. Aigrain, P. Richard, and U. Rouziés (Paris, 1924), col. 105.

But William Ziezulewicz, "Etude d'un faux monastique à une période réforme: une charte de Charles le Chauve pour Saint-Florent-de-Saumur (8 juin 848)," *Cahiers de civilisation médiévale* 28 (1985), pp. 204–209, believes that the bishop of Nantes exercised his episcopal authority over the Mauges in the mid-eleventh century (op. cit., p. 204). His evidence for this is Bishop Walter of Nantes' consecration of the church of Saint-Lourent-du-Mottoy in the Mauges, for St. Florent in 1041, which Ziezulewicz portrays as "un acte routine annuelle" (p. 205). However, the source for this information makes it clear that Bishop Walter was return-

light on the timing of this transfer of the Mauges into Hubert's diocese. One, a bull supposedly given by Pope John XVIII, stressed the dependence of St. Florent on the counts of Blois and exempted the monastery from all returns claimed by the bishop of Angers except for the sinodal tax.[26] The other false act, probably fabricated after the bull, is a charter whereby Charles the Bald, at the request of the bishops of Nantes and Poitiers, purportedly exempted the churches belonging to St. Florent (-le-Vieil) located within their dioceses from the sinodal tax.[27]

These two forgeries must have been produced at St. Florent between 1004 and 1044, and it is generally held that it was after 1026, and that these two acts formed part of St. Florent's struggle in resistance to Fulk's domination of the monastery after his capture of Saumur in that year.[28] However, once Fulk seized Saumur and the surrounding region, his followers replaced the Blésois forces in their benefices there, including the *castrum* of Saumur. This was a political reality that made any effort on the part of St. Florent to defy Angevin supremacy in the Saumurois futile.

Moreover, Abbot Frederick of St. Florent is not known to have pressed any claim of the monastery's dependence on the count of Blois during this time, and Bishop Hubert exercised his episcopal control over St. Florent even before Fulk's conquest of the region. Both Saumur and St. Florent

---

ing from his participation in the dedication of St. Florent's new monastery (see below, Part II, No. 40) and lodged at the monastery of Saint-Florent-le-Vieil in the Mauges, and the monks simply took advantage of the occasion to ask him to consecrate the church ("Histoire de l'abbaye royale de Sainct Florent près Saumur," Archives départementales de Maine-et-Loire, H 3716, fol. 58 v). On the question of the movement of the Mauges into the diocese of Angers, see also below, note 31.

[26] For an edition of the manuscripts of the forged bull, see William Ziezulewicz, "A Monastic Forgery in an Age of Reform, a Bull of Pope John XVIII for Saint-Florent-de-Saumur (April 1004)," *Archivum Historiae Pontificae* 23 (1985), pp. 38–42. All the manuscripts carry the clauses that exempt St. Florent from any episcopal ban of excommunication and provide for a judgment of two or three bishops if its abbot should be charged with any *calumnia* or *crimen*. The provision concerning episcopal taxation is found in only one copy, Archives départementales de Maine-et-Loire, H 1836, no. 6, edited in Marc Saché, *Inventaire-sommaire des Archives départementales antérieures à 1790, Maine-et-Loire, Archives ecclésiastiques, Série H*, vol. 2 (Angers, 1926), pp. 6–7. However, both Johannes Ramackers, "Papsturkunden in Frankreich," *Abhandlungen der Akademie des Wissenschaften in Göttingen*, Philologisch-Historische Klasse, dritte Folge, no. 35 (1956), p. 32, and H. Zimmermann, *Papstregesten 911–1024* (Vienna, 1969), p. 392, suggest that this manuscript is the original, apparently because it was executed in a style imitating the script of the papal chancery. Ziezulewicz dismisses this argument without presenting a case against it (op. cit., p. 13) and prefers Archives Maine-et-Loire, H 1837, no. 1, as the pseudo-original, but again without an argument to support his decision. He admits that the relationship of the oldest copies, H 1836, no. 6, and 1837, nos. 1, 2 and 3, has not been determined (op. cit., p. 39). At present, the question of which manuscript ought to be preferred would appear to be open, and the clause concerning episcopal taxation in ms. 1836, no. 6, cannot be dismissed.

[27] *Recueil des actes de Charles II, le Chauve*, ed. Georges Tessier (Paris, 1952), no. 470. On the inauthenticity of these two acts, see A. Giry, "Etude critique de quelques documents angevins de l'époque carolingienne," *Mémoires de l'institut national de France, Académie des inscriptions et belles-lettres*, vol. 36, part 1, 1901, pp. 222–243; Lemarignier, *Privilèges d'exemption*, pp. 98–110; Tessier, *Rec. Charles II*, pp. 556–557; and Guillot, *Comte d'Anjou*, 1: pp. 230–232.

[28] See Giry, Lemarignier, Tessier, and Guillot, cited above, note 27.

were firmly in Angevin hands after 1026 and Frederick could have had no hope for success in attempting to break free of Angevin political or ecclesiastical domination after 1026.[29]

Since a principal intent of the forged papal bull was to gain an exemption from episcopal authority, it was most likely meant for a new bishop who would be unsure of the exact nature of his rights for a relatively brief period following his ordination. Abbot Robert had nothing to fear from his ally Bishop Renaud II of Angers, but after the latter's death a new bishop, acting in concert with Count Fulk, presented a very real threat to St. Florent and its possessions. The two forgeries, therefore, were probably intended to be used against Hubert, the one to claim an exemption from episcopal taxation over the monastery and the other from the sinodal tax for its lands in the Mauges. Hence the forgeries were probably executed under Abbot Robert ca. 1005–1006.[30]

---

[29] Bachrach, "Robert of Blois," p. 143, n. 2.

[30] Ibid., pp. 142–143. Ziezulewicz, "A Monastic Forgery in an Age of Reform," pp. 17–36, argues that the papal bull was fabricated between 1060 and 1062. However, this is based solely on the provisions of the bull stressing St. Florent's being under the *dominium* of the house of Blois, which was an effort to claim the monastery's freedom from any lay *dominium* (Ziezulewicz, p. 31). Therefore the bull would have been forged only after the Angevin conquest of the Saumurois in 1026 (ibid., p. 31). Ziezulewicz preferred the years 1060–62 for the forgery on the basis of the instability in Anjou following the death of Count Geoffrey Martel and the accession of his nephew Geoffrey the Bearded in 1060, which resulted in the latter's abandonment of many of his rights at Saumur and over St. Florent (op. cit., pp. 31–32; Guillot, *Comte d'Anjou*, 2: no. 241), in part based on the fear of a papal anathema. Ziezulewicz interprets the mention of the pope as a reference to this forged bull. While it may be so, it provides only a *terminus ad quem* for the forgery.

In his argument for a date of 1060–62 for the bull, Ziezulewicz fails to take into account the provisions in the bull that claim juridical and perhaps fiscal independence from the bishop of Angers. Since Eusebius Bruno was bishop from 1047 to 1081, it is difficult to understand how such new claims by St. Florent, made fifteen years into his episcopate, would have been successful, especially being based on a document that ostensibly had been in the monastery's possession for over half a century.

The bull's prohibition of St. Florent's ever leaving the *dominium* of the house of Blois and its freeing the abbey from certain areas of episcopal authority would appear to come from a period when St. Florent felt threatened by Anjou both politically and ecclesiastically. Therefore, Bachrach's dating of the forgery to ca. 1005–1011 ("Robert of Blois," pp. 141–143) seems to take better account of all the contents of the bull. Moreover, the catalogue of St. Florent's lands that were confirmed in the bull apparently reflect the monastery's holdings around the mid-tenth century (Ziezulewicz, "A Monastic Forgery," p. 25), which would support an earlier rather than a later date for the bull. Also, during Bishop Renaud's last year, 1004–1005, Abbot Robert of St. Florent was interested in obtaining administrative and judicial exemption from the bishop of Angers (Bachrach, "Robert of Blois," pp. 135–136; for Renaud's charter for St. Florent, see Archives départementales de Maine-et-Loire, H 3715, Livre rouge, fol. 29 v-30 r). Bishop Renaud granted Robert freedom "ab omni descensu et procuratione episcopi et clericorum Andegavensium." Thus a forgery produced after the death of the friendly Bishop Renaud in 1005, to be presented if necessary to the new bishop of Angers, along with other, authentic exemptions from episcopal jurisdiction and authority gained just at the end of Renaud's life, would have had the best chance for success. The date carried by the bull, April 1004, when Abbot Robert was in Rome (Ziezulewicz, "A Monastic Forgery," p. 34), reinforces the interpretation that it was Abbot Robert who produced the forgery and claimed that he had obtained it while on his pilgrimage.

Since the forged royal charter, attempting to free St. Florent's churches in the Mauges from a sinodal tax imposed by Bishop Hubert, was supposedly based on a request by the bishops of Nantes and Poitiers, it is clear that the forger believed that his work would be more effective if those bishops had given up that right. So ca. 1005–1006 the Mauges were not considered to be in the diocese of Angers, or else a forgery based on a surrender by one of Hubert's predecessors at Angers probably would have been produced. But it was either under a grave threat of being brought under Angevin jurisdiction or it was in the process of such a transfer. Thus a forgery based on the previously existing juridical condition, with the Mauges under the bishop of Nantes or Poitiers, was thought to comprise the best case. The most likely date for the beginning of the incorporation of the Mauges into the diocese of Angers is very early in Hubert's episcopacy, at the same time that Fulk's *milites* were being placed in the Mauges to bring it under his direct control. With the county of Nantes in hostile hands, would Fulk have left the Mauges under the ecclesiastical jurisdiction of the bishop of Nantes?[31]

Not only did Hubert's policy towards the Mauges—acceptance of Fulk's seizure of Renaud's patrimony and incorporation of the Mauges into the diocese of Angers—have the effect of increasing his own episcopal powers, but it also struck a blow at St. Florent, whose holdings pertaining

---

[31] Ziezulewicz, "Etude d'un faux monastique," denies that the Mauges was under the bishop of Angers until the episcopate of Eusebius Bruno, 1047–1081 (for part of this argument, see above, note 25). Between 1047 and 1055, Bishop Eusebius brought nine rural parishes of Saint-Florent-le-Vieil under his authority and subjected them to the synodal tax (*Cart. noir de la cathédrale,* no. 47). They had been "per multa jam annorum tempora nulli omnino diocesi assignatae vel subditae, sed ab omni pontificali regimini incertum quonam eventu destitutae." Ziezulewicz claims that this act concerned the parishes of Saint-Florent-le-Vieil, although the charter deals with only nine churches, so its significance for the Mauges as a whole is limited. His assertion, on the basis of this charter, that Eusebius was the only bishop of Angers to collect the *synodus* from the churches of Saint-Florent-le-Vieil (p. 209) is certainly an argument from silence.

Ziezulewicz argues that the royal charter was forged in 1081, at the death of Bishop Eusebius, in order to free the churches of Saint-Florent-le-Vieil from the synodal tax. It is difficult to believe that such a forgery made at that time could have succeeded. The *synodus* had been collected from those churches for at least twenty-five years and perhaps even longer. Even if the new bishop of Angers would have been unaware of that fact, the diocesan administration, especially the archdeacons, would have known, and a document that was supposed to have been in the monastery's possession since 848 would have been rather suspect. Where had it been for the twenty-five or more years while Bishop Eusebius had been collecting that tax?

The accession of Bishop Hubert, the unclear diocesan status of the Mauges, the seizure of Bishop Renaud's patrimony in that district and the resulting extension of Count Fulk's direct power in the Mauges, and the consequent uncanonical ecclesiastical takeover of the Mauges in a piecemeal fashion by Bishop Hubert would have provided the best chances for a successful forgery in that atmosphere of transition and confusion. Thus the period after 1005 produced the political and ecclesiastical threat to St. Florent that favored the forging of the royal charter. The incorporation of the Mauges into the diocese of Angers should be seen as a long process that followed the territorial advances of the count of Anjou, not as an act accomplished at a single stroke. For example, note how Bishop Hubert regained parts of Bishop Renaud's patrimony seized by Count Fulk, see below, notes 33–35.

to St.-Florent-le-Vieil lay in the Mauges and were now under Hubert's diocesan authority. By the death of Bishop Renaud II and the appointment of Bishop Hubert, St. Florent and Abbot Robert had lost an ally and gained a bishop whose faithfulness to Count Fulk now placed the monastery in a more politically isolated position than ever before.

Abbot Robert attempted to thwart Bishop Hubert by producing the two forgeries, but soon the pressure of political realities forced him to change the direction of his policy towards Anjou. Count Odo II of Blois was unable to act on behalf of St. Florent because of his war with Duke Richard II of Normandy, but Gelduin of Saumur was still attempting to dominate the monastery. Facing opponents on all sides and without the episcopal support formerly supplied by Renaud II, Abbot Robert struck the best bargain available to him under the trying circumstances. He temporarily recognized Count Fulk as his *senior*.[32]

With the blessings of Count Fulk and later his son Count Geoffrey Martel, Bishop Hubert's long-range policy in the Mauges was to restore much of Bishop Renaud's inheritance to the power of the original church establishment from which Fulk had taken it, and to place the family of Emma and Radulfus IV, his heirs, into the leading position in the Mauges. Sometime before 1031, Bishop Hubert obtained a judgment from Fulk's court that allowed him to repurchase the villa of Champigné-sur-Sarthe. Earlier it had been given to St. Serge by Bishop Renaud, but then it had been taken away and granted out as a benefice. Upon his repurchase of the villa, Hubert restored it to St. Serge.[33] Similar restorations seem to have been made to the cathedral of St. Maurice of Angers by Bishop Hubert by 1025.[34]

Bishop Hubert's niece Emma came to possess half of the *curtis* and the church of St.-Rémy-en-Mauges. That church had earlier been given to St. Serge by Bishop Renaud, but then it had been taken away by Count Fulk and given to his *milites*. When Bishop Hubert's niece came to possess it from him, the count's *milites* were left in their holdings.[35] The family of Emma and Radulfus came to possess both Fulk's fortress of Montrevault and the vicontiel title to it.[36] This arrangement could have been achieved only with the support of the counts of Anjou. As Olivier Guillot remarked, it is very exceptional that the bishop of Angers appeared to dominate the hierarchy of the Mauges juridically, while the count was virtually absent.[37]

---

[32] Bachrach, "Robert of Blois," pp. 138–139.

[33] See below, Part II, No. 23.

[34] Fulk took away what Renaud had given to the cathedral (see below, Part II, No. 81). In August 1025, Bishop Hubert made a number of restorations to the canons of the cathedral, whom he pitied and hoped to help because for a long time they had borne poverty due to the oppression of the counts (below, Part II, No. 10). The obituary notice for Bishop Hubert recorded by the canons also refers to the thanks given him for restoring the position of the canons of the cathedral, who had fallen on hard times due to the oppression of "tyrants" and the neglect of the preceding bishops (see above, chap. 1, n. 2).

[35] See below, Part II, No. 81.

[36] See above, chap. 2, n. 89.

[37] Guillot, *Comte d'Anjou*, 1: p. 241.

But Count Fulk and Geoffrey Martel could afford to place the Mauges in the hands of Hubert and his family and to turn their active attention elsewhere, for that strategic region was under the control of trustworthy *fideles*.

Hubert or his heirs brought in inhabitants from the Vendômois to possess lands around Montrevault and to control the Mauges.[38] Hubert, thanks to the counts of Anjou, stepped into some of the former possessions belonging to Viscount Renaud and his son Bishop Renaud, including half of the church of St.-Rémy-en-Mauges and the association with the family of Roger of Loudun at Montrevault.[39]

Because of Hubert's own kinship with the vicontiel–episcopal families of Le Mans, Fulk's actions in choosing him as bishop of Angers were probably motivated in part by the long Angevin tradition of attempting to dominate the county of Maine. Geoffrey Greymantle allied with Bishop Segenfredus, who was also assisted by Bouchard the Venerable of Vendôme. Count Fulk continued this policy and he could count Geoffrey of Sablé, son and brother to viscounts of Le Mans, among his supporters.[40] By 1023, the viscount of Le Mans and his son even appeared in Vendôme with Fulk, Bishop Hubert, and other members of the Vendômois branch of Hubert's family.[41]

Hubert himself maintained contact with his relatives in Maine during the early years of his episcopate. He was present at the gift of the church of Solesmes to St. Pierre of Couture by Geoffrey of Sablé. Also in attendance were Bishop Avesgaudus of Le Mans and Geoffrey's two brothers Viscount Radulfus and Odo.[42] A fourth brother Ivo became archdeacon of the cathedral of Le Mans and yet another, named Hubert, was its treasurer, thus continuing the intimate connections between the vicontiel and episcopal families of Le Mans.[43]

Since Hubert lacked a male heir, he went back to the Maine branch of the family to find a husband for his heiress Emma, the daughter of his sister Hadeburga. The marriage was arranged with Radulfus IV, the son and heir of Viscount Radulfus III (or Roscelinus), by 1026 at the latest. Bishop Hubert appears to have taken the lead in this alliance, for the meeting in Vendôme in 1022 of Radulfus III, his son Radulfus IV, Bishop Hubert and many members of his family, and Count Fulk seems to have been for the purpose of settling the negotiations. Viscount Hubert, Hadeburga, and her husband Stephen were not present at that time, and Bishop

---

[38] Ibid., 1: pp. 239–241.

[39] Roger of Loudun, also known as Roger of Montrevault (see Guillot, *Comte d'Anjou*, 1: p. 240 n. 167), held lands from Viscount Renaud (Halphen, *Comté d'Anjou*, p. j. no. 1), and either he or his son Roger was closely allied with Hubert's family at Montrevault (Guillot, *Comte d'Anjou*, 1: p. 240 n. 167). And see below, Part II, No. 81.

[40] Bachrach, "Geoffrey Greymantle," p. 26; *Cart. St.-Aubin*, no. 85.

[41] See below, Part II, No. 7.

[42] See below, Part II, Nos. 3, 4.

[43] See above, chap. 2, n. 67.

Hubert appears to be the representative of his family. His later actions towards Emma and Radulfus IV certainly bear out this impression.[44]

Hubert brought Emma and her husband into the family's position in the Vendômois and promoted them in the Mauges as well. The viscounts of Le Mans were now, through their connection to Hubert, fully enmeshed in the Angevin political network. When Count Fulk imprisoned Count Herbert Wake-Dog of Maine in 1025 and held him in captivity for two years, he was supported by Bishop Hubert and his Maine kinsfolk, who included the viscount of Le Mans.[45] Another relative, Bishop Avesgaudus of Le Mans, was already an opponent of the count of Maine.[46]

Radulfus IV and Emma and their sons were as consistent in support of the Angevin cause as was Bishop Hubert. No doubt with the favor of the counts of Anjou, Hubert's heirs dramatically increased their possessions and thus their wealth. Radulfus himself carried the title of viscount of Vendôme, and he and his son Radulfus Paganus both were very influential there. The Mauges were dominated by the family from the *castrum* of Montrevault, and its vicontiel title was eventually carried by Radulfus Paganus. Radulfus IV and his son Hubert were viscounts of Lude, and their holdings there must have come from the counts of Anjou. The loyalty of the family of Hubert's heirs was most clearly demonstrated by the energetic and almost legendary defense of Maine led by Hubert's grand-nephew Viscount Hubert of Ste.-Suzanne against the Norman attempts to bring that county into the control of William the Conqueror.[47]

Hubert and his family were not only involved in promoting Angevin interests in the Vendômois and in Maine, but they also were active in the endemic warfare between Count Fulk and his forces and those of the count of Blois–Tours–Chartres and his allies. This support of his count led Hubert to violate the legal limits of his episcopal office while remaining true to the allegiance that he honored towards Fulk and King Robert II. Warfare between Anjou and Blois erupted again in 1016, which culminated in the battle of Pontlevoy on 6 July. The Angevins had the victory after a bitter struggle that came to have a terrible reputation for the blood that was shed. Fulk was able to follow up his success by moving even more deeply into Blésois territory and establishing a fortress at Montboyau only a short distance from Tours.

We know of Hubert's actions during this warfare[48] from a letter written to him in the name of Archbishop Hugh of Tours, an important supporter

---

[44] See below, Part II, No. 7; and see above, chap. 2, nn. 71, 76.

[45] Halphen, *Comté d'Anjou*, pp. 66–68.

[46] See Latouche, *Comté du Maine*, pp. 22–23, 84, and the letter of Fulbert of Chartres to Archbishop Ebalus of Reims in support of Bishop Avesgaudus against Count Herbert, *Letters and Poems of Fulbert of Chartres*, no. 87.

[47] On these points, see above, chap. 2, nn. 83, 89, 91, 94.

[48] On the dating of Hubert's warfare against Archbishop Hugh, see Fanning, "La lutte entre Hubert."

of Count Odo II and an ally of Gelduin of Saumur, one of Fulk's worst opponents on the Anjou–Touraine frontier. This letter, however, is in the collection of letters of Bishop Fulbert of Chartres,[49] another of Count Odo's adherents, and it is safe to assume that it was Fulbert who actually composed it. Since it was Hubert's father and other relatives who ten years earlier had ignored Fulbert's threats of excommunication and interdict if they did not recognize his, and thus indirectly Count Odo's, overlordship, he may have enjoyed a measure of revenge in assisting Archbishop Hugh in this manner.[50]

From the letter it is clear that a number of messages were passed between Hubert and his archbishop before and after the fighting. Hubert, called a "leader of so many arms," had taken action against Odo's "evil" at the command of King Robert and Count Fulk (who was sarcastically referred to as "tuus diuus"). The archbishop had ordered him not to attack Count Odo. But instead Hubert had threatened fire, sword, and death, defied Hugh's command, and laid waste part of the Touraine, including vines that belonged to the cathedral of Tours. So Hubert had not only fought against Count Odo, but he had also attacked the archbishop's lands as well.

Lacking a military response to the Angevin victory, Archbishop Hugh then excommunicated Hubert and placed him under a personal interdict against saying the divine service. Hubert did not give the appearance of being especially concerned at this censure. He replied to Hugh in his own defense. He countercharged against Hugh, saying that the archbishop had acted rashly and that Hugh had not given him forty days in which to respond to the first summons. Changing tactics, Hubert then claimed that he had been justified in going to war because he had been ordered to do so by King Robert. Therefore, since he felt that he was innocent of wrongdoing, Hubert would ignore the excommunication and interdict.

Archbishop Hugh then sent the actual letter that survives. He reviewed the above communications, and then refuted Hubert's defense. The destroyed vines of the cathedral proved Hubert's guilt, he claimed, and he denied that he had acted rashly. The letter previously sent to Hubert by Hugh had been sufficient summons, and thus the interdict was reasonable and according to canon law. Hubert's defense that he had acted by royal command, whether true or not, was not sufficient justification for flouting the orders of his archbishop. As Pope Gregory the Great had written, the pastor ought to be obeyed whether his actions are just or unjust. Hugh closed by stating that Hubert was afflicted by pride, contempt, and presumption, and only by submitting to Hugh's decrees could he be cured.[51]

It is not known when the excommunication and interdict were lifted

---

[49] *Letters and Poems of Fulbert of Chartres,* no. 71.
[50] See above, n. 17.
[51] *Letters and Poems of Fulbert of Chartres,* no. 71.

from Hubert, but by September 1022 he was on reasonably good terms with Count Odo II. At that time Hubert ordained Frederick, Odo's choice as abbot of St. Florent,[52] and it is difficult to imagine such cooperation between Hubert and Odo if Hubert were still an excommunicate for his successes against Odo and Hugh.

It may be an exaggeration to say along with Louis Halphen that Hubert was perhaps more expert in wielding the sword than in praying to God, but this single known episode in Hubert's career as *dux armatorum* demonstrates where his loyalties lay. His allegiance to his secular lord far outweighed any obedience that he felt towards his ecclesiastical superior who was as deeply in the service of Count Odo as Hubert was in that of Count Fulk.[53]

No other act so clearly political is known in Hubert's career, but his adherence to Count Fulk continued unabated. Throughout the 1020s, the bishop and the count were on good terms. Around December of 1020, Hubert dedicated Fulk's monastery of St. Nicholas.[54] In 1023 Fulk was present in Vendôme with Bishop Hubert and several members of Hubert's family, a meeting that was probably for the purpose of arranging the marriage of Hubert's niece Emma to the son of the viscount of Le Mans.[55] In 1025, doubtlessly with Fulk's approval, Bishop Hubert made a number of restorations to the canons of the cathedral of St. Maurice of Angers on the occasion of its dedication.[56] And in 1028, Hubert was a major participant, along with Count Fulk and his family, at the dedication of the convent of Ronceray.[57]

Hubert's only known contacts with King Robert II indicate cooperation. The king confirmed Hubert's grants to St. Serge,[58] and Hubert fought against Count Odo II and Archbishop Hugh at least in part in the name of the king. What role, if any, Hubert played in the conflict within the royal family ca. 1027, concerning the cooption of young Henry by Robert, is unknown. It has been argued that Hubert joined with Count Odo II and Henry against Fulk and King Robert because Hubert and Odo appear together in Vendôme in 1029.[59] However, whatever difficulties there were

---

[52] See below, Part II, No. 6.
[53] Fanning, "La lutte entre Hubert," p. 32.
[54] See below, Part II, No. 5.
[55] See below, Part II, No. 7.
[56] See below, Part II, No. 10.
[57] See below, Part II, No. 15.
[58] See below, Part II, No. 23.
[59] Guillot, *Comte d'Anjou*, 1: p. 244, concerning the charter below, Part II, No. 21. On this Capetian family clash, see Guillot, ibid., pp. 34–38, and Dhondt, "Sept femmes et un trio de rois," pp. 50–51. The sole evidence produced by Guillot to sustain his argument that Odo and Henry fought against Fulk and Robert is Count Odo's attack on Sulpicius of Amboise in 1027 (recorded in *Annales de Vendôme*, in *Recueil d'annales angevines et vendômois*, p. 61; see Guillot, *Comte d'Anjou*, 1: pp. 34–35, and Léonce Lex, "Eudes comte de Blois, de Tours, de Chartres, de Troyes et de Meaux [995–1037] et Thibaud, son frère [995–1004]," *Mémoires de la Société de l'Aube* [1891], p. 228). However, the entry in the *Annales de Vendôme* makes it clear that Odo's intention was to emend "quasi superioris fortunam," and the entry in the

between Fulk and Odo must have been resolved by early 1028 when the two appear together with King Robert.[60] In July 1028, Hubert and Fulk were together for the dedication of the convent of Ronceray, which was the special project of Fulk's wife, Countess Hildegardis.[61] The struggle over the royal succession was over by 1028, and Hubert's action with Count Odo in 1029 cannot have been related to it. Nor does it indicate that Hubert broke with Count Fulk over that issue.

The annals and chronicles of Anjou and Vendôme report that the 1030s saw a serious conflict between Count Fulk and his son Geoffrey Martel.[62] It is variously described as a *bellum* or *dissensio*, or in Lucan's colorful phrase to mean a war among kinsmen, a *bellum plus quam civile*.[63] The annals give no consistent chronology of this family dispute, for it may have begun between 1032 and 1037, and lasted until 1038 or 1042. The source of the conflict, when it is given, is reported to be Geoffrey Martel's marriage to Agnes, the widow of Count William the Great of Poitou, and his imprisonment of her stepson Count William the Fat.[64]

Such a war between father and son would have been a horror for all the *fideles* of the count of Anjou, to have to choose between support of Fulk or of his only son, who would succeed him one day. But it was especially so for Bishop Hubert and the other Angevin supporters of the Vendômois. By around January 1032, Geoffrey Martel had been made count of Vendôme by his father.[65] So these magnates would have had to take the side of the man who was now their count, or that of his father, with whom they had been allied since the end of the tenth century and who was still probably recognized as the real power in Vendôme despite his son's carrying the comital title. To make matters even worse for Vendôme, Bishop Gervais took advantage of Geoffrey's distraction due to this conflict to attack the Vendômois. The two were quarreling over the succession to the county of Maine, with Geoffrey supporting Herbert Bacon and Bishop Gervais backing Herbert's grandnephew Hugh III.[66] Vendôme was now caught in a three-way struggle. Not to stand with Count Geoffrey would invite depredations by Bishop Gervais, and to stand with him would alienate Count Fulk, to whom Vendôme had intense and durable ties of loyalty.

---

same annal for the year 1026 relates Odo's failure to take the fortress of Montboyau and Fulk's capture of Saumur. Thus Odo's attack in 1027 was an outcome of his personal conflict with Count Fulk and was probably not related to the royal feud. At any rate, the conflict between Fulk and Odo was over by early 1028, when they appear together with King Robert (see below, n. 60).

[60] Guillot, *Comte d'Anjou*, 1: p. 36 and n. 179; William Mendel Newman, *Catalogue des actes de Robert II, Roi de France* (Paris, 1937), no. 72.

[61] See below, Part II, No. 15.

[62] On the sources for this conflict, see Bachrach, "Henry II and the Angevin Tradition of Family Hostility," pp. 119–121.

[63] *De bello civile*, I. 1; this was repeated in Isidore of Seville's *Etymologies* (*Isidori Hispalensis episcopi Etymologiarum sive originum*, ed. W. M. Lindsay [Oxford, 1911], XVIII. 1).

[64] Bachrach, "Angevin Tradition," p. 121.

[65] Guillot, *Comte d'Anjou*, 1: p. 45.

[66] Ibid., pp. 54–55; Halphen, *Comté d'Anjou*, pp. 69–70; Latouche, *Comté du Maine*, pp. 26–28.

It has recently been argued that there was no serious warfare between Fulk and Geoffrey, that there was more of a period of disagreement or discord between them, and no known battle was fought in this so-called war.[67] But there certainly was trouble between the two. There was a serious misunderstanding over Geoffrey's grant of the *fructus* of the church of Mazé to a certain Geoffrey Malramnus,[68] and Geoffrey Martel enticed Renaud, abbot of Fulk's monastery of St. Nicholas at Angers, to leave that house without permission to become abbot of his own monastery of Trinité de Vendôme.[69] More compelling than these events to indicate a very serious clash between Fulk and Geoffrey is the record of its consequences for two of Geoffrey's supporters in the Vendômois, people who were also close to Bishop Hubert.

Hersendis was the daughter of Aremburgis, who held land from the family estates of Bishop Hubert.[70] She wrote to Count Geoffrey, complaining that because he had been busy dealing with his father's anger and could not give her assistance, Bishop Gervais had been able to seize part of her patrimony.[71] Likewise, we know that Salomon of Lavardin, with whom Bishop Hubert had close ties, had suffered losses in the war with Bishop Gervais.[72] It is difficult to imagine that Geoffrey would allow his position in the Vendômois to be damaged and for his loyal supporters there to sustain serious losses at the hands of Bishop Gervais unless his conflict with his father were even more dangerous than his warfare with the bishop of Le Mans. Neglect of one's *fideles* could only be a response to a quarrel of great proportions. The "bellum plus quam civile" must have been real, and it must have been serious.

The losses incurred by Hersendis and Salomon indicate that Hubert's circle did not abandon Geoffrey, but an almost complete lack of details of the conflict between Fulk and Geoffrey makes it impossible to assess the stance taken by Bishop Hubert and the other great figures of the Vendômois. There is no sign that he was opposed to either father or son in the 1030s. In December 1032 Hubert, his archdeacons, and Count Fulk acted together to extend the rights of Fulk's monastery of St. Nicholas,[73] while in December of 1036 Hubert assented, along with Fulk, to the choice of Walter as abbot of St. Aubin.[74] Sometime in 1036 Hubert acted with Geoffrey Martel to consecrate and grant privileges to St.-Maur-sur-Loire,[75] and between 1031 and 1037 Hubert appeared with both Fulk and Geof-

---

[67] Bachrach, "Angevin Tradition," pp. 121–125.
[68] *Cart. Trinité de Vendôme*, no. 44, and below, Part II, No. 1.
[69] See below, Part II, Nos. 32, 35.
[70] See below, Part II, Nos. 19, 20; on Hersendis as the daughter of Aremburgis and Teduinus, see *Cart. Trinité de Vendôme*, nos. 19, 20, 111.
[71] *Cart. Trinité de Vendôme*, no. 19.
[72] Ibid., nos. 62, 63, 68.
[73] See below, Part II, No. 24.
[74] See below, Part II, No. 25.
[75] See below, Part II, No. 26.

frey at a grant to Marmoutier.[76] Additionally, between 1031 and 1039, Hubert, Fulk, and King Henry participated in a charter that set out the rights to be exercised by the count over the lands of the cathedral canons at Longchamps.[77]

One of the advantages available to Fulk in choosing Hubert to head the diocese of Angers in 1006 was the traditional relationship of the Vendômois to the Touraine, dominated by the Blésois rivals of Anjou. The great monastery of Marmoutier at Tours, whose abbots were selected by the counts of Blois-Tours-Chartres,[78] was the target of Angevin interest from the end of the ninth century. Count Fulk Nerra had, upon occasion, extended his largess towards that prestigious abbey despite its Blésois connections.[79] But his wooing of Marmoutier became more intense starting in 1020 when he sought from Marmoutier the first abbot of his new monastery of St. Nicholas. Baudricus was chosen, but he preferred the religious life at Marmoutier and left St. Nicholas. Not deterred by this failure, in the 1030s Fulk again sought a monk of Marmoutier to head St. Nicholas and Abbot Albert provided Renaud. But Renaud, too, fled from Count Fulk and became the first abbot of Geoffrey Martel's new monastery of Trinité de Vendôme. Exasperated at last, Fulk turned to St. Aubin at Angers for an abbot of St. Nicholas.[80]

Marmoutier had long been the favorite monastery of the Vendômois, however, and Hubert and his family and friends were accustomed to extend their favor to that house. The only known gifts to ecclesiastical establishments by Hubert's father and grandfather were in favor of Marmoutier.[81] Bishop Hubert's efforts at gaining influence at Marmoutier seem to have been more successful than those of Count Fulk. When Hubert consecrated Frederick as abbot of St. Florent in 1022, Abbot Ebrardus of Marmoutier was also present, even though the affair was solely a concern of the diocese of Angers.[82]

But with the accession of Albert of La Ferté to the abbotship of Marmoutier, Hubert's relations with that monastery became much closer. Albert was from the Vendômois and perhaps was even related to Hubert.[83] Hubert's cousin Vulgrinus took up the monastic life at Marmoutier (another indication of the family's attachment to that house), and it was under Abbot Albert that he rose to be prior, thus Albert's assistant, of the mon-

---

[76] See below, Part II, No. 27.

[77] See below, Part II, No. 34.

[78] Ferdinand Lot, *Etudes sur le règne de Hughes Capet et la fin du Xe siècle* (Paris, 1903), p. 433.

[79] Guillot, *Comte d'Anjou*, 2: nos. 5, 8, 55–57(a).

[80] See below, Part II, Nos. 8, 32, 35; Guillot (*Comte d'Anjou*, 1: p. 177) may well be right in seeing these incidents as proof of the weakness of Angevin monasticism and the prestige of Marmoutier, but Fulk's political intentions must not be ignored.

[81] *Livre des serfs de Marmoutier*, no. 1; and see below, Part II, No. 9.

[82] See below, Part II, No. 6.

[83] See above, chap. 2, n. 99.

astery.[84] With Albert and Vulgrinus controlling Marmoutier during the 1030s and 1040s, Hubert naturally found his influence there increased, and Angevin political ambitions in the Touraine had the path smoothed before them.

Except for his episcopal monasteries of St. Maurille and St. Serge and his own cathedral of St. Maurice, Hubert made personal grants to only one ecclesiastical establishment—Marmoutier.[85] In 1046, when Hubert "asked" Abbot Albert to select an "apt person" to become abbot of St. Serge, unsurprisingly Albert found that his prior, Hubert's own cousin Vulgrinus, was the best man for the task.[86] Hubert's warm relations with Marmoutier under Abbot Albert must have been well known and re-spected, for it was only after Hubert's death that certain monks of St. Serge pillaged the oratory of St. Vincent at Chalonnes-sur-Loire that Hubert had given to Marmoutier.[87]

Hubert's penetration of the Touraine is also seen at Tours itself. He opened ecclesiastical offices in Anjou to important churchmen at Tours, as in the case of Berengerius, the famous Berengar of Tours who was involved in the eucharistic conflict with Lanfranc in the mid-eleventh century. Ber-engar was from the Touraine and held the position of master of the cathe-dral school of Tours. But before 1039 he was associated with the church of St. Martin at Angers, and Hubert appointed him one of the three archdea-cons of his diocese by 1040. He made Berengar the cathedral treasurer ca. 1045–1046, an office that was particularly close to Hubert.[88] Thus when Count Geoffrey Martel made himself master of the Touraine in 1044,[89] the region had been drawn close to Anjou by means of the Angevin church under Bishop Hubert. Moreover, Marmoutier under Abbot Albert had been controlled by men of the Vendômois for over a decade. Thanks to Bishop Hubert, the count of Anjou already had many friends in the church of the Touraine.

By the time that Fulk departed Anjou on his last pilgrimage to Jerusalem sometime in 1039,[90] he and Bishop Hubert had been closely allied for thirty-two years. Although Hubert was not part of Fulk's retinue, they had fought together and had supported each other's political and ecclesiastical policies. Hubert and Fulk worked together on at least two occasions to settle disputes between ecclesiastical establishments,[91] and twice Fulk gave

---

[84] See above, chap. 2, nn. 98–100.

[85] See below, Part II, Nos. 52, 61, 68, 79.

[86] See below, Part II, No. 53.

[87] See below, Part II, No. 61.

[88] See below, chap. 4, nn. 49–50.

[89] Jacques Boussard, "L'éviction des tenants de Thibaut de Blois par Geoffroy Martel, comte d'Anjou, en 1044," *Moyen Age* 69 (1963), pp. 141–149; and Halphen, *Comté d'Anjou*, pp. 46–49.

[90] Halphen, *Comté d'Anjou*, pp. 217–218; Bachrach, "Pilgrimages of Fulk Nerra," p. 211.

[91] See below, Part II, Nos. 2, 34.

judgments that protected the bishop and promoted his efforts to rehabili-
tate St. Serge as well as the cathedral of Angers.[92]

Towards Count Geoffrey Martel, Bishop Hubert showed the same fidelity and cooperation that he had to Count Fulk Nerra. Geoffrey became
count of Vendôme ca. January 1032, and Hubert's position as a seigneur in
the Vendômois immediately placed him in a secular relationship with
Count Geoffrey. Hubert, his family, and his friends gave their support to
Geoffrey in his warfare with Bishop Gervais of Le Mans, and in endowing
the count's new monastery of Trinité de Vendôme.[93] With the approval of
the House of Anjou, Viscount Radulfus IV, husband of Hubert's niece
Emma, also came to hold the vicontiel title of Vendôme, and he and his
younger son Radulfus Paganus maintained a strong position in the
Vendômois throughout the eleventh century.[94]

From the time that Geoffrey Martel exercised the comital powers of
Anjou (by the end of 1039), until Bishop Hubert's death in March of 1047,
there is a continual record of harmony and cooperation between the count
and the bishop. Hubert led the Angevin clerical delegation at the dedication of Trinité de Vendôme in May of 1040.[95] Hubert and Geoffrey were
witnesses to the testament of Bishop Gervais of Le Mans to his cathedral
chapter around the same time.[96] In 1040 Hubert was involved in the
generale placitum held by Geoffrey at Angers.[97] In 1041 Geoffrey and
Hubert were together at Chardonnet for the dedication of St. Florent's new
church.[98] In 1045 Bishop Hubert was among sixteen witnesses to Count
Geoffrey's confirmation of Count Fulk's grants to Ronceray.[99] He was also
a witness to Geoffrey's confirmation of his father's gifts to St. Nicholas and
to Geoffrey's own donations to that monastery.[100]

Count Geoffrey and Hubert acted together to authorize the granting of
lands and customs to St. Serge by Burchardus the treasurer.[101] Geoffrey

---

[92] See below, Part II, Nos. 29, 23.

[93] The family of Hersendis was allied with Bishop Hubert (see above, n. 70). Salomon of
Lavardin, with whom Hubert was close (see below, Part II, No. 74), was a strong supporter of
Count Geoffrey during the war with Bishop Gervais (see above, n. 72). Bishop Hubert
cooperated with Countess Agnes in the transaction that eventually resulted in the countess's
giving Villerable to Trinité de Vendôme (see below, Part II, No. 71). Present at the dedication
of Trinité de Vendôme were Bishop Hubert (see below, Part II, Nos. 36, 37), Salomon of
Lavardin (*Cart. Trinité de Vendôme*, no. 35), an Ingelbaldus (ibid., no. 35), who was probably
Ingelbaldus Brito, the husband of Bishop Hubert's cousin Hildegardis (see above, chap. 2, n.
41), and perhaps Viscount Radulfus, the husband of Hubert's niece Emma (*Cart. Trinité de
Vendôme*, no. 36, and see below, Part II, No. 37, where he appears among the witnesses). On
the monastery of Trinité de Vendôme, see Penelope D. Johnson, *Prayer, Patronage and Power:
the Abbey of la Trinité, Vendôme, 1032–1187* (New York and London, 1981).

[94] See above, chap. 2, nn. 81–84.

[95] See below, Part II, Nos. 36, 37.

[96] See below, Part II, No. 38.

[97] See below, Part II, No. 39.

[98] See below, Part II, No. 40.

[99] See below, Part II, No. 42.

[100] See below, Part II, Nos. 49, 50.

[101] See below, Part II, No. 44.

cooperated with Hubert in the dedication of Toussaint,[102] and he approved of the appointment of Vulgrinus as abbot of St. Serge.[103] Between 1044 and 1047, Hubert participated with Count Geoffrey in resolving the dispute between Eudo of Blaison and the canons of St. Lézin.[104] Even after Hubert's death, Geoffrey continued to support the ecclesiastical restorations of Bishop Hubert by giving his permission for the prebend of St. Maurice to be regained by St. Serge.[105] In addition, the loyalty of Hubert's family continued to be rewarded. In 1056 Geoffrey appointed Vulgrinus to the bishopric of Le Mans.[106]

Hubert's steady allegiance to the Angevin counts during the last two decades of his life was mirrored by his persistent good relations with King Henry I, the son and successor of Robert II. Count Geoffrey Martel was constantly friendly with King Henry through 1047,[107] the year of Hubert's death. In addition to the resolution of the dispute concerning the cathedral canons' lands at Longchamps by Fulk, Hubert, and King Henry,[108] the king confirmed no less than three of Hubert's grants to ecclesiastical establishments between 1031 and 1047.[109] Hubert maintained his family's tradition of loyalty to the Capetians that stretched back even before the royal accession of Hugh Capet. Hubert's record of acts with King Henry also indicates that the king was not as much of a stranger to a territorial principality like Anjou as has usually been thought. Hubert obviously considered it worthwhile to seek out and obtain royal confirmations of many of his donations.[110]

In Bishop Hubert, the counts of Anjou had a true *fidelis*. There is no indication of any quarrel or dispute between Hubert and either Fulk or Geoffrey Martel during the almost forty-one years of his episcopacy. Hubert loyally supported Angevin politics, as was the tradition of his family, and he in turn found the counts willing to promote his ecclesiastical and family policies. This comital favor was also extended to the family of Hubert's niece Emma and to his cousin Vulgrinus. While it may be true that "il n'existe au 11e siècle que des intérêts et pas des fidélités,"[111] it was clearly in the interest of Hubert and his family to be faithful to the Angevin counts. Not even excommunication and interdict could dislodge Hubert

---

[102] See below, Part II, Nos. 57–58.

[103] See below, Part II, No. 53.

[104] See below, Part II, No. 76.

[105] See below, Part II, No. 80.

[106] See above, chap. 2, nn. 101–107.

[107] Jan Dhondt, "Henri Ier, l'Empire et l'Anjou (1043–56), *Revue belge de philologie et d'histoire* 25 (1946–47), pp. 99–101.

[108] See below, Part II, No. 35.

[109] See below, Part II, Nos. 68–70; and see Steven Fanning, "Charters of Henry I of France Concerning Anjou," *Speculum* 60 (1985), pp. 111–114.

[110] Fanning, "Charters of Henry I," pp. 113–114.

[111] Jan Dhondt, "Une crise du pouvoir capétien (1032–1034)," *Miscellanea Mediaevalia in memoriam Jan Frederik Niermeyer* (Groningen, 1967), p. 148.

from his position as a devoted follower of his count. Archbishop Hugh could derisively refer to Count Fulk as Hubert's *divus Fulco*.[112]

No doubt Fulk, after his difficulties with Bishop Renaud II, found that his selection of the son of the viscount of Vendôme was a wise and happy choice. The Vendômois, dominated by Hubert's clan, never failed to support the Angevin cause. The marriage of Hubert's niece to Viscount Radulfus of Le Mans helped to further the Angevin domination of Maine and the political isolation of the count of Maine within his own county. Hubert and his family worked to pull Marmoutier within the Angevin sphere of influence. And the Angevin church, under Hubert's direction, was always in harmony with comital politics. Hubert was unflinchingly loyal to Fulk Nerra and Geoffrey Martel, and they in turn fully cooperated with him. Loyalty was very much a mutual relationship.

The policies of Bishop Renaud, at variance with those of the count, ended in utter failure, while Bishop Hubert's policies, forged in alliance with the counts of Anjou, were eminently successful. For Hubert, political loyalty was an enduring element of his ecclesiastical and seigneurial careers.

---

[112] *Letters and Poems of Fulbert of Chartres,* no. 71, p. 122.

IV. THE ECCLESIASTICAL WORLD

Just as there were immediate political crises facing Hubert when he was ordained bishop of Angers in June of 1006, there were other severe problems awaiting his attention. Although Anjou and its surrounding regions experienced the general economic and population growth common to western Europe in the eleventh century, and the conquests of Fulk Nerra and Geoffrey Martel added considerable territory and power to the Angevin position, life in Anjou was still insecure. Two major fires raced through Angers within one-third of a century, there was major famine in the years 1043–1044, and almost constant warfare throughout this period visited its attendant misfortunes on all classes of society and disrupted the region's economy.[1]

The ecclesiastical life of Anjou also was not on a sound footing. The abbey of St. Aubin at Angers had been revived in the tenth century because of the interest and generosity of the counts of Anjou, as had the monastery of St. Florent under the counts of Blois. However, the remaining establishments of the diocese had not experienced a similar renaissance. The cell of St. Maurille was in ruins, the monastery of St. Serge had been wrecked by the Viking raids of the ninth and tenth centuries and was without monks, and the priory of St.-Maur-sur-Loire at Glanfeuil had also been destroyed by the "pagans" and was again plundered after being restored.[2] The church of St. Martin at Angers was so reduced that only two priests served there.[3] And the cathedral of St. Maurice at Angers had been ruined by the fire of the year 1000, was decrepit due to its age, and its canons had suffered from the neglect of the bishops and the depredations of the counts.[4] Conditions that were condemned by the eleventh-century reformers were common throughout the diocese. Simony, a married clergy, proprietary churches, and proprietary monasteries were to be found everywhere in Anjou.[5]

---

[1] Jacques Boussard, "La vie en Anjou aux XIe et XIIe siècles," *Moyen Age* 56 (1950), pp. 29–35; Jean-Marc Bienvenu, "Pauvreté, misères et charité en Anjou aux XIe et XIIe siècles," *Moyen Age* 72 (1966), pp. 389–424, 73 (1967), pp. 5–34, 189–216, esp. 72 (1966), pp. 389–410.

[2] See below, Part II, Nos. 22, 53, 26.

[3] B. n., D. H. II¹, no. 407; and see Forsyth, *Church of St. Martin at Angers*, pp. 104–105, n. 134.

[4] See below, Part II, No. 10; *Annales de Saint-Aubin*, p. 3; and see the obituary of Bishop Hubert, cited above, chap. 1, n. 2.

[5] Jean-Marc Bienvenu, "Les caractères originaux de la réforme grégorienne dans le diocèse d'Angers," *Bulletin philologique et historique du Comité des travaux historiques et scientifiques,*

Bishop Renaud II (973–1005) had attempted to restore both St. Maurille and St. Serge. At the latter he reestablished monks, and he made substantial endowments out of his own patrimony both to it and to the canons of the cathedral.[6] However, in doing so he came into opposition with Count Fulk, with the result that the domains of both establishments were plundered by the count.[7]

Warfare also struck hard at the church. For example, the prestigious monastery of St. Florent was burned when Fulk Nerra captured Saumur in 1026.[8] Church lands and offices were commonly diverted to secular purposes. The political interest of the bishops could bring about the secular retribution of the plundering of church lands, as occurred when Bishop Hubert fought against Archbishop Hugh of Tours in 1016.[9]

When Hubert became the bishop of Angers, therefore, his diocese was in a state of disruption and he was to face many difficulties throughout his episcopate. At Hubert's accession the most visible symbol of the delapidation of the diocese was his ruined cathedral. The fire of 1000 severely damaged the basilica, which was already in poor condition because of its age.[10] The restoration of the cathedral became the major work of the first half of Hubert's episcopate. He and his parents devoted considerable energy and expense to rebuild it from its foundations. This labor required twenty years, and neither of Hubert's parents lived to see the completion of the project. When the work was done, Hubert invited neighboring prelates to attend the dedication ceremonies on 16 August 1025. At that time he also provided for the welfare of the cathedral canons by returning to them rights that he had exercised over some of their lands. He retained only his customary episcopal rights. Hubert promoted the independence of the canons by conceding them the control of their own domains.[11]

In 1032 another fire, worse than the first, devastated Angers.[12] A Poitevin chronicle relates that everything within the city walls was burned, including the cathedral. Although the cathedral's walls withstood the flames, the remainder of the building was gutted,[13] and there is no record

---

1968, vol. 2, pp. 545–546; Madeleine Dillay, "Le régime de l'église privée du XIe au XIIIe siècle dans l'Anjou, le Maine, la Touraine," *Revue historique de droit français et étranger*, 4th series, 4 (1925), pp. 253–294; and C. Van de Kieft, "Une église privée de l'abbaye de la Trinité de Vendôme au XIe siècle," *Moyen Age* 69 (1963), pp. 157–168, esp. pp. 157–159. On the similar state of the Norman church in this period, see David Douglas, "The Norman Episcopate," pp. 101–102.

[6] See below, Part II, Nos. 22, 53.

[7] See above, chap. 3, n. 24.

[8] See below, Part II, No. 31.

[9] See above, chap. 3, nn. 48–51.

[10] See above, n. 4.

[11] See below, Part II, No. 10; and *Letters and Poems of Fulbert of Chartres*, no. 102. Some idea of the great effort involved in building a cathedral can be gained from Henry Kraus, *Gold Was the Mortar: the Economics of Cathedral Building* (London, Henley and Boston, 1979), even though it deals with the Gothic cathedrals of a later age.

[12] *Annales de Saint-Aubin*, p. 3.

[13] *Chronicon Sancti Maxentii Pictavensis* in *Chroniques des églises*, ed. Marchegay and Mabille (Paris, 1869), p. 391. Some Angevin loyalists have denied that the fire of 1032 damaged the

of the efforts made by Hubert during the last fifteen years of his life to repair St. Maurice once again.[14]

The welfare of his cathedral canons, as demonstrated in his grants to them when the cathedral was dedicated, was a concern of Hubert.[15] The lands pertaining to the canons and those to the bishop had probably been in the process of forming separate domains (*mensae*) from the end of the ninth century,[16] and Hubert's concession to the canons at the dedication of 1025 demonstrates that he favored this process.[17] Nevertheless, he maintained his control over the cathedral chapter, frequently attending its meetings and perhaps even presiding over them.[18]

The actual record of Hubert's donations to the cathedral gives little evidence that he was especially interested in its canonry, for it consists only of the restorations of 1025 and a no longer extant royal confirmation of another donation to the cathedral.[19] Moreover, Bishop Hubert had cooperated with Count Fulk when the latter overturned Bishop Renaud II's grants to St. Serge and to the cathedral, acts which must have caused great harm to the economic well being of the canons.[20] However, this meager record belies the fact that Hubert was active on behalf of the canons and that he earned their respect and admiration. The school master Bernard wrote that Hubert was "orderly in his habits and a young man of outstanding goodness."[21] To the canons, Hubert was far superior to his predecessors.[22]

Bishop Renaud II had gained from Fulk Nerra a concession of economic rights (bridge tolls) and the remission of *malae consuetudines*.[23] He restored to the cathedral chapter two churches that had been usurped by his family.[24] And he gave much of his own patrimony in the Mauges to the cathedral, the act which led to his bitter conflict with Count Fulk and to his

---

cathedral. See Thorode, *Notice de la ville d'Angers*, ed. Emile Longin (Angers, 1897), pp. 61–62, and see Longin's own comments, p. 62 n. 1. However, the fact of the cathedral's having been burned was effectively demonstrated by Ch. Urseau, "La cathédrale d'Angers, a-t-elle été incendiée en 1032?" *Bulletin monumental* 86 (1927), pp. 103–111. See also Paul de Farcy, "Construction de la cathédrale d'Angers," *Congrès archéologique de France* 38 (1871), pp. 252–254; Louis de Farcy, "Les fouilles de la cathédrale d'Angers," *Bulletin monumental* 66 (1902), pp. 488–498; Ch. Urseau, *La cathédrale d'Angers* (Paris, 1930), pp. 7–10; and André Mussat, *Le style gothique de la France (XIIe–XIIIe siècles)* (Paris, 1963), pp. 173–179.

[14] But it is not likely that Hubert would have allowed his cathedral to have remained in ruins with no effort made at repair during his last fifteen years.

[15] On the life of the canons during Hubert's episcopate and before, see Gerard Robin, "Le problème de la vie commune au chapitre de la cathédrale Saint-Maurice d'Angers du XIe et XIIe siècle," *Cahiers de civilisation médiévale* 13 (1970), pp. 305–322.

[16] Ibid., pp. 309–310.

[17] See below, Part II, No. 10.

[18] See below, Part II, No. 56.

[19] See below, Part II, Nos. 10, 69.

[20] See above, chap. 3, n. 24.

[21] *Liber Miraculorum Sancte Fidis* I, p. xxxiv, "Quorum dominus meus Hugbertus, hujus Andecavine urbis episcopus, satis compositis moribus, et egregie bonitatis juvenis . . ."

[22] See below, n. 28.

[23] *Cart. noir de la cathédrale d'Angers*, no. 22.

[24] Ibid., no. 23.

own virtual exile from Anjou.[25] But when Renaud died, the cathedral's obituary carried only the laconic entry, "12 June—Renaud, distinguished, venerable, and generous bishop of Angers died, in the year of salvation 1005, in the year of his ordination 31."[26]

But the cathedral's obituary entry for Bishop Hubert, whose grants to the canons have been regarded by a modern scholar as being of little significance when compared to those of Bishop Renaud,[27] is nothing less than effusive, and his care for both the cathedral and its canons is specifically contrasted favorably with that shown by his predecessors.[28]

When the sparse evidence presented by the surviving *diplomata* is supplemented by this eulogy, a much altered view of Hubert's relationship to his canons emerges. To the cathedral chapter, Hubert was an outstanding benefactor and a bishop worthy of veneration. Perhaps the brief obituary entry for Renaud II was due to his difficulties with Count Fulk, which made it impolitic for the canons to expend much praise for or lamentation on the bishop, or perhaps the comital wrath that fell on the cathedral because of Renaud's donations made the canons wish that he had not been quite so generous. Nevertheless, it is true that Hubert gained the sincere thanks of his cathedral chapter for his efforts on their behalf and for the general nature of his episcopate.

It is natural, then, that when the canons, led by the chanter Girard, desired to found an oratory to help care for the physical and spiritual needs of the poor, and they sought Bishop Hubert's approval,[29] he readily agreed and ordered that worthy priests be chosen for it so that the needs of the poor might be cared for honestly.[30] Hubert then dedicated the oratory in honor of All Saints, Toussaint, between 1040 and 1046, and Count Geoffrey Martel joined in the dedication to make a number of grants to the new foundation.[31]

Under Bishop Hubert the organization of the cathedral became more complex. As under his predecessors, Bishop Hubert's cathedral was administered by a dean, three archdeacons, a treasurer (who under Hubert was always one of the archdeacons), and a chanter.

The triple archidiaconate of the diocese dated back at least to 966,[32] and Hubert maintained this system. Guy, Burchardus, and Joscelin were archdeacons in 1025.[33] Burchard, Berengar, and Renaud were serving in

---

[25] Ibid., no. 24 (Halphen, *Comté d'Anjou*, p. j. no. 4).

[26] *Obituaire de la cathédrale d'Angers*, p. 23.

[27] Guillot, *Comte d'Anjou*, 1: p. 238, "La seule donation qu'ait faite l'évêque Hubert aux chanoines de Saint-Maurice pendant tout son épiscopat a été peu de chose à côté de celles qu'avait accordées, on l'a vu, son prédécesseur Renaud . . ."

[28] *Obituaire de la cathédrale d'Angers*, pp. 7–8, and see above, chap. 1, p. 1.

[29] See below, Part II, Nos. 54, 56.

[30] See below, Part II, Nos. 55, 56.

[31] See below, Part II, No. 57.

[32] Urseau, *Cart. noir de la cathédrale d'Angers*, p. xl; Jean-Marc Bienvenu traces it back to 886–888 (*Angers*, p. 17).

[33] See below, Part II, No. 10.

1040,[34] and Berengar, Renaud, and another Joscelin were archdeacons in March of 1046.[35] The diocese had been divided into distinct territories pertaining to each of the archdeacons perhaps as early as 929,[36] but it certainly seems to have been so during Hubert's episcopate. It is known that there were specific lands that pertained to Berengar's archidiaconate.[37]

Hubert seems to have had an especially close relationship with his archdeacon–treasurer. Guy and Burchardus may have been related to him.[38] Burchardus became an archdeacon no later than 1025 and obtained the office of treasurer by 1028.[39] He held both posts until sometime between October 1045 and March 1046.[40] Burchardus was the only major clerical officeholder who was a permanent part of Hubert's entourage. He witnessed Hubert's charter for the cathedral canons in 1025, helped him establish the parochial boundaries of Ronceray, and along with the bishop he witnessed donations to that convent by Count Fulk and Countess Hildegardis.[41] He was also present at the dedication of Trinité de Vendôme in 1040.[42] Along with Hubert and the dean Joscelin, he witnessed Geoffrey Martel's confirmation of Count Fulk's gifts to Ronceray.[43] Burchardus and Hubert were the only two clerics who witnessed Count Geoffrey Martel's confirmation of Fulk's donations to St. Nicholas.[44]

At some point in 1045 or 1046, Bishop Hubert made a substantial change in the office of archdeacon–treasurer. Guy and Burchardus had both been married and had children. They had been deeply involved in secular affairs, and in his old age Burchardus had grown weary of the wars he had fought for the counts of Anjou.[45] Between October of 1045 and March of 1046, Hubert made the archdeacon Berengar the treasurer of St. Maurice as well.[46] Better known as the heresiarch Berengar of Tours, he had been educated under Bishop Fulbert of Chartres, and had been the master of the cathedral school of Tours.[47] Berengar's association with the Angevin church was probably partly political in nature,[48] yet it was also part of a mild reform of the clergy of the Angevin diocese.

---

[34] They were among the Angevin witnesses to Part II, Nos. 36, 37.

[35] See below, Part II, No. 53.

[36] *Cart. noir de la cathédrale d'Angers*, no. 33, note k, and pp. xxxix–xl.

[37] Ibid., no. 52, "guerpivit Marchoardus pater et Marchoardus filius terram sancti Mauricii pertenentem ad archidiaconatum Berengerii . . ."

[38] See above, chap. 2, n. 111.

[39] See below, Part II, No. 15.

[40] See below, Part II, No. 53, which follows Guillot, *Comte d'Anjou*, 2: no. 91.

[41] See below, Part II, Nos. 10, 15.

[42] He was among the witnesses to Part II, Nos. 36, 37.

[43] See below, Part II, No. 42.

[44] See below, Part II, Nos. 49, 50.

[45] See below, Part II, No. 41, "ego Burchardus clericus et thesaurarius Sancti Mauricii matris Ecclesiae Andecavensis . . . ac per hoc sub iisdem bellicosissimis principibus multis defatigatus bellorum et laborum negotiis . . ."

[46] See below, Part II, No. 53.

[47] See below, Part II, No. 55.

[48] See above, chap. 3, n. 88.

Even though Berengar divided his time between Angers and Tours, Hubert kept up a close relationship with his learned archdeacon–treasurer. Berengar was at Hubert's side when the bishop granted land at Grand Launay to Marmoutier to smooth the way for Hubert's cousin Vulgrinus to be appointed abbot of St. Serge.[49] The man who held the office of arch-deacon–treasurer of the cathedral of Angers was more closely associated with Hubert than any other cleric. It seems that Hubert relied heavily on the archdeacons and it is possible that he used the archdeacons Berengar and Renaud as his representatives to judgments to determine ecclesiastical conflicts, as in the dispute between St. Aubin and St. Florent over Saugé-aux-Moines.[50]

In addition to the change that Hubert instituted in the office of arch-deacon–treasurer, he was also the first bishop of Angers known to have had a personal chaplain.[51] Fulcodius *capellanus episcopi* was a witness to Hubert's charter of 1 March 1046,[52] and it may well have been he who witnessed Hubert's 1025 charter as Fulcoius *presbyter*.[53]

The most important innovation concerning the cathedral carried out by Hubert during his episcopacy came in the area of education. It is under Hubert that a cathedral school, the forerunner of the University of Angers, is first known to have existed at Angers.[54] The foundation of such schools in the west of France was common during the later tenth and eleventh centuries.[55] This development, in which Bishop Fulbert of Chartres played a major role,[56] was shared by Angers.

Probably around 1012, Bishop Hubert called Bernard, a former pupil of Fulbert, to direct the school of Angers.[57] Bernard, who was a native of

---

[49] See below, Part II, Nos. 52, 53.

[50] *Cart. St.-Aubin,* no. 198, dated to 27 June 1040–15 August 1052 by Guillot (*Comte d'Anjou,* 2: no. 127).

[51] Urseau, *Cart. noir de la cathédrale d'Angers,* pp. lvii–lviii.

[52] See below, Part II, No. 53.

[53] See below, Part II, No. 10.

[54] Urseau, *Cart. noir de la cathédrale d'Angers,* pp. lviii–lvix.

[55] On the school, see Pierre Rangeard, *Histoire de l'Université d'Angers,* ed. Albert Lemar-chand (Angers, 1872), 1: pp. 8–33; Hastings Rashdall, *The Universities of Europe in the Middle Ages,* new ed. by F. M. Powicke and A. B. Emden (Oxford, 1936), 2: pp. 151–152; Léon Maitre, *Les écoles épiscopales et monastiques en Occident avant les universités (768–1180)* (Paris, 1924), pp. 85–86; Emile Lesne, *Histoire de la propriété ecclésiastique en France,* vol. 4, *les écoles de la fin du VIIIe siècle à la fin du XIIe* (Lille, 1940), pp. 121–123; Jean-Marc Bienvenu, "Les caractères originaux," p. 547; and Jean Vezin, *Les 'scriptoria' d'Angers au XIe siècle,* Bib-liothèque de l'Ecole des hautes études, IVe section—Sciences historiques et philologiques, fasc. 322 (Paris, 1974), pp. 8–9.

[56] Rashdall, *Universities of Europe,* 1: pp. 29–31; Maitre, *Les écoles épiscopales,* pp. 64–65; and Behrends, *Letters and Poems of Fulbert of Chartres,* pp. xxxiv–xxxv.

[57] *Liber Miraculorum Sancte Fidis,* letter to Bishop Fulbert of Chartres, p. 2, "Interea causa extitit qua ad urbem Andecavensem, ab ipsius urbis episcopo exoratus, transmigrarem." On the date of Bernard's going to Angers, see P. Calendini, "Bernard Ier, scholastique d'Angers," *Dictionnaire d'histoire et de géographie ecclésiastiques* 8, col. 579. This dating seems to be confirmed by Bernard's description of his first stay at Angers (*Liber Miraculorum,* p. 2; see below, n. 60). In the intitulation of his letter, Bernard describes himself as *scolasticus, Ande-cavine scola magister.*

Anjou,[58] established good relations with the relatively young Hubert, and when the bishop restored the cathedral of Angers, he dedicated an altar in it to St. Foi,[59] whose miracles were recorded by Bernard in the work for which he is best known, the *Liber Miraculorum Sancte Fidis.* Bernard had originally planned to stay at Angers for only three years, but Hubert apparently convinced him to remain longer. During the conflict of 1016 between Hubert and Archbishop Hugh of Tours, Bernard was caught in a difficult position. Bishop Fulbert, Bernard's mentor, was allied with Archbishop Hugh and Count Odo II, but Bernard was in Angers and supported Bishop Hubert, Count Fulk, and King Robert. Hubert may have prevailed upon his *scolae magister* to help him in the exchange of polemics with Hugh and Bishop Fulbert. But then he permitted Bernard to escape further entanglements by leaving Angers and visiting Conques to do research on St. Foi's miracles.[60] After the conflict was resolved, Bernard returned to Angers to resume the direction of the school.[61]

By 1025, however, Hubert had named Bernerius as the master of the school,[62] where he had earlier been associated with Bernard.[63] By 1039 Hubert had appointed another of Fulbert's students, Renaud, as the *magister.*[64] This Renaud also became an archdeacon and a chancellor, and he wrote numerous charters for the counts of Anjou. He was head of the cathedral school until around 1075, and he was the author of the *Annales dites de Renaud.*[65]

Bishop Hubert saw to it that some of the masters of the school became closely involved in the office of chancellor. Under Bishop Renaud II the chancellor's office was held by an archdeacon.[66] Hubert continued this practice in the first half of his episcopate. In 1025, for example, Burchardus

---

[58] Bouillet, *Liber Miraculorum,* p. xi.

[59] *Liber Miraculorum,* 1: xxxiv, p. 87.

[60] *Liber Miraculorum,* 1: p. 2; 2: vii; and see Fanning, "La lutte entre Hubert," p. 32.

[61] *Liber Miraculorum,* 1: p. 2; 2: vii, vol. 1, p. 87.

[62] See below, Part II, No. 10.

[63] *Liber Miraculorum,* 1: xiii.

[64] See the witness list to B. n., D. H. II¹, no. 407, "hoc donum viderunt et audierunt Beringerius grammaticus, Magister Rainaldus . . ." Guillot (*Comte d'Anjou,* 2: no. 61) dates this act only between 1000 and 1039, but since Renaud is the *magister* here, it must have occurred after Bernerius was the head of the school in 1025, thereby giving chronological *termini* of 16 August 1025–1039. On Renaud's association with Fulbert, see *Historia Sancti Florentii* in *Chroniques des églises d'Anjou,* p. 287.

[65] Urseau, *Cart. noir de la cathédrale d'Angers,* p. lvi. The *scolasticus* John who was present at the dedication of Trinité de Vendôme (witness list to Part II, Nos. 36, 37) on 31 May 1040 was not a master of the school. Renaud was already *magister* by 1039 (see above, n. 64). Moreover, at this period in Angers, *scolasticus* is not always synonymous with master of the school. For example, as noted above, end of n. 57), Bernard called himself by both titles at once, *scolasticus, Andecavine scola magister,* and later in the *Liber Miraculorum* he referred to Bernerius as *scholasticus meus* (vol. 1, xiii). Therefore the meaning of *scholasticus* here seems to be only the general term "schoolman" or teacher. See also Halphen, *Recueil d'annales angevines et vendômoises,* pp. xxxii–xxxiii.

[66] *Gallia Christiana* 14, Instrumenta, c. 62, for Hildemannus (and see *Cart. noir de la cathédrale d'Angers,* no. 27); for Burchardus, see *Cart. St.-Aubin,* no. 21.

was archdeacon and chancellor.[67] However, at the same time, school personnel were already being given a role in the actual drawing up of *diplomata*. During the early eleventh century it was common in France for a school master to perform the duties of a chancellor. Sometimes he would carry the actual title of chancellor, as at Chartres, Tours, Cambrai, and Liège.[68] The title *levita*, or Levite, was also intimately associated with one who served as a scribe.[69] This was the case at Chartres, Tours, Fleury, Cluny, and Angers during this period.[70] It was also often paired with the title of master of the school.[71]

Under Bishop Hubert this same phenomenon occurred at Angers. In 1025 Bernerius was called *levita et scholae magister*. The actual writer of that charter was named Renaud, who was acting *ad vicem Burchardi archidiaconi et cancellarii*.[72] As has been seen, a Renaud succeeded Bernerius as master of the cathedral school,[73] and it appears that it was he who served as scribe in this charter and went on to function as a comital scribe for forty years.[74]

---

[67] See below, Part II, No. 10.

[68] For Chartres, see A. Clerval, "Les écoles de Chartres au moyen-âge du Ve au XVIe siècle," *Mémoires de la Société archéologique d'Eure-et-Loir* 11 (1895), pp. 22–23, 47–48; for Liège and Cambrai, see Godefroid Kurth, *Notger de Liège et la civilisation au Xe siècle* (Paris, 1905), p. 259; for Tours, see Edouard Favre, *Eudes Comte de Paris et Roi de France (882–898)* (Paris, 1893), p. j. no. 4, and Emile Mabille, "Les invasions normandes dans la Loire et les pérégrinations du corps de Saint Martin," *Bibliothèque de l'Ecole des chartes*, 6th series, 5 (1869), p. j. no. 8; see also *Cart. St.-Julien de Tours*, no. 1; and for Marmoutier, see *Cartulaire de Marmoutier pour le Dunois*, ed. Emile Mabille (Châteaudun, 1874), no. 52.

[69] This has been noted for southern France and Spain by Henri Leclercq, "Levita," *Dictionnaire d'archéologie chrétienne et de Liturgie* 8, ed. Fernand Cabrol and Henri Leclercq (Paris, 1929), col. 2993.

[70] For Chartres, see *Cartulaire de l'abbaye de Saint-Père de Chartres*, 2 vols., ed. Guérard (Paris, 1840), 1: no. iii; 3: no. vii; 6: no. iv; for Tours, see de Grandmaison, "Fragments de chartes," no. 36; Favre, *Eudes comte de Paris*, p. j. no. 4; Mabille, "Invasions normandes," p. j. no. 14; *Cart. St.-Julien de Tours*, nos. 1, 10; for Marmoutier, see *Marmoutier, Cartulaire blésois*, ed. Ch. Métais (Blois, 1891), no. 4; for Fleury, see *Recueil des chartes de l'abbaye de Saint-Benoît-sur-Loire*, Documents publiés par la Société historique et archéologique du Gâtinais, vol. 5 (Paris, 1900–1907), nos. 52, 59, 53, 57, 58. For Cluny, there is an overwhelming abundance of information in *Recueil des chartes de l'abbaye de Cluny*, ed. Auguste Bernard and Alexandre Bruel, 6 vols. (Paris, 1876). In the first volume alone one can find twenty-three *levitae*–scribes during the period 863–953. For the scribal activities at Cluny at the end of the tenth century by Aldebald, who was also called *levita*, see Bernard de Vregille, "Aldebald the Scribe of Cluny and the Bible of Abbot William of Dijon," tr. Frideswide Sandleman and Maria Boulding, *Cluniac Monasticism in the Central Middle Ages*, ed. Noreen Hunt (Hamden, Conn., 1971), pp. 85–97, esp. 92–93. For Angers, see *Cart. St.-Aubin*, nos. 18, 21, 394, 211, 282.

[71] At Tours, this was true from Archanaldus (Mabille, "Invasions normandes," p. j. no. 8, 14), and Adalmarus (Grandmaison, "Fragments de chartes," no. 38, and Emile Mabille, *Chroniques des comtes d'Anjou, Introduction* [Paris, 1856–57], no. 10; this is also true for Aregarius at Chartres (René Merlet and Abbé Clerval, *Un manuscrit chartrain du XIe siècle* [Chartres, 1893], p. 169).

[72] See below, Part II, No. 10.

[73] See above, n. 65.

[74] On the subject of comital scribes, see Guillot, *Comte d'Anjou*, 1: pp. 418–420. However, he does not identify Renaud the scribe with Renaud the archdeacon, although he does suggest that the scribe might be Renaud the chancellor (ibid., p. 420). In discussing Fulk's

As noted above, both Berengar and Renaud were associated with the comital church of St. Martin at Angers before 1040.[75] It seems probable that it was they who were assigned the task by Fulk Nerra of writing down the tale of the count's difficulties in finding an abbot for St. Nicholas.[76] Renaud also became the cathedral chancellor,[77] so he held the related offices of school master and chancellor. It was probably this same Renaud who wrote several comital charters ca. 1049–1073 and is called variously *levita, notarius,* and *archidiaconus.*[78]

Prebends from the church of St. Martin at Angers appear to have provided the financial compensation for those who wrote on behalf of the counts of Anjou. Berengar *grammaticus* and *magister* Renaud were clerics at St. Martin,[79] and Count Fulk ordered the *domini* Berengar and Renaud to write a document for his monastery of St. Nicholas.[80] Berengar wrote numerous letters for Count Geoffrey Martel,[81] and Renaud *levita* served as a comital scribe for almost forty years.[82] Thus it seems that the Renaud who was *magister, archidiaconus,* and *cancellarius* was also the Renaud who was called *levita* during the same period.

Therefore there was a modest reform in the office of chancellor of the cathedral under Bishop Hubert. Just as Guy and Burchardus were succeeded as treasurer by Berengar, so Burchardus was also followed as chancellor by the school master Renaud, who actually fulfilled the functions of that office until the last years of his life.

Hubert's relationship with the regular clergy of his diocese varied with

---

scribes, Guillot states that the count ordered two cathedral canons to draw up an act for him. But in the citation of his source for that assertion (p. 419 n. 352 #1), he made an ellipsis of five words, which greatly altered the meaning of the quotation. Guillot cited Le Peletier's *Epitome* (*Rerum Scitu Dignissimarum a Prima fundatione Monasterii S. Nicolai Andegavensis ad hunc usque diem, Epitome, Nec non eiusdem Monasterii Abbatum series* [Angers, 1635]), p. 5; no. 50 in Guillot's catalogue d'actes, Part II, No. 24 below, which reads, with his ellipsis supplied here and italicized, "Haec autem decreta Rotbertus atque Lambertus, duo uterini fratres canonici sancti Mauricii, *sculpenda in ipsius eclesiae parite,* ut diu servata essent, depinxerunt." Thus Robert and Lambert served here as stone carvers, not scribes.

[75] See above, n. 64.

[76] See below, Part II, No. 35, where Fulk ordered Berengar and Renaud to record the events.

[77] Among the witnesses to the charter in Le Peletier, *Epitome,* p. 18 (Guillot, *Comte d'Anjou,* 2: no. 192), are Bishop Eusebius, the dean Joscelin, the chancellor Renaud, and Berengar *grammaticus.* Since this Renaud appears here surrounded by members of the cathedral hierarchy, and given the common association of the offices of chancellor and master of the school (see above, nn. 64, 65, 67), and of those of chancellor and archdeacon at Angers (see above, nn. 65, 72), it seems that this identification is correct.

[78] *Cart. St.-Aubin,* nos. 77, 198; *Cart. Trinité de Vendôme,* no. 159; Le Peletier, *Epitome,* pp. 16–18 (Guillot, *Comte d'Anjou,* 2: no. 192), and Le Peletier, *Breviculum Fundationis et Series Abbatum Sancti Nicolai Andegavensis* (Angers, 1616), p. 17; *Cart. Trinité de Vendôme,* no. 88 (Guillot, 2: no. 122); and see above, n. 74.

[79] B. n., D. H. II[1], no. 407.

[80] See above, n. 76.

[81] Jean de Montclos, *Lanfranc et Brenger, la controverse eucharistique du XIe siècle,* Université catholique de Louvain, Spicilegium Sacrum Lovaniense, Etudes et documents, fasc. 37 (Leuven, 1971), pp. 15–16.

[82] See above, n. 78.

the status of his monastic house. He was not especially close to most of the comital abbeys of Anjou. His episcopal position was respected, but those monasteries were largely left to the direction of the counts. However, during Hubert's episcopate a measure of reform came to them, just as it had to the cathedral and the episcopal abbeys under his supervision.

The monastery of St. Aubin was the principal monastic house that was in the power of the counts of Anjou at the time when Hubert became bishop of Angers. (St. Florent came under Fulk's domination only in 1026 when he captured Saumur.) In the eleventh century St. Aubin was firmly in the hands of the counts of Anjou, forming part of their comital *honor*.[83] The designation of the abbot was exercised by the count, although the charters make it clear that at times the bishop had some role in the abbatial appointment.[84]

The first abbatial vacancy at St. Aubin during Hubert's rule of the Angevin church occurred in 1027, and the charter relating the designation of Primaldus to that office, which is found in St. Aubin's twelfth-century cartulary, is mutilated in such a fashion that it is impossible to determine if a reference to a role played by Bishop Hubert in Primaldus's selection was originally included.[85] But since Hubert was on good terms with Count Fulk in 1027 and 1028, it is probable that he ordained Primaldus as abbot of St. Aubin.[86]

The appointment of Walter as abbot in 1036, however, clearly demonstrates that by then Hubert was involved in the selection of St. Aubin's abbot. Following a formula first used in the charter of the election of the first abbess of Ronceray in 1028,[87] the 1036 charter of St. Aubin changed the wording to state that Walter's selection was made "through the assent of Lord Bishop Hubert and through the favor of Lord Count Fulk, with the assent of noble clerics and laics and outstanding persons of both sexes."[88] On this occasion, the charter, following Ronceray's formula, went on to state that the monks had given their unanimous consent to Walter's legitimate election.[89] These two elements, the prominent role of the bishop and

---

[83] Guillot, *Comte d'Anjou*, 1: pp. 138–154.

[84] *Cart. St.-Aubin*, nos. 21–22, 24–26, in which the counts "delegated" the abbots. These five acts follow the same formula, but the lines carrying the counts' title of archabbot of St. Aubin were gauged out in its cartulary during the twelfth century by a monk who found the absence of proper abbatial elections by the monks too offensive (Guillot, *Comte d'Anjou*, 1: pp. 445–452). In the charter of 970 (no. 21), it is evident that the mutilator also obliterated a portion of the lines that concern those who agreed to the appointment of Abbot Albert, for the text resumes with "———sis episcopi vel etiam nobilium personarum nostrorum fidelium . . . ." The original document must have read "Nefingi Andegavensis episcopi," etc., perhaps preceded by "una cum consensu" since nos. 24–26 resume after the mutilation with those words. No. 25 specifically mentions participation by Bishop Renaud II, "———una cum consensu Rainaldi Andecavensis episcopi . . ." Therefore some role by the bishop in abbatial appointments seems to have been ordinary.

[85] *Cart. St.-Aubin*, no. 26.

[86] See above, chap. 3, nn. 57, 61.

[87] *Cart. Ronceray*, no. 15.

[88] See below, Part II, No. 25.

[89] Loc. cit.

the election of an abbot, rather than his delegation by the count, mark a major change in the relationship of St. Aubin to the count. Henceforth the preponderant voice of the bishop in abbatial selections at St. Aubin is standard.[90]

While Hubert was not deeply involved in the management of St. Aubin, he did perform his normal episcopal functions towards it. He collected his episcopal revenues from its parishes,[91] he probably participated in the division of St.-Rémy-la-Varenne between St. Aubin and St. Lézin in 1014,[92] and he had a role in appointing its abbots.[93] He may have indirectly helped resolve the dispute over Saugé-aux-Moines between St. Aubin and St. Florent.[94] The resolution of this conflict occurred between 1040 and 1052.[95] The name of the bishop of Angers at the time of the settlement is not given, but Berengar the archdeacon and Renaud *levita* (who was also an archdeacon)[96] were present. Since Bishop Hubert was especially close to Berengar, perhaps on this occasion the two archdeacons served as his representatives at the judgment.

The dispute between St. Aubin and Trinité de Vendôme over the church of St. Clement at Craon perhaps also dates from Hubert's pontificate. Count Geoffrey and Countess Agnes removed that church from St. Aubin's power and gave it to Trinité.[97] The latest possible date for the transfer is 27 June 1047,[98] only three months after Bishop Hubert's death. Therefore, some of the "many synods of the bishop of Angers"[99] at which the monks of St. Aubin failed to regain St. Clement could have been held by Hubert.

The abbey of St. Nicholas was founded by Count Fulk Nerra and Bishop Hubert dedicated it around 1 December 1020.[100] Twelve years later, Hubert and the archdeacons cooperated to make a decree allowing more people to be buried in its cemetery so long as they paid the proper dues to their own parish.[101] This provision was responsible for a dispute ca. 1073–1077 between Ronceray and St. Nicholas over the attempt to bury the young man Piscis in the latter's cemetery.[102] Following Fulk's death,

---

[90] *Cart. St.-Aubin*, nos. 28–31.

[91] See below, Part II, No. 64, and see below, n. 155.

[92] See below, Part II, no. 2.

[93] See above, n. 88.

[94] *Cart. St.-Aubin*, no. 198, and see above, n. 50.

[95] Guillot, *Comte d'Anjou*, 2: no. 127.

[96] See above, n. 78.

[97] *Cart. Trinité de Vendôme*, no. 98.

[98] The church of St. Clement at Craon appears among the possessions of Trinité de Vendôme in Pope Clement II's confirmation of that date (*Cart. Trinité de Vendôme*, no. 76).

[99] Ibid., no. 98.

[100] See below, Part II, No. 5.

[101] See below, Part II, No. 24.

[102] See below, Part II, No. 17. On this dispute and others of a similar nature, see Jean-Marc Bienvenu, "Les conflits de sépulture en Anjou aux XIe et XIIIe siècle," *Bulletin philologique et historique du Comité des travaux historiques et scientifiques*, vol. 2, 1966, pp. 673–685.

Bishop Hubert witnessed Count Geoffrey Martel's confirmation of his father's grants to St. Nicholas as well as his own gifts to the monastery.[103]

No charters of abbatial appointments for St. Nicholas still exist, but it is obvious that Count Fulk maintained full control over the selection of the abbots.[104] Since Hubert had a role in the selection of St. Aubin's abbot and he ordained Frederick of St. Florent, who was the nominee of Hubert's old opponent Count Odo II of Blois, it is probable that he ordained St. Nicholas's abbots as well.[105]

The convent of St. Mary of Charity, better known now as Ronceray, was also a comital establishment. The surviving documents show that Hubert was more closely involved there than in the other abbeys under the control of the counts. Ronceray was founded by the comital family of Anjou, but it was principally a project of Fulk's wife, Countess Hildegardis. Hubert dedicated Ronceray on 14 July 1028 and played a major role in establishing the arrangements between the nuns and the priests who served their church. He constituted the parish of St. Mary and confirmed the grants made to the convent. After the dedication, vine lands near the church, meadows near Fosse, an alod with a mill at Chauvon, an alod at Sémelon, and one-fourth of the mill in the river Sarthe at Morannes were given to Ronceray but were still held by Hubert.[106] This was perhaps an indication that Hubert was the donor of these gifts, a suggestion reinforced by Countess Hildegardis's grant of a mill at Morannes returning the *census* to the bishop, since it is known that Hubert had possessed a mill at Morannes but he had cooperated with the countess in giving it to Ronceray.[107] In addition to these direct actions to Ronceray's benefit, Hubert also gave his consent to the widow Aremburgis to donate the land and coliberts at Coëmont, which she held as a benefice from him, to that convent when she and her daughter entered it.[108]

The charter of the election of Leoburga as the first abbess of Ronceray does not mention Hubert, but it does mark the initiation of monastic reform in Anjou. In that diploma, given in 1028, it is recorded that all the sisters gave their consent to the legitimate election of Leoburga,[109] and that charter became the model for the election of Abbot Walter of St. Aubin in 1036.[110] Despite the silence of this charter concerning Hubert, his prominent role in the foundation, dedication, and endowment of Ronceray makes it likely that he also ordained Leoburga as abbess.

A fourth Angevin monastery came into comital hands with the capture of Saumur by Fulk Nerra in 1026. Under Abbot Robert (985–1011), the

---

[103] See below, Part II, Nos. 49, 50.
[104] See below, Part II, No. 8.
[105] See below, Part II, Nos. 25, 6.
[106] See below, Part II, No. 15.
[107] See below, Part II, Nos. 14, 18.
[108] See below, Part II, No. 20.
[109] *Cart. Ronceray,* no. 15.
[110] See above, nn. 87–89.

abbey of St. Florent had been allied with the House of Blois. Bishop Renaud II of Angers had broken with Count Fulk and joined Abbot Robert and the counts of Blois. However, the accession of Fulk's *fidelis* Hubert as bishop of Angers endangered Robert's position. In an effort to break free of Hubert's episcopal power, which was sure to be exercised on Fulk's behalf, Abbot Robert produced two forged *diplomata* aimed at exempting St. Florent from normal diocesan taxation. Robert's machinations against Anjou failed, however, and he was forced by events to recognize Fulk as his *senior*.[111] Bishop Hubert set about incorporating the Mauges, containing many lands pertaining to St.-Florent-le-Vieil, into his diocese. After he had successfully weathered the crisis of 1016, Bishop Hubert was able to exercise his episcopal authority over St. Florent. In September 1022 he ordained Frederick, the choice of Count Odo of Blois, as its abbot.[112]

With Fulk's capture of Saumur in 1026 and the associated burning of the monastery of St. Florent,[113] both the *castrum* and the *monasterium* were in firm Angevin hands. Now the records of Hubert's direction of the diocesan affairs of St. Florent are more abundant. He reestablished the burned out church of St. Florent within Saumur.[114] In 1040 he participated in the resolution of a dispute over the customs of that church in Count Geoffrey's *placitum*.[115] In 1041 he assisted in the dedication of St. Florent's new monastery.[116] Perhaps, through his archdeacons, he helped resolve the quarrel between St. Florent and St. Aubin over Saugé-aux-Moines.[117]

In addition to these other monasteries, the abbey of St. Lézin at Angers was in the count's power. Fulk Nerra was its archabbot,[118] and Hubert had few contacts with it. In 1014 he was probably a participant in the division of the *curtis* of St.-Rémy-la-Varenne between St. Lézin and St. Aubin carried out by Fulk.[119] Hubert's only other known contact with St. Lézin was when he assisted Geoffrey Martel in resolving a dispute between its canons and Eudo of Blaison between 1044 and 1047.[120]

Of the monastic houses in the power of the bishop of Angers, Hubert was in complete control. The little cell of St. Maurille, located at Chalonnes-sur-Loire, had been in the hands of the bishops of Angers for two centuries,[121] and Bishop Renaud II had undertaken its restoration, but he died before the project could be completed.[122] Hubert continued Renaud's

---

[111] Bachrach, "Robert of Blois," p. 143.

[112] See below, Part II, No. 6.

[113] See below, Part II, No. 31.

[114] Loc. cit.

[115] See below, Part II, No. 39.

[116] See below, Part II, No. 40.

[117] See above, nn. 50, 94.

[118] *Cart. St.-Aubin*, no. 1.

[119] See below, Part II, No. 2.

[120] See below, Part II, No. 76.

[121] *Rec. de Charles le Chauve*, no. 32, where it is listed among the possessions confirmed to the cathedral of Angers by Charles the Bald.

[122] See below, Part II, No. 22.

work and dedicated the cell's church, and he and several of his *fideles* made donations to St. Maurille.[123] During the course of his episcopacy, he also was able to remove Renaud of Château-Gontier and his family from their position in St. Maurille by means of an exchange of lands.[124] He also bought vine lands from various sources and gave them to the cell.[125] Then, on 1 March 1046, he gave St. Maurille to the only other monastery in the diocese that was an episcopal establishment, St.-Serge d'Angers.[126]

The abbey of St. Serge, located just outside the north wall of Angers, had originally been given to Bishop Raino of Angers and his successors by Alan the Great of Brittany around the beginning of the tenth century.[127] Bishop Renaud II had also taken a great interest in repairing the damage done to that abbey by Viking raids and other depredations.[128] He is said to have restored St. Serge in the year 1000,[129] and he sent monks into the monastery.[130] Perhaps he installed one of his kinsmen as its abbot,[131] and he made a number of grants to it. He attempted to exempt its *burgus* from all episcopal and comital customs,[132] and he gained a royal confirmation for his restorations and grants to St. Serge from his own patrimony in the Mauges.[133]

As has been seen, this patrimony was claimed by the comital house of Anjou. Count Fulk took matters into his own hands and pillaged Renaud's grants to St. Serge in the Mauges and elsewhere. He began the construction of his *castrum* of Montrevault, and his *milites* received benefices from the lands given to the abbey by Renaud. This action was carried out either directly by Fulk himself or indirectly by the canons of the cathedral, since the chapter could exercise the bishop's functions *sede vacante*.[134] At this time, the monks were probably removed from St. Serge and replaced with canons.[135] Thus Renaud's efforts towards St. Serge came to nothing be-

---

[123] Loc. cit.

[124] See below, Part II, No. 48.

[125] See below, Part II, No. 62.

[126] See below, Part II, No. 53.

[127] *Cart. noir de la cathédrale d'Angers,* no. 12.

[128] See below, Part II, No. 53.

[129] *Chronicon Sancti Sergii Andegavensis* in *Chroniques des églises d'Anjou,* p. 134.

[130] See below, Part II, No. 53.

[131] See above, chap. 2, n. 110.

[132] B. n., ms. lat. 5446, p. 239, no. 16.

[133] *Recueil des historiens de France* 10, p. 583.

[134] Robert L. Benson, *The Bishop-Elect: a Study in Medieval Ecclesiastical Office* (Princeton, N. J., 1968), p. 85.

[135] Renaud placed monks there (see below, Part II, No. 53), and he also donated the villa of Champigné-sur-Sarthe to St. Serge (Part II, No. 23). But Hubert also established monks at St. Serge (Part II, No. 77), and when he restored Champigné-sur-Sarthe to the monastery, it was related that the villa had been granted to "someone" in a charter when the canons were living there (Part II, No. 23). Thus it seems that Renaud placed monks at St. Serge and made his donations from his patrimony to it. Then, due to Fulk, canons replaced the monks and the land that Renaud had given the abbey was granted out as benefices. Hubert then repurchased some of these lands and reestablished monks at St. Serge.

cause of his conflict with the power of Count Fulk. In 1006, St. Serge must have presented a lamentable appearance to the new bishop.

Upon his ordination, Hubert began to practice a policy of cooperation with Fulk, and he was able to resume the restoration of St. Serge and to promote the welfare of his own family. Hubert, ever faithful to Fulk, was careful to get the count's permission to repurchase some of these controversial lands. By 1031 Hubert had begun to restore a portion of the recovered lands to St. Serge,[136] but a part he kept in his own power and eventually gave to his niece Emma.[137] As has been seen, Hubert's family became the most prominent and powerful group in the Mauges. Just as Viscount Hubert of Vendôme was able to convince Count Fulk that his son would be a valuable supporter and thus obtained for Hubert the episcopal seat of Angers, so too Bishop Hubert was able to persuade Fulk that he and his family could be trusted to control the Mauges.

After the dust of the Mauges controversy had settled, Hubert reestablished monks at St. Serge[138] and appointed a certain Hubert, perhaps related to him, as its abbot.[139] At this time, Hubert's favor towards St. Serge became evident. One of his own *fideles*, John of Jalesne, became a member of St. Serge and gave to it the land at La Prellé that he held in *beneficium* from Bishop Hubert. Not only did the bishop give his authorization for this gift, but he also ordered others having an interest in that land to give their permission for the grant to be made.[140]

On 1 March 1046 Hubert installed as abbot of St. Serge his cousin Vulgrinus, previously the prior of the monastery of Marmoutier.[141] The bishop was obviously interested in promoting his own cousin, but he also wanted an abbot who would govern St. Serge religiously and with discipline, so that the monastic rule might be observed there more firmly.[142] Hubert was as interested in the welfare of St. Serge as he was in the advancement of Vulgrinus's career.

At the same time that he named Vulgrinus to head St. Serge, Bishop Hubert also gave that abbey the cell of St. Maurille, thus combining both of his monasteries under the same management.[143] Count Geoffrey was present for this grant and for the blessing of Vulgrinus as abbot. There is no record of any comital interference in the affairs of St. Serge after Hubert became bishop of Angers.

---

[136] See below, Part II, No. 23.

[137] See below, Part II, No. 81. At the same time he made other grants to St. Serge from his patrimony, Renaud also gave half of the church of St.-Rémy-en-Mauges (*Rec. des historiens de France*, 10, p. 583), which came to be possessed by Emma (see below, Part II, No. 81).

[138] See below, Part II, No. 77.

[139] See above, chap. 2, n. 109.

[140] See below, Part II, No. 46.

[141] See below, Part II, No. 53; and see above, chap. 2, nn. 98–100.

[142] See below, Part II, No. 53.

[143] Loc. cit.

During the last year of his life, March of 1046 to March of 1047, Hubert also made a number of remissions of customs to St. Serge. He freed it of the *vicaria* and all the customs that he held in its lands, in addition to a remission of all the customs that he had over St. Maurille, so long as they were not subsequently alienated.[144] He also conceded that whatever was given either to St. Serge or to St. Maurille would be free of all customs or revenues that pertained to the bishop unless, again, they should later be alienated by those establishments.[145] In addition to these and other grants that he had made to St. Serge and to St. Maurille, virtually at the moment of his death Hubert restored one prebend of the cathedral to the possession of St. Serge.[146]

The cell of St.-Maur-sur-Loire, located at Glanfeuil, was a priory of St.-Maur-des-Fossés and had been involved in a series of disputes with St. Florent during the episcopate of Renaud II, whose favoritism towards St. Florent was a feature of his break with Count Fulk.[147] As has been seen, Hubert's accession ended Abbot Robert of St. Florent's cozy relationship with the bishop of Angers,[148] and the monks of St. Florent ceased bringing suits against St. Maur for the bishop's judgment. The only contact that Hubert is known to have had with St. Maur was his consecration of its rebuilt monastery in 1036, at the request of Abbot Odo of St.-Maur-des-Fossés. A sign that the old conflicts of Bishop Renaud's time were over was the presence of Abbot Frederick of St. Florent at this consecration.[149]

Because most of the documents that have survived for this period belonged to cathedral and monastic archives, little is known of Hubert's relations with his secular clergy other than the cathedral personnel. However, some information exists concerning the church of St. Martin at Angers,[150] which was restored by Count Fulk and Countess Hildegardis, a work that Hubert was also involved with. The actual rebuilding must have been underway by 1012, when Bishop Hubert found the remains of St. Lupus, a seventh-century bishop of Angers, under a sarcophogus in that church.[151] Thirteen canons were established at St. Martin,[152] and its domains were increased to give it sounder financial support. The best known case of this support was when Count Fulk and Countess Hildegardis took

---

[144] See below, Part II, No. 77.

[145] See below, Part II, No. 78.

[146] See below, Part II, No. 80.

[147] Bachrach, "Robert of Blois," pp. 128–130.

[148] See above, chap. 3, nn. 25–30.

[149] See below, Part II, No. 26.

[150] On the archaeological history of this church and especially its rebuilding in the eleventh century, see Forsyth, *Church of St. Martin at Angers,* esp. pp. 103 ff.

[151] Ibid., p. 108 and p. 45 n. 80 for the text, "Hic sunt reliquiae B. Lupi episcopi Andegavensis et confessoris, repertae a venerabili Huberto Andegavensi episcopo, in quodam subgrondrio sub sarcophogo magno, reperto in ecclesia S. Martini, anno incarnationis millesimo duodecimo, XI⁰ kalendarum aprilis, rege Francorum regnante Roberto." However, Forsyth incorrectly translates "XI⁰ kalendarum aprilis" as April 11.

[152] B. n., D. H. II¹, no. 407.

away from St. Aubin one-sixth of various revenues pertaining to St.-Rémy-la-Varenne and three unfree inhabitants there and gave them to the church of St. Martin in 1029. Abbot Primaldus and the monks of St. Aubin protested the transfer but found no relief from either the count or the bishop, and they handed over the revenues.[153] Two of Hubert's key cathedral clerics were also closely associated with St. Martin, an indication of his continuing interest in that church and of his cooperation with the counts in its welfare. Both of the archdeacons Berengar and Renaud were clerics there.[154]

It is certain that Bishop Hubert exacted fixed sums from some of the individual churches pertaining to St. Aubin, in the form of *sinodi* and *circadae*.[155] Additionally, the two forgeries produced at St. Florent ca. 1005–1007 demonstrate that the monastery was anticipating that Hubert would attempt to impose the *sinodus* on its churches within his diocese.[156] Other customs known to have been held at individual churches by Bishop Hubert include burials (*sepulturae*), bread (*panis*), candles (*candelae*), oblations (*oblationes*), tithes (*decimae*), *census,* and *vicariae.*[157] While it seems certain that Hubert held diocesan synods, the only documentary reference to them may lie in the charters concerning the protests of St. Aubin over Geoffrey Martel's and Agnes's transferral of the church of St. Clement at Craon to Trinité de Vendôme.[158]

The "regime of the private church,"[159] the *Eigenkirche* of Stutz's memorable work,[160] was vigorous during Hubert's episcopate, and he made no attempt to eliminate it. Both Hubert and his family were traffickers in private churches.[161] He gave churches to monasteries, but others of his family held them from him as well.[162] Even the archdeacon–treasurer Burchardus held the church of St. Marcel at Briollay jointly from Hubert and the count of Anjou.[163]

The existence of monasteries in private hands, the *Eigenklöster,* was also the rule in Anjou and was tolerated without qualm by Bishop Hubert, who himself was the proprietor of St. Maurille and St. Serge.[164] St. Aubin, St. Nicholas, St. Lézin, and Ronceray were in the hands of the counts of Anjou. St. Florent was under the domination of the counts of Blois until

---

[153] See below, Part II, No. 2.
[154] See above, n. 79.
[155] See below, Part II, No. 64.
[156] See above, chap. 3, nn. 26–27.
[157] See below, Part II, Nos. 22, 60, 23.
[158] See above, nn. 97–99.
[159] The phrase is from the title of the article by Madeleine Dillay, "Le régime de l'église privée."
[160] U. Stutz, *Die Eigenkirche als Element des mittelalterlich-germanischen Kirchenrechts,* 1895.
[161] See below, Part II, Nos. 1, 65, 67.
[162] See below, Part II, Nos. 65, 67, 71, 81.
[163] See below, Part II, Nos. 30, 43, 44.
[164] See above, nn. 121–146.

1026, when it came under the control of Fulk Nerra. Hubert had numerous contacts with these comital *Eigenklöster*.[165]

Simony and a married clergy, or nicolaitanism, two of the cardinal evils according to the reformers who were already active in Italy, were common in Anjou and were accepted by Hubert. He himself had gained the bishopric of Angers by a simoniacal exchange carried out by his father and Count Fulk.[166] Although there is no sign that Hubert was married, he made no effort to enforce the celibacy or even chastity of his diocesan clergy. His first two archdeacon–treasurers were married and had children,[167] while a priest with children held lands from Hubert.[168]

However, the beginnings of some degree of reform in the ecclesiastical life of Anjou can be seen during Hubert's rule.[169] At Ronceray the abbesses were elected rather than appointed. Election also became institutionalized at St. Aubin beginning in 1036, along with a major role of the bishop in selecting its abbots.[170] Also, towards the end of his career, Bishop Hubert appointed celibate clerics of recognized ability to his cathedral's archidiaconate.[171] Hubert also founded the cathedral school and supplied well-trained masters to direct it.[172] And the first episcopal chaplain is found during Hubert's episcopate.[173]

Clerical life underwent a great expansion in Anjou under Hubert. St. Nicholas and the oratory of Toussaint were founded to help the poor,[174] and Ronceray was the first abbey in the diocese dedicated to the spiritual welfare of women.[175] Both St. Maurille and St. Serge were restored and Hubert established the monastic rule at St. Serge after canons had been sent in. St. Florent and St.-Maur-sur-Loire were rebuilt and Hubert did the same to his cathedral.

Under Hubert's direction a complex organization had been developed for the management of his episcopal estates, a development in advance of the comital administration of Anjou.[176] The episcopal fisc was organized on a geographical basis, with definite sets of estates under the direction of a seneschal. The seneschal Renaud administered those around Cha-

---

[165] See above, nn. 83–120.
[166] See above, chap. 1, nn. 58–61.
[167] See above, chap. 2, n. 111.
[168] See below, Part II, Nos. 47, 52.
[169] J.-M. Bienvenue, "Les caractères originaux," p. 547: "le trait le plus marquant de son épiscopat fut le brillant renouveau du monachisme bénédictine dans le diocèse." And see Guillot, *Comte d'Anjou*, 1: pp. 245–247.
[170] See above, nn. 87–90, 109.
[171] See above, nn. 45–58.
[172] See above, nn. 54–65.
[173] See above, nn. 51–53.
[174] See below, Part II, Nos. 24, 54–58; J.-M. Bienvenu, "Pauvrété, misères, et charité," *Moyen Age* 73 (1967), pp. 5, 13–14.
[175] Jean Verdon, "Les moniales dans la France de l'Ouest aux XIe et XIIe siècles, Etude d'histoire sociale," *Cahiers de civilisation médiévale* 19 (1976), pp. 247–264.
[176] Guillot, *Comte d'Anjou*, 1: p. 420.

lonnes-sur-Loire,[177] while Algerius was in charge of those at Morannes,[178] where Hubert had a major episcopal residence.[179] In addition to his seneschals, Hubert also had a marshal, *prepositi*, a butler, chamberlains, and hunters in his administration.[180]

Unlike his predecessor and successor,[181] Hubert's ecclesiastical horizons were rather narrow. He is not known to have had any contacts with the papacy or to have attended any provincial synods. There are records of only four face-to-face meetings between Hubert and his archbishop.[182] He is known to have been only within the central complex of the counties of Anjou, Vendôme, Maine, and the Touraine. Bishop Hubert's few contacts with non-Angevin monasteries can be explained by reasons of family or politics, rather than by ecclesiastical concerns. His controversy with Archbishop Hugh of Tours in 1016 demonstrated that for a strong, independent bishop like Hubert, who was supported by his secular lord, not even the most severe church penalties were to be feared.

The picture drawn here of Bishop Hubert is one of a vigorous and active prelate who worked well within the existing ecclesiastical environment of Anjou while at the same time initiating some reforms within his diocese. He restored his own cathedral and invigorated his canons. He completed the restoration of St. Maurille and St. Serge, dedicated new comital monasteries of St. Nicholas and Ronceray, assisted at the dedication of the

---

[177] For Renaud the seneschal, see below, Part II, No. 79. He apparently served only Hubert and not his successor Bishop Eusebius, for under the latter he was called *senescallus Huberti episcopi*, while he was followed in a witness list by *Gausfredus senescallus Eusebii episcopi* (B. n., ms. lat. 12878, fol. 82 v). He is called the seneschal of Chalonnes when he gave to Marmoutier his alod at Rigny in the Vendômois (*Cart. Marmoutier pour le Vendômois*, no. 122), so this was undoubtedly the same Renaud whose gift of his alod at Rigny to Marmoutier was witnessed by Bishop Hubert (see below, Part II, No. 75).

[178] Algerius the seneschal was a witness to three acts of Bishop Hubert (see below, Part II, Nos. 77–79). He was probably in charge of the estates of Morannes, since he was usually called Algerius of Morannes, and Hubert had extensive lands at Morannes (see below, Part II, Nos. 10, 14, 15, 16, 18, 23, 47, 72). He was close to Hubert's family after the bishop's death. He was a witness to Viscount Radulfus's restoration of St.-Rémy-en-Mauges to St. Serge in 1058 (see below, Part II, No. 81), along with Bishop Eusebius and Renaud the seneschal. Algerius remained close to Bishop Eusebius, appearing with him on this occasion and on another (*Cart. St.-Aubin,* no. 263).

[179] See below, Part II, No. 15, "apud Morennam, scilicet, sedem episcopalem . . ."

[180] For Mainard the marshal, see below, Part II, No. 77. On the *prepositi* Ingelbaldus and Bernard, see Part II, Nos. 77, 79. The Hilduinus who was a witness to Part II, No. 53, was the *prepositus* of Angers (Guillot, *Comte d'Anjou,* 1: pp. 410–415. For the butler Hubert, see Part II, Nos. 77, 79. For the chamberlains Renaud, Isenardus, and Warinus, see Part II, No. 79. For the hunters Jovinus and Peter, see Part II, Nos. 78, 79.

[181] Renaud II obtained a papal confirmation of his grants to the cathedral of Angers (*Cart. noir de la cathédrale d'Angers,* no. 26) and he cooperated with Pope Sylvester II in granting privileges to the monastery of St. Peter of Bourgueil (Migne, *Patrologia Latina,* 139, cols. 285–286). For the activities of Bishop Eusebius, see M. Cappuyns, "Eusèbe Bruno," *Dictionnaire d'histoire et de géographie ecclésiastiques,* vol. 15, ed. R. Aubert and E. Van Cauwenbergh (Paris, 1963), cols. 1435–1436, and by the same author, "Bérenger de Tours"; Halphen, *Comté d'Anjou,* pp. 120–126; and Guillot, *Comte d'Anjou,* 1: pp. 249–252.

[182] See below, Part II, Nos. 21, 36, 37, 38, 40.

rebuilt monastery of St. Florent, and consecrated the rebuilt priory of St.-Maur-sur-Loire. He dedicated his own cathedral, the church of the cell of St. Maurille, and the oratory of Toussaint, as well as the church at Baracé, whose three altars he authorized.[183] He established the parochial boundaries of Ronceray and assisted in the restoration of the church of St. Martin at Angers. Bishop Hubert ordained Abbot Frederick of St. Florent, had a major voice in the selection of Abbot Walter of St. Aubin, and maintained control over the abbotship of St. Serge.

Hubert participated in numerous decisions involving questions of ecclesiastical justice. In 1014 he played a role in the division of St.-Rémy-la-Varenne between St. Aubin and St. Lézin. By 1031 he had obtained a judgment from Count Fulk's court that allowed him to repurchase lands taken from St. Serge by Fulk. Hubert, Fulk, and the archdeacons extended St. Nicholas's burial rights. Sometime before 1039 Hubert was supported by Fulk in the almost comical affair concerning the theft of the bishop's laundry box.[184] Along with the count and the king, Hubert assisted in the determination of Fulk's customs at Longchamps.[185] The bishop was a major participant at Count Geoffrey's *placitum* concerning the customs over St. Florent's parish of St.-Georges-Châtelaison, and ca. 1044–1047 Hubert had a role in resolving the dispute between St. Lézin and Eudo of Blaison. Perhaps Hubert acted through his archdeacons to settle a quarrel between St. Aubin and St. Florent over Saugé-aux-Moines, and he may have held synods that considered the claims of St. Aubin to the church of St. Clement at Craon.[186]

In addition to this record of foundations, dedications, consecrations, and judgments, it was due to Hubert's cooperation with Count Fulk that the extensive territory of the Mauges was incorporated into the Angevin diocese early in his episcopate. Backed by the power of the count, Hubert removed the Mauges from the jurisdiction of the bishop of Nantes and placed it in his diocese as part of a campaign directed against Abbot Robert of St. Florent and his policy of opposition to Anjou. This transferral added greatly to Hubert's economic and spiritual power, and supported as he was by comital authority, his control over the diocese made him one of the most powerful figures in Anjou.

The affair of the laundry box, "derisive"[187] as it may have been, illustrates this point well. The thugs who broke into the laundry and pilfered Hubert's clothes box did so only after they believed that the laundry had left the bishop's hands. It is noteworthy that Fulk fully supported Hubert and punished his *ministri* who committed the theft by forcing them

---

[183] See below, Part II, No. 41.
[184] See below, Part II, No. 29.
[185] See below, Part II, No. 34.
[186] Therefore there were at least five judicial decisions in which Hubert participated with Count Fulk, and two to four under Geoffrey Martel. Guillot (*Comte d'Anjou*, 1: p. 239) found only a total of two for all of Hubert's episcopate.
[187] Guillot, *Comte d'Anjou*, 1: p. 239.

to undergo the humiliation of returning Hubert's box to him upon their necks.[188]

This view of the respect shown towards Hubert is reinforced by the history of the oratory of St. Vincent at Chalonnes-sur-Loire, which Hubert had given to Marmoutier. The "impious" monks who raided the oratory acted only after Hubert's death.[189] The implication is that while Hubert lived, the monks would not have dared to overturn his gift.

This ensemble of Hubert's actions as bishop of Angers illustrates that he was a busy prelate who was zealous for the welfare of his diocese and who gained the respect of his contemporaries. The effusive eulogy for Hubert left by the canons of his cathedral appears to be the common view of him at the time of his death. It shows that there was far more to Hubert than a cleric who was better at fighting than at praying. Forsyth's description of Hubert as a "bellicose church-building bishop"[190] comes closer to the total view of Hubert's ecclesiastical career. But Dom Liron has presented the most accurate appraisal of Hubert's life as a bishop, saying that he was "one of the bishops of Angers who was the most loved and who was the most mourned after his death. Indeed, he was honest, charitable, generous, and he did as much good as he could for everyone." Liron reproached Hubert only for the affair surrounding his excommunication.[191]

Hubert was out of favor with his archbishop for only a short time, and even then he seems not have been hindered in the execution of his office. As a bishop, Hubert was not an actor on the larger stage of church life, nor did he challenge the socio-political structure of the world around him. But he was strong, active, effective, respected, and beloved. He demonstrated that the reform and welfare of the church could be achieved by a simoniacal bishop who had once been excommunicated and who tolerated proprietary churches and monasteries and a married clergy. Anjou was much sounder and better endowed at his death than it had been at his accession, and Hubert directly had much to do with this progress.

---

[188] See below, Part II, No. 29.
[189] See below, Part II, No. 61.
[190] Forsyth, *Church of St. Martin at Angers,* p. 108 n. 150.
[191] *Bibliothèque d'Anjou* (Nantes, 1897), p. 24.

V. CONCLUSION

One of the most striking features of Bishop Hubert's career is its apparent ordinariness. In most respects, Hubert was a very typical bishop in the west of France in this period. His social and geographical origins are what one would anticipate.[1] He counted bishops and viscounts among his close relatives, and he was from the region of his diocese. The military nature of his political career is certainly not out of the ordinary in an age of fighting bishops. He gained office in a simoniacal exchange at a time when simony was widespread, and he was appointed bishop by the count of Anjou in a period of lay investiture in the secularized, "feudalized" church. His diocese was well acquainted with married priests as well as proprietary churches and monasteries. Even two of Hubert's greatest accomplishments as bishop are in keeping with the general trends of his time. He founded the cathedral school of Angers in a period of the founding of cathedral schools,[2] and he rebuilt the cathedral of St. Maurice of Angers during a time of cathedral building. For example, during this time most of the Norman dioceses received new cathedrals,[3] as did Chartres and Poitiers.[4] Therefore, Hubert's career is illustrative of that of so many of his fellow bishops during this age, the prelates who were not prominent literary or educational figures, or important secular administrators. Moreover, his diocese was in the heart of an important, powerful, and growing territorial principality in the mainstream of the political, social, and economic developments of Neustria and its surrounding regions in the tenth and eleventh centuries. Thus much of what is learned of Hubert's world can be applied to the bishoprics that shared these same characteristics, that were in regions that were shaping the course of French secular and ecclesiastical history. At first glance, Hubert may have seemed to have done only what any bishop would have done.

However, at the same time it is obvious that Hubert was an extraordinary bishop to his contemporaries. The lavish epitaph left by his cathedral canons,[5] the account of his grand funeral at St. Serge,[6] and the warm praise given to him by Bernard, the former master of his cathedral school,[7]

---

[1] Fanning, "Family and Episcopal Election," pp. 40–42.
[2] See above, chap. 4, nn. 54, 55.
[3] Bates, *Normandy Before 1066*, pp. 209, 213–214, 298.
[4] *Letters and Poems of Fulbert of Chartres*, pp. xx, lxxxvii, no. 107.
[5] See above, chap. 1, n. 2.
[6] See above, chap. 1, n. 74, and below, No. 81.
[7] See above, chap. 4, n. 21.

present a consistent picture of a bishop who was exceptionally loved and respected by those who knew him best—his canons, his school master, his neighboring bishops and the abbots under his diocesan authority, and the *fideles* of the church of Angers. What this shows is that Hubert was a very successful bishop to those around him, those who felt obliged to perpetuate his memory. He was much more than a bishop who was merely competent.

Modern historians who view his career with derision have evidently not understood Hubert's role in his own society, nor have they caught a glimpse into the values against which Hubert was judged by his contemporaries, both clerical and lay. To understand why Hubert's life was seen to have been crowned with such success will allow us more fully to appreciate Hubert's world on its own terms and standards. We can begin to see what it believed was important in the making of a "good" bishop, in the actions of the leader of the spiritual life of the diocese of Angers.

It is obvious that all Hubert's enterprises were successful. He cooperated fully with the laity when ecclesiastical matters were involved. He accepted Fulk's actions in the Mauges, and when he wanted to regain some of those lands, he did so with the approval of the count's *curia,* and then he purchased the lands from their possessors. When he wanted to give certain lands held by Renaud of Château-Gontier and his family to one of his monasteries, he made an exchange of lands with them.[8] A legacy of this spirit can be seen in the return of St.-Rémy-en-Mauges to St. Serge by Radulfus IV. It was stipulated that the *milites* who held tenements there should continue to hold them as fiefs, *beneficialiter,* and to do service for them. Hubert went to war with his own archbishop in order to serve his count and his king, and he was undeterred by the punishments of excommunication and interdict.

Hubert's aim of assisting his family and promoting its interests was a notable achievement. His family was able to hold its position in the Vendômois and it gained extensive lands in the Mauges. His niece Emma and her husband and children could thank Hubert for much of their prosperity. His cousin Vulgrinus came out of the abbey of Marmoutier to head Hubert's monastery of St. Serge, and then he became bishop of Le Mans largely due to his kinship with Hubert and Radulfus IV. It becomes obvious why a family would want one of its members as a bishop and why it would pay to gain such an office. It could mean great prosperity for many of its other members.

Hubert's cooperation with the laity is especially clear when it concerns the count of Anjou. Hubert and his family were consistent *fideles* of Fulk Nerra and Geoffrey Martel, and in return they were supported and promoted by the counts. Fidelity was a mutual relationship. The case of Bishop Renaud II demonstrates what can happen when a bishop worked

---

[8] See below, Part II, No. 48.

against the count. He was virtually exiled from his diocese and his family, which had been one of the most prominent dynasties of the lower Loire and could number counts, viscounts, and bishops among its members, disappeared from the power structure of the region and the viscountship of Angers, which had formerly belonged to it, was suppressed. But Hubert's family thrived, and so much of its success was dependent on comital favor. They could not have held the viscountships of Vendôme, Lude, and Montrevault without the consent of the count of Anjou, Hubert could have regained the lands in the Mauges only with Fulk's permission, and Vulgrinus could have attained the bishopric of Le Mans only by the nomination of Geoffrey Martel.

Hubert was able to effect a considerable reform of his diocese. A cathedral school with well-qualified masters was begun, celibate clerics slowly replaced married men with families in the archidiaconate, an episcopal chancery was developed, the monasteries of St. Maurille and St. Serge were restored, the abbot of St. Aubin and the abbess of Ronceray were elected, and he regained, in part for the church, many of the lands in the Mauges that had been despoiled by Count Fulk. The cathedral of Angers was rebuilt, and the poor were better provided for by the church. Anjou fairly bristled with new monasteries and churches.

Perhaps Hubert was not as generous to the cathedral of Angers as Renaud II had been, but the epitaphs of the two bishops are convincing evidence that the canons were far more appreciative of Hubert. Renaud's generosity came to them at the cost of his incurring the wrath of the count and their lands were plundered. Twenty years later the memory of the "oppression of the counts"[9] was still green, and forty years later the canons recalled the "oppression of tyrants."[10] But under Hubert their cathedral was rebuilt, some of the lands were recovered, and they could enjoy the general prosperity that came to the diocese. Renaud's generous defiance of the count had brought them ruin, but Hubert's perhaps more parsimonious cooperation with the count allowed them to recover and to flourish. The canons felt a great obligation to remember Hubert and to appreciate the prosperity that they came to know under his episcopacy.

What we can see in Hubert's career is that there was no necessary sharp distinction between the world of the laity and that of the clergy. Indeed, such a demarcation was impossible in this age. As Boussard put it, "l'Eglise est inextricablement mêlée à la société féodale."[11] Hubert appeared to understand this fact, to sympathize with it, to work within it. As a result, the Angevin church experienced unprecedented growth and prosperity. Bishop Renaud seemed to forget this essential point, and his church suffered grievous losses. It is ironic that the church of Anjou indeed flourished and experienced significant reform and renewal under a bishop who is

---

[9] See below, Part II, No. 10.
[10] See above, chap. 1, n. 2.
[11] "Les évêques en Neustrie," p. 186.

generally scorned by modern historians for his secular interests and care-
lessness regarding the church.

Hubert was a member of a large and influential family, and he never
was isolated from it. He continually concerned himself with its welfare,
and it also prospered. He was inextricably involved in the affairs of the
world and he never questioned his secular obligations. As bishop of
Angers, Hubert was active in the promotion of the establishments over
which he had direct control—St. Maurille, St. Serge, the cathedral of St.
Maurice and its personnel, the diocesan organization—and he encouraged
and presided over the reform and growth brought about by others. He
played an important role in the continued Angevin control of Vendôme
and expansion into the Touraine. This loyalty in turn led to the support of
the counts of Anjou for his family and ecclesiastical policies.

Thus Hubert's world was a unified whole. His family, the church, his
loyalty and responsibility to the counts of Anjou, were all facets of his life
and mutually supported each other. When Anjou prospered, so did his
family and his diocese. Hubert recognized his interests and responsibilities
and he defended them. He was a *defensor domus, defensor ecclesiae, defensor
comitis.* Hubert was a success because he understood his world, worked
within its mentality, and was attached to the politics of a successful principality. He was seen by his contemporaries as a success, and it seems that
he fit the spirit of his times extraordinarily well and understood the values
and expectations of his world, which indeed were his own. This examination of Hubert's career illustrates what his society wanted from its bishops,
for he was able to satisfy its desires. What emerges from this study is the
portrait of a very extraordinary ordinary bishop, and why he was so successful.

This study permits us to see a side of the episcopate that is rarely in view
because it is rarely looked for in our research. In the first place, we can
observe that Bishop Hubert indeed had his own policies that were independent of those of the count. While Hubert supported Anjou's politics, he
also had his own family policy, as well as a program for the reform and
recovery of his diocese, that were apart from the plans of Fulk Nerra and
Geoffrey Martel.

In the second place, this view of Hubert's career presents us with a
picture of a bishop and a church less feudalized, less secularized, less
dominated by lay politics than we are accustomed to see. Hubert was
deeply involved in the affairs of the church, but he also was a bishop who
took his ecclesiastical duties seriously and could meet them without clash-
ing with the world around him. Hubert's life makes it clear that church
reform and a strong lay influence in the church were not incompatible.

In the third place, this detailed study allows us to look behind the scenes
of Hubert's episcopal appointment, and to understand the reasons for
Fulk's choice of the son of the viscount of Vendôme in 1005 or 1006. By
discovering the full extent of Hubert's family in Maine and in Vendôme,
and by being fully appreciative of the political circumstances, we can see

Hubert as more than a type—a bishop of a certain class and from a certain region—and instead see him as an individual. We can learn why particular men were chosen to be bishops of particular sees at particular times. These same considerations are discerned in the appointment of Hubert's cousin Vulgrinus to be bishop of Le Mans in 1056. Thus the life of both the church and the world comes more fully alive with this awareness.

In the fourth place, a nuance of the meaning of *fidelitas* is brought into focus in this glimpse of Hubert and his family. Hubert was a *fidelis* par excellence. He never swerved from his loyalty to the count of Anjou. He became bishop of Angers because of his family's demonstrated loyalty to Anjou, he prospered in office as he continued to support the counts of Anjou even if church lands were sometimes plundered and he was once excommunicated, and his family maintained its loyalty to Fulk and Geoffrey during his lifetime and after his death, and thus its continued prosperity was ensured. There is no feeling that this faithfulness was coerced or given merely out of a sense of duty. Instead it seems to have been genuine and deeply felt. Hubert and his family faced risks in the demonstration of their loyalty to Anjou. They defied the legitimate claims of the bishop of Chartres to Vendôme, they worked against the count of Maine in his own territory, he himself accepted ecclesiastical censure and opprobrium. Had Anjou failed, they could have suffered the losses of lands, positions, and offices that accompanied such failures. One has only to think of the disgrace and exile of Bishop Renaud II, the dispossession of the men of Thibaud of Blois when Geoffrey Martel captured the Touraine,[12] and the exile and embarrassment of Bishop Gervais of Le Mans after his defeat by Anjou. Fidelity entailed risks in this age of political struggle in the west of France. But Hubert and his family remained firmly attached to the House of Anjou, and they flourished along with Angevin fortunes in the reigns of Fulk Nerra and Geoffrey Martel.

In the fifth place, the continuing strength of the family is amply demonstrated by Hubert's career, which is comprehensible only in a family setting. Family considerations were vital in his selection as bishop, and his family policy was a major focus of his activity and energy as bishop. An understanding of Hubert's family clarifies so much of comital actions in this period—the nature of Angevin penetration of Maine, the means of the Angevin hold on Vendôme, the disposition of the Mauges, the Angevin expansion into the Touraine, the rise of Viscount Radulfus IV, the episcopal appointment of Vulgrinus, and Geoffrey Martel's power network in Maine to oppose the Norman threat. In "feudal society," the family was still of paramount importance and to ignore it is to overlook one of the most significant aspects of that society, one that helped determine the shape of lives and the course of events.

---

[12] See Jacques Boussard, "L'éviction des tenants de Thibaut de Blois par Geoffroy Martel, comte d'Anjou, en 1044," *Moyen Age* 69 (1963), pp. 141–149.

The importance of undertaking extensive studies of bishops such as Hubert can readily be seen by comparing the picture of Bishop Hubert presented here with those in the two previous discussions of him of any length or originality, those of Jacques Boussard and Olivier Guillot. When research is squarely focused on one particular bishop instead of on a brief synthesis of the characteristics of the bishops of five sees over the period of a century, or on the count of Anjou and those in power around him from the late tenth to the early twelfth centuries, a different and far more complex picture of Hubert and his career emerges.

Boussard devoted five pages to Hubert in his review of the bishops of Neustria (Angers, Tours, Orléans, Le Mans, and Chartres) in the period 950–1050, the most extensive treatment given to any of the bishops he studied.[13] The attention devoted to the bishops of Angers by Guillot is unusual, for by far he gives the fullest and most detailed of all of the regional studies that concern France in the period. Hubert's predecessor is the subject of twenty-four pages, and Hubert himself has twenty-six, while the bishops from 1047 to 1109 are investigated in thirty-one pages.[14] Hubert is extraordinarily fortunate in being the subject of these two scholars' work, for most bishops are far less known than is he. One can learn more of Hubert than of virtually any of his fellow bishops of France in this period.

Boussard noted Hubert's parents and thus he was aware of his social and geographical origins. But Boussard incorrectly believed that Hubert was closely related to his predecessor Renaud II, which led him to invalid conclusions concerning the nature of the Angevin bishopric as well as the means by which Hubert's niece Emma came to hold lands in the Mauges. In addition, he mistakenly identified a reference to Emma's husband Radulfus as an allusion to a brother of Hubert by that name.

In looking at Hubert's actions as bishop, Boussard was able to examine only his role towards monasticism, and this concerned only St. Serge and St. Aubin. Other than his generosity towards his cathedral, Hubert's role towards his secular clergy was not mentioned. Hubert's own policies, or the reforms that he carried out in his diocese, or the extent and firmness of his loyalty to the counts of Anjou, or the true nature of his family network are unknown in Boussard's brief glance at Hubert. One gains little more than an indistinct profile or silhouette of Bishop Hubert, rather than a portrait of him.

Guillot's great study has its focus on the count of Anjou, and it is unsurprising that it presents Bishop Hubert as a figure thoroughly dominated by the count. Guillot examined only fourteen charters concerning Hubert that did not involve the count of Anjou (and only four of these

---

[13] "Les évêques en Neustrie," pp. 166–171, and see above, chap. 1, p. 13.
[14] *Le comte d'Anjou*, 1: pp. 195–279, and see above, chap. 1, pp. 14–15.

were unpublished). He was scarcely able to see Hubert's career in its own right, in either its political, religious, or family setting.

In the Mauges, Guillot saw Hubert as a passive loyalist, tamely carrying out the will of the count. The nearly complete juridical absence of the count from the Mauges in the decades that followed was unexplained.[15] Thus Guillot could not see Hubert's own policy of regaining some of those disputed lands and firmly placing his heirs in the territory.

In attempting to explain the disappearance of Hubert's non-existent brother William, Guillot was led to the theory that the counts of Anjou would appoint a bishop who was the last scion of a vicontiel house and then extinguish the line. In this manner, Count Fulk was able to substitute the viscount of Le Mans at Vendôme.[16] But it is now clear that there was no such Viscount William,[17] and that Emma and her husband Viscount Radulfus were already the heirs to the viscountship of Vendôme and to Hubert's patrimony. While it is inconceivable that Radulfus would have become viscount of Vendôme without Count Fulk's approval, his inheritance of that office and the patrimonial lands and position in the Vendômois was an entirely natural occurrence and had nothing to do with a grand design by the count of Anjou. It was primarily a part of the internal policies of Hubert's family. Guillot's judgment of Hubert as more of a duped prelate than a great seigneur[18] must be discarded.

In the Vendômois, Guillot's limited examination of the documents led him into believing that Hubert was only "more or less" faithful to the count of Anjou, and he suggested that Hubert actually opposed Count Fulk and King Robert and allied with Count Odo and young King Henry.[19] But a study of all the evidence demonstrates that one of the principal foci of Hubert's career and one of the enduring policies of his family was constant loyalty to the counts of Anjou, in the Vendômois, in Anjou, in the Mauges, and in Maine as well.

Guillot's assessment of Hubert's episcopal career was almost totally negative. In his view, Bishop Renaud II had reestablished the juridical position of the bishop within his diocese, but Hubert did practically nothing. From 1006 to 1040, Guillot knew of only one judgment involving Hubert, the "derisive" event when his laundry box was stolen.[20] Guillot failed to see that so many of Renaud's judgments were given in favor of St. Florent as part of his break with Count Fulk, and with the accession of Hubert, a firm Angevin loyalist, St. Florent would have ceased taking its disputes before a hostile bishop.[21] The cessation of synodal judgment has far more to do with the politics between Anjou and Blois–Tours–Chartres

---

[15] Ibid., pp. 224, 239.
[16] *Le comte d'Anjou*, 1: pp. 234, 236.
[17] See above, chap. 2, nn. 33–34.
[18] *Le comte d'Anjou*, 1: p. 224.
[19] Ibid., pp. 239, 242–244; and see below, Part II, No. 21.
[20] *Le comte d'Anjou*, 1: p. 239, and see below, Part II, No. 29.
[21] Bachrach, "Robert of Blois," pp. 126–130, 135–138; and see above, chap. 3, pp. 71–74.

than "la déficience de l'évêque Hubert."[22] Moreover, a focus on Hubert's career shows that there were at least five judicial decisions made by Bishop Hubert in the period 1006–1040, not the one that Guillot knew him to have been involved with.

Thus the general picture of Hubert is much different. Instead of Guillot's fumbling, confused, and timid figure of divided loyalties who neglected his episcopal authority, we can see Hubert as a man pursuing distinct secular and religious policies independent of those of the count whom he served with unswerving loyalty throughout his life, and in the end the bishop, his family, and his church prospered.

This review contrasts the impression of Hubert's career gained from a focus on the count and an inability to devote careful attention to all the documents concerning the bishop, with one based on an orientation solely towards this particular bishop. Guillot's treatment of the individual bishops of Angers in this period is far more extensive and well researched than those in other regional studies, or indeed in most studies of bishops in their own right. It is obvious that so little of Hubert's career—in its familial, seigneurial, political, or ecclesiastical aspects—has been understood up to this point. Since our knowledge of Bishop Hubert, one of the most extensively studied bishops of this period in one of the most thoroughly studied regions of France, has been so incomplete and error-riddled, with no real appreciation of him as a bishop with his own mind, interests, and policies, what must be the state of our understanding of the many other bishops of this time or of their societies?

Thus we really know very little of the French episcopate in the post-Carolingian period, a time when it is acknowledged that the bishops were among the most powerful figures of that society. Without further full-length studies of other bishops in this region and in this time, we shall continue to have only an impression of society, politics, and the church in this decisive period of French history. Our focus needs to be sharpened and brought to bear on Hubert and his episcopal colleagues. We need to be able to determine if a bishop like Hubert was better able to wield the sword than pray to God, or a bellicose church-building bishop, or a duped seigneur, or the very model of a successful bishop before the Gregorian Reform. We need to understand how modern views of Bishop Hubert have been at such variance from those of his contemporaries.

---

[22] *Le comte d'Anjou,* 1: p. 239.

PART TWO

CATALOGUE OF ACTS OF BISHOP HUBERT
OF ANGERS

INTRODUCTION

This diplomatic and paleographic study of the acts pertaining to Bishop Hubert of Angers includes all extant acts known to the author in which Bishop Hubert participated or acted as a witness, or in which actions taken by him or concerning him are mentioned. An effort has also been made to establish and discuss acts in which Bishop Hubert participated, for which documentation is lacking but other evidence suggests once existed. Diplomas that refer to Hubert only to make a chronological reference but do not indicate an action taken by him are not included here. Likewise, entries in chronicles and annals are not placed in this study unless they indicate that charterial material was probably the source for that information. For the same reasons, notices concerning Hubert in monastic and cathedral obituaries are omitted from these investigations, as is the information concerning Hubert's discovery of the remains of St. Lupus. This study is composed of entries based on charters known or believed once to have been issued, that indicate an action taken by Bishop Hubert or concerning him.

Frequently the information concerning Hubert is included in a later document, which thus provides us with knowledge of several different acts stretching over many years. When this is so, a full description of the document as it stands today is provided in the catalogue, but the entries are classified according to the data concerning Bishop Hubert. The study is arranged on a chronological basis. Each entry is headed by the date at which or the time span during which the act of or concerning Hubert occurred. When the time during which an act took place is known only for a range of years, the entry is placed at the end of that range. For example, entry No. 3 fell between 13 June 1006 and 1016, so it follows No. 2, which occurred in 1014. The places where the acts were executed, if known, follow the dates.

Following each description of an act or of its parts is a list of participants and witnesses involved in the act. The known manuscript tradition is then given in chronological order, indicated by capital letters. Printed editions of the texts are then indicated in order of appearance, denoted by Roman numerals. Then there are references to the act in previous catalogues, lists and inventories, as well as significant diplomatic or paleographic discussions of the act in scholarly literature, listed in chronological order by Arabic numerals. Then follow discussions of the texts, evaluating their authenticity, studying the diplomatic problems presented, and making arguments for the dating of the acts. When known, the modern forms of place names are given, along with their locations in current French style. Unless otherwise stated, all the sites are in the modern *département* of Maine-et-Loire.

SUMMARY OF THE CONTENTS OF THE CATALOGUE

Bishop Hubert authorizing grants to monasteries, Nos. 13, 20, 44, 46, 59, 72.

Bishop Hubert and clerical arrangements, Nos. 15.I, 34, 64.

Bishop Hubert confirms lands held from him, Nos. 19, 43, 45, 57.

Bishop Hubert confirms lands held from others, No. 37.

Bishop Hubert dedicating his cathedral, No. 10.

Bishop Hubert dedicating churches, Nos. 5, 15.I, 40, 41.

Bishop Hubert dedicating monasteries, Nos. 15.I, 22, 24, 26.

Bishop Hubert dedicating an oratory, Nos. 57, 58.

Ecclesiastical payments to Bishop Hubert, Nos. 15.IV, 16.

Bishop Hubert establishing burial rights, No. 24.

Bishop Hubert establishing parochial boundaries, No. 17.

Bishop Hubert exchanging lands, No. 48.

Bishop Hubert giving permission for establishing an oratory, Nos. 54–56.

Bishop Hubert's grants to family members, Nos. 65, 67.

Bishop Hubert's grants to laymen, Nos. 14, 45, 66.

Bishop Hubert's grants to a priest, No. 47.

Bishop Hubert's grants for a sale of lands held from him, No. 71.

Holdings from Bishop Hubert, Nos. 19, 29.

Bishop Hubert reestablishes a church, No. 31.

Royal confirmations of Bishop Hubert's grants, Nos. 23, 68, 69, 70.

Bishop Hubert and the selection and ordination of abbots, Nos. 6, 25, 32, 35, 53.

Sinodus and *circada* paid to Bishop Hubert, No. 64.

Bishop Hubert as a witness:

> to acts of his family, Nos. 7, 73.
>
> to clerical acts, No. 2.
>
> to confirmation of grants to monasteries, Nos. 37, 42, 49, 51, 73.
>
> to dedication of a church, No. 12.
>
> to gifts to monasteries, Nos. 2, 3, 11, 15.III, 27, 33, 36, 50, 74, 75.
>
> to grants to a cathedral, No. 38.
>
> to settlement of customs over monastic lands, No. 39.
>
> to settlement of ecclestiastical disputes, Nos. 28, 76.
>
> other, No. 21.

References to Bishop Hubert in acts of his father, Nos. 1, 9.

Reference to Bishop Hubert's burial, No. 81.

ABBREVIATIONS USED IN PART II

Angot—Abbé Angot, "Les vicomtes du Maine: Cartulaire," *Bulletin de la Commission historique et archéologique de la Mayenne* 30 (1914), pp. 321–342.

Arch. Maine-et-Loire—Archives départementales de Maine-et-Loire, Angers.

Bibl. d'Angers—Bibliothèque municipale d'Angers.

B. n.—Bibliothèque nationale, Paris.

B. n., D. H.—Bibliothèque nationale, Paris, Collection Touraine-Anjou (Dom Housseau).

BPF—*Catalogue générale des manuscrits des bibliothèques publiques en France*, vol. 31.

Bertrand de Brouissillon, *Craon* no.—*La maison de Craon*, cartulaire de Craon.

Bertrand de Brouissillon, *Laval* no.—*La maison de Laval*, cartulaire de Laval et de Vitré.

Bréquigny—M. de Bréquigny, *Table chronologique des diplômes, chartes, et imprimés, concernant l'histoire de France*, 2 vols.

Château-du-Loir—*Cartulaire de Château-du-Loir*, ed. Eugène Valée.

Davis and Whitwell—*Regesta Willelmi Conquestoris et Willelmi Rufi, 1066–1100*.

Durville—A. Durville, *Le cartulaire de Saint-Serge d'Angers*.

Guillot—Olivier Guillot, *Le comte d'Anjou et son entourage au 11e siècle*, 2 vols.

Guillot no.—*Le comte d'Anjou*, vol. 2, Catalogue d'actes, entry numbers.

Halphen—Louis Halphen, *Le comté d'Anjou au XIe siècle*.

Halphen no.—*Le comté d'Anjou*, catalogue d'actes, entry numbers.

Hogan no.—Richard Hogan, "The Angevin Church in the First Feudal Age," Part Two.

Latouche no.—Robert Latouche, *Le comté du Maine*, catalogue d'actes.

Lebrun, *Dict. Maine-et-Loire*—François Lebrun, *Paroisses et communes de France, Dictionnaire d'histoire administrative et demographique, Maine-et-Loire*.

Levron—Jacques Levron, *Répertoire numérique des Archives départementales de Maine-et-Loire antérieures à 1790, Archives ecclésiastiques, Série H.*

Lex—Léonce Lex, "Eudes comte de Blois," catalogue d'actes.

Mabille—Emille Mabille, *Catalogue analytique des diplômes . . . relatifs à l'histoire de Touraine contenus dans la collection de Dom Housseau*.

Marchegay, *Livre noir*—"Le livre noir de Saint-Florent de Saumur," *Archives d'Anjou*, vol. 3.

Newman no.—William Mendel Newman, *Catalogue des actes de Robert II, Roi de France*.

Pfister no.—Christian Pfister, *Robert le Pieux*, catalogue des diplômes.

Port—Célestin Port, *Dictionnaire historique, géographique et biographique de Maine-et-Loire*, 3 vols.

Port, G—Célestin Port, *Inventaire des archives départementales, archives ecclésiastiques, série G, clergé seculier.*

Port, H—Célestin Port, *Inventaire des archives départementales, archives ecclésiastiques, série H, clergé regulier.*

Round, *CDF*—J. Horace Round, *Calendar of Documents Preserved in France Illustrative of the History of Great Britain and Ireland,* vol. 1.

Saché—Marc Saché, *Inventaire sommaire des Archives départementales antérieures à 1790, Maine-et-Loire, Archives ecclésiastiques, Série H,* vol. 2.

Soehnée—Frédéric Soehnée, *Catalogue des actes d'Henri Ier, Roi de France.*

Thorode—*Notice de la ville d'Angers.*

Tresvaux—François Marie Tresvaux du Fraval, *Histoire de l'église et du diocèse d'Angers.*

Vallée—Eugène Vallée, *Dictionnaire topographique du département de la Sarthe.*

Ziezulewicz no.—William Ziezulewicz, "The Monastery of Saint-Florent-de-Saumur," Part Two.

No. 1

12 June 1005–13 June 1006.

Notice: Viscount Hubert of Vendôme gives the *curtis* and church of Mazé[1] to Count Fulk Nerra, from whose *fevum* he had held it, to obtain the bishopric of Angers for his son HUBERT.

Participants: two: Viscount Hubert and Count Fulk.

This information is included in the first part of a larger document relating how Count Geoffrey Martel came to give the church of Mazé to the monastery of Trinité de Vendôme. The other transactions in this document are: (2) Count Fulk then gives the *curtis* of Mazé to Lancelinus of Beaugency and the church to the cleric Anastasius of les Hayes. (3) Anastasius dies without legitimate heirs and his brother Roscelinus is given the church. (4) Roscelinus defies Fulk in the war of Plastulfus Renaldus and the count disinherits him and ejects him from the church. (5) Count Fulk holds the church for a while and then gives it to his son Geoffrey (Martel), who had asked for it, but Fulk stipulates that his son can give it to no one else, but must hold it in demesne. (6) Geoffrey Martel gives the *fructus* to Geoffrey his *juvenis,* the brother of Malramnus, until the former should decide to resume it himself. (7) Count Fulk hears of the grant and, believing that his son has violated their agreement, takes back the church. (8) But when Fulk learns that Geoffrey Martel had not contradicted the agreement, he returns the church to his son, who returns the *fructus* to Geoffrey Malramnus. (9) Then Geoffrey Malramnus gives half the church, with all the land of the altar, to Sienfredus, son of Geoffrey of Lude. (10) When Sienfredus dies, Geoffrey Malramnus gives the half-church to the former's brother Lancelinus, but Count Geoffrey Martel gives his consent to neither grant. (11) After the death of Geoffrey Malramnus, Count Geoffrey Martel refuses to grant the church to Lancelinus, who asked for it, but lets him hold it on the same fructuary terms that Geoffrey Malramnus had held it from him. (12) Then Count Geoffrey gives the church in its entirety to Trinité de Vendôme.

Participants in parts 2–11: eight are named: Count Fulk, Lancelinus of Beaugency, Anastasius of les Hayes, Roscelinus, Geoffrey Martel, Geoffrey Malramnus, Sienfredus, Lancelinus his brother; and the monks of Trinité de Vendôme.

Manuscripts: A. Original redaction, lost. B. Copy, cartulary of Trinité de Vendôme, no. 197, fol. 76 v, lost. C. Copy of the seventeenth century, B. n., coll. Baluze, vol. 47, fol. 253 v, and extract in vol. 139, p. 242. D. Copy of the seventeenth century, Cheltenham, mss. Philips, no. 25058, fol. 119. E. Copy of the seventeenth century, B. n., coll. Decamps, vol. 103, fol. 134 v. F. Extract of the seventeenth century, B. n., ms. lat. 12700, fol. 272 v. G. Copy of the eighteenth century, B. n., D. H. II[1], no. 350, and XIII[1], no. 10836.

Edition: *Cart. de la Trinité de Vendôme*, no. 44.

References: 1. C. van de Kieft, "Une église privée de l'abbaye de la Trinité de Vendôme au XIe siècle," *Moyen Age* 69 (1963), pp. 157–168. 2. Guillot no. 196 (parts 5–12).

Viscount Hubert's return of the *curtis* and church of Mazé must have occurred between the death of Bishop Renaud II (12 June 1005) and the ordination of Bishop Hubert (13 June 1006). Parts 2–4 must have occurred after 12 June 1005, but completed by 1039 (for by the end of that year Fulk left for his last pilgrimage to Jerusalem, never to return to his county; see Halphen, *Le comté d'Anjou*, pp. 217–218). Parts 5–8 fall into the period when both Fulk Nerra and Geoffrey Martel were active. The earliest that it is likely that Geoffrey would be acting as an adult is at age fifteen, 14 October 1021. The *terminus ad quem* is 1039, Fulk's last exit from Anjou. Parts 9–11 fall between Geoffrey's coming of age, 14 October 1021 and his death, 14 November 1060 (*Annales de Vendôme*, p. 63), for it is not clear if Count Fulk had died or left Anjou during these events. Part 12, Count Geoffrey's grant of the church of Mazé to Trinité de Vendôme, must have occurred after 31 May 1040, since Mazé is not enumerated among the possessions of the monastery in its authentic foundation charter of that date (*Cart. de la Trinité de Vendôme*, no. 35), but the donation must have been made by Count Geoffrey's death, 14 November 1060.

---

[1] Mazé, canton Beaufort, arr. Baugé (Port II, p. 632).

No. 2

1014.

Notice: BISHOP HUBERT witnesses Count Fulk Nerra's division of the *curtis* of Chirriacus (St.-Rémy-la-Varenne[1]) between St. Aubin and the canons of St. Lézin, but they still share the *decima*, *cimiteriae*, and those things that pertain to the altar; this was done in 1014 when HUBERT was bishop of Angers and his contemporary Hubert was abbot of St. Aubin and Thebaldus the Old was abbot of the canons of St. Lézin.

Participant: one: Count Fulk.

Witnesses: three: Bishop Hubert, Abbot Hubert and Abbot Thebaldus.

The date of this partition is given in the text. This act is the third part of a much longer document. The other sections are:

I. (929; down to "Herveo cathedre Andegavensi presidente"): Count Fulk the Red gave the *curtis* of Chyrriacus to the churches of St. Aubin and St. Lézin when Herveus was bishop of Angers.

Participant: one: Count Fulk the Red.

Witness: one: Bishop Herveus.

II. (987–1014; down to "benigne perdonavit"): the two churches held the *curtis* without diminution for thirty-seven years, until Count Geoffrey Greymantle ejected canons from St. Aubin and placed monks there, for another eight years until Bishop Nefingus died and was succeeded by Renaud, and to the twenty-eighth year of Fulk Nerra's rule (1014); Count Fulk gave St. Aubin *vicariae* and other customs that he had in the lands of St. Aubin.

Participant: one: Count Fulk Nerra.

IV. (21 July 1028–20 July 1029; after "partiri fecit"): three years after Count Fulk took Saumur, in the forty-second year of his rule, at the instigation of his wife Hildegardis, he violently took away from St. Aubin and gave to Ronceray the *curtis* of Cepia (Seiches[2]) and to the canons of St. Martin of Angers the returns from that part of Chirriacus belonging to St. Aubin, namely a sixth part of the *decimae, census, terragium,* and *vinagium*. The canons also received three brothers from that part, who were freed for their service. One, Alcherius, was sent beyond the Loire to receive these returns, while two, Berengisius and Hubert, served the canons at Angers. The other things remained with St. Aubin. Abbot Primaldus and the monks of St. Aubin vehemently protested this act, to no avail.

Participants: fifteen: Count Fulk and Hildegardis, and Abbot Primaldus and the monks of St. Aubin who made the protest: Hamericus, Boso, Robert, Walter, Hildinus, Fromundus, Letardus, John, Haimo, Mainardus, Segbaldus, Lawrence.

Manuscripts: A. Original redaction, lost. B. Copy of the twelfth century, cartulary of St. Aubin, Bibl. d'Angers, ms. 829 (745), fol. 63 v. C. Copy of the eighteenth century, B. n., D. H. II[1], no. 401, after B.

Edition: *St. Aubin,* no. 197.

References: 1. George H. Forsyth, Jr., *The Church of St. Martin at Angers,* pp. 106–107. 2. Guillot no. 45 (part IV only). 3. Hogan no. 30.

The list of monks named in Part IV are also the first twelve monks, named in exactly the same order, who witnessed the selection of Walter as abbot of St. Aubin in 1036 (see below, No. 25). Thus Guillot suspects the act's authenticity. However, the accuracy of the other information in the document supports the veracity of the information that is the primary concern of the redactor—the story of how first Count Fulk divided

St.-Rémy-la-Varenne between St. Aubin and St. Lézin, and then gave part of its revenues and Seiches to St. Martin and Ronceray.

The chronological information in this document, down to Fulk Nerra's gift of customs in the lands of St. Aubin, appears to be taken from the *Annales de Saint-Aubin,* whose first four items record Fulk the Red's gift of Chirriacus to St. Aubin and St. Lézin in 929 (Part I of this act), and that entry was taken from St. Aubin's charter for the donation (*Cart. St. Aubin,* no. 177); Geoffrey Greymantle's ejection of the canons from St. Aubin and their replacement by monks in 966; the death of Bishop Nefingus in 973; the succession of Bishop Renaud in 974; and the death of Geoffrey Greymantle in 987.

Part II, Fulk Nerra's grant to St. Aubin of the *vicaria* and "many customs" that he had in the lands of St. Aubin, is based on two inauthentic charters (*St. Aubin,* nos. 4 and 4 bis; Guillot nos. ⟨3⟩ and ⟨3 bis⟩) which purport to relate Fulk's remission of customs that he held in St. Aubin's lands, including the middle part of the *curtis* of St.-Rémy-la-Varenne, namely the *bannum, carruacum, corvatae, biduanum,* and the *vicaria,* and every custom.

Part III, Fulk's division of the *curtis* between the two establishments, is based on a notice of the act in the first part of the document drawn up when Count Geoffrey Martel settled a further dispute over the lands formerly shared by St. Lézin and St. Aubin (*St. Aubin,* no. 178), which states that for the peace and quiet of the churches, Fulk divided the *curtis* of Chirriacus between the monks of St. Aubin and the canons of St. Lézin, except for the *decimae, cimiteria,* and those things that pertained to the altar, which remained in common. Guillot interpreted *St. Aubin,* no. 178, as meaning that by this division, Chirriacus was given to St. Aubin and Chamilchiriacus (another *curtis* in dispute), was accorded to St. Lézin, and he noted that those terms differ from the ones related in Part III of No. 2 here (see Guillot no. 30).

However, Guillot used too narrow a definition of *curtis* to conclude that one *curtis* was given to St. Lézin and another to St. Aubin, for *St. Aubin,* no. 178, actually states that Abbot Tetbaldus first divided the "wholeness" of both *curtes* and then established Girbertus's road as the boundary between the portions. Then Abbot Hubert gave the territory *towards* Chamilchiriacus to St. Lézin while keeping the part *towards* Chirriacus washed by the Loire. Based on this context, it is clear that *curtis* as used here does not denote a hamlet, but rather a hamlet and the lands pertaining to it. Thus when Abbot Tetbaldus made his division along the road, all the land towards the hamlet of Chamilchiriacus went to St. Lézin while the lands towards Chirriacus went to St. Aubin. Both houses then held lands which formerly had belonged to each hamlet, but not with each hamlet itself going to a different abbey.

Therefore there is no difference between the two accounts of the division of Chirriacus. *St. Aubin,* no. 178, is more detailed in its discussion of the partition, but No. 2 here is also correct—St. Lézin received part of the lands pertaining to the hamlet of Chirriacus. That is, it shared in the *curtis* of Chirriacus although it did not receive that hamlet itself. *St. Aubin,* no.

178, agrees with No. 2 here that the *decimae, cimiteria,* and other things pertaining to the altar were not divided.

It is assumed that Bishop Hubert was a witness to Part III, for the text mentions that he was bishop of Angers at the time of the division, while Hubert was abbot of St. Aubin and Tetbaldus headed St. Lézin. Tetbaldus and Abbot Hubert are both mentioned in the text of the later document of Geoffrey Martel, but the witness list of the charter of the original division was omitted. In the other cases of this act, however, when mention is made of a bishop presiding over the diocese at the time of an act concerning Chirriacus, it is known that the bishop appeared as a witness to the deed. In Part I, Fulk the Red gave Chirriacus to St. Aubin and St. Lézin, "Herveo cathedre Andegavensi presidente," and in the charter of that grant (*St. Aubin,* no. 177), one finds the subscription "S. Hervei episcopi." Part II states that Geoffrey Greymantle sent monks into St. Aubin "sub Nephingo episcopo," and among the subscriptions to the charter of that act (*St. Aubin,* no. 2) appears "S. Nefingi Andecavorum episcopi." Based on these examples, it is likely that the reference to Bishop Hubert in Part III of No. 2 was based on the redactor's use of the original charter of the division of Chirriacus, which Bishop Hubert either witnessed or subscribed.

The gift of Seiches to Ronceray by Count Fulk in Part IV is confirmed by the notice in the Ronceray cartulary (no. 126) reporting Fulk's gift made at the suggestion of the countess. As Forsyth pointed out (pp. 85–86), the authenticity of this gift of one-sixth of the specified returns is strengthened by the passage in the *Chronica de gestis consulum Andegavorum* in *Chroniques des comtes d'Anjou* (p. 34), which tells of Fulk the Red's original gift of Chirriacus to the two abbeys. At some later time, the two congregations called the clerics of St. Martin into a sixth part of the *curtis* of Chirriacus. Therefore, this gift to St. Martin by Fulk and Hildegardis was actually a restoration of the church's former rights.

Part IV states that Fulk made his gifts to Ronceray and St. Martin in the third year after he took Saumur and in the forty-second year of his countship. Since his father died 21 July 987 (*Annales de Saint-Aubin,* p. 2), Fulk's forty-second year ran from 21 July 1028 to 20 July 1029. This corresponds to the information on Saumur, which was taken by Fulk in the summer of 1026 (Halphen, *Comté d'Anjou,* p. 41 and n. 2) and the third year after its capture was summer 1028–summer 1029.

Despite the suspicious nature of the list of monks in Part IV, this act can be taken for authentic (excluding Part II, which relied on an inauthentic charter), because Parts I, III, and IV are based on authentic events.

---

[1] St.-Rémy-la-Varenne, canton les Ponts-de-Cé, arr. Angers (Port III, p. 448).
[2] Seiches, canton Seiches-sur-le-Loire (Lebrun, *Dict. Maine-et-Loire,* p. 395).

No. 3

13 June 1006–1016.
Charter: BISHOP HUBERT witnesses gifts of Geoffrey of Sablé to St. Pierre of Couture. He gives the church of Solesmes near the *castrum* of Sablé,[1]

with all its appurtenances, arable and non-arable lands, meadows, vines, and mills; two hamlets pertaining to it, Chantemesle[2] and Rocheteau[3]; the *vicus* Melleray[4] and the alod l'Abbaye Bousse[5] with everything pertaining there and with the freedom of enlarging in the woods; the *vicus* les Valières[6] with all its appurtenances, which he acquired by service to Count Hugh of Maine; the part of Bossé[7] with the *vicaria*, which Primaldus, who gave up the world to follow God, possessed; all the burials of the *castrum* of Sablé; the custom of guarding the *castrum*; the alod of les Brenières[8], beyond the Mayenne; all the customs from these lands conceded, *viz.*, *vicaria, foresta, venatio, bannum, carredum*; neither his vicars, foresters, dog-keepers, nor dogs shall have the right of the *gîte* in these lands. Count Hugh of Maine and Geoffrey's wife Adeleis and son Drogo confirm the concessions.

Participants: four: Geoffrey, Adeleis, Drogo and Count Hugh.

Witnesses: nineteen: Viscount Radulfus, his brother Odo, Patrick, Hugh the vicar, William Three-Lances, Aimery, Renaud the youth, Count Hugh, Geoffrey of Sablé, his wife Adelaidis (*sic*), their son Drogo, Rainandus Crasselus, Bishop Avesgaudus of Le Mans, Bishop Hubert of Angers, Abbot Ingelbaldus, Robert *grammaticus*, Guarinus (who wrote this charter), the monk Garnerius, the monk Rambertus.

II. *Vidimus:* at the request of Abbot Renaud, King William (I) of the English confirms the charter above.

Participants: two: King William and Abbot Renaud.

Witnesses: seven: the *barones* Geoffrey son of Liziardus, Gauterius the *miles*, Orricus the *praepositus*, Rannulfus son of Hugh the vicar, Herbert *miles* son of Guimbertus, Solomon son of Normannus, Patrick.

Manuscripts: A. Original, lost. B. Vidimus of 1073, lost. C. Vidimus of 1408, Arch. de l'abbaye de Solesmes.

Editions: I. Ménage, *Hist. de Sablé* I, pp. 25–26. II. Dom Piolin, *Hist. Eglise du Mans* III, p. j. XIII, pp. 639–641. III. *Cart. St.-Pierre de la Couture,* no. 8.

References: 1. Round, *CDF,* no. 1424 (part II only). 2. Davis and Whitwell, *Regesta Regum Anglo-Normannorum* I, no. 67 (part II only). 3. Angot nos. 18, 21 (part I only).

Geoffrey of Sablé's gift must fall between Bishop Hubert's ordination and the death of Count Hugh of Maine, perhaps by 6 July 1016 (Halphen, *Comté d'Anjou,* pp. 66–67, n. 5 on p. 66, nn. 1–2 on p. 67). The document now exists as a *vidimus* of King William I of England confirming Geoffrey's donation, on 30 March 1073 at Bonneville-sur-Touques (Calvados).

---

[1] Sablé, commune and canton, arr. La Flèche, Sarthe (Guillot 2: p. 340).
[2] Chantesmesle, hamlet, commune Solesmes (Vallée, p. 201).
[3] Rocheteau, commune Solesmes (Vallée, p. 1043).
[4] Melleray, commune of canton Montmirail, Sarthe (Vallée, p. 592).
[5] L'Abbaye Bousse, chef-lieu, commune de Bousse, Sarthe (Vallée, p. 1).
[6] For the identification of Vileras with les Valières, see *Cart. de Couture.* p. 10.
[7] Bossé, dép. Sarthe (Vallée, p. 981).
[8] For the identification of Brenerias with les Brenières, see *Cart. de Couture,* p. 11.

No. 4

13 June 1006–1016.

Charter: BISHOP HUBERT witnesses Count Hugh of Maine's confirmation of the gifts of Geoffrey of Sablé to St. Pierre of Couture. The terms of the gifts given here are the same as in No. 3 above, with the following differences: in the *vicus* of Solesmes, also given are two *formarii* under the monastery on the Sarthe; the two hamlets of Chantemesle and Rocheteau are specified as having been borrowed by Geoffrey from his brother Viscount Radulfus; it is mentioned that Count Hugh's confirmation was made in the presence of Bishop Avesgaudus of Le Mans and BISHOP HUBERT of Angers.

Participants: four: Count Hugh, Geoffrey of Sablé, Drogo his son, and Adelaidis his wife.

Witnesses: twenty-one: the same as in the first part of No. 3 above, with these exceptions: not subscribing this act but subscribing No. 3 is Bishop Hubert; subscribing this act but not No. 3 are Geoffrey of Sablé's other sons Burchardus and Liziardus, and Abbot Renaud.

II. *Notice:* Count Geoffrey (the Bearded) of Anjou confirms the first part above and renounces the *vicaria,* alods, and all customs that he held there justly or unjustly.

Participant: one: Count Geoffrey.

Witnesses: twenty-three: Count Geoffrey, Fulk (Réchin), Aimery de Tienns, Geoffrey Crassis, Fulk de Boeria, Geoffrey de Pliaco, Isembardus Bardo, Robert the *prepositus,* Fulk the chaplain, the canons of St. Laud Gerbertus, Simon, Hugh, and Ebo; Bishop Erbaldus, Anianus the cleric, Guiternus Castor, Martin son of Ingellundus the cleric, Renaud the cleric of Vetula Auricula, Guy the butcher and *villanus,* Hubert Ribola, William son of Constantine, Rochetus Calamus, Guarinus the cleric.

III. *Vidimus:* King William (I) of the English confirms Count Hugh's confirmation.

Participant: one: King William.

Witnesses: fourteen: King William, Bishop Arnaldus of Le Mans, Bishop Hugh of Lisieux, Abbot Renaud of St. Peter of Solesmes, William the monk, Herbert the monk, Gaudebertus the cleric; Geoffrey son of Liliardus [*recte* Liziardus?], Walter the *miles,* Otricus the *prepositus,* the *miles* Herbert son of Gumbertus, Salomon son of Normandus, Patrick, Ranulphus son of Hugh the Vicar.

It is unsure if the following six witnesses belong to Part II or Part III: Abbot Adelaidis [*sic,* for Adelardis], Frogerius the prior, Frederick the monk, Girardus the monk and cantor, Breverius the monk, William the monk.

Manuscripts: A. Original, lost. B. Vidimus of 1073, lost. C. Vidimus of 1408, Arch. de l'abbaye de Solesmes. C. Vidimus of 1415, Arch. de l'abbaye de Solesmes. D. Copy of the seventeenth century by Gaignières, B. n., ms. lat. 17123, p. 187, after A.

Edition: *Cart. de St.-Pierre de la Couture*, no. 9, after B.

References: 1. Round, *CDF* no. 1425 (Part III only). 2. Halphen no. 204 (Part II only). 3. Latouche no. 17 (Part I only). 4. Davis and Whitwell no. 68 (Part III only). 5. Angot nos. 19, 22 (Part I only). 6. Guillot no. 259 (Part II only).

For the dating of Count Hugh's confirmation, see the dating of Geoffrey of Sablé's grant, Part I of No. 3 above. Geoffrey the Bearded gave his confirmation between 14 November 1060 and 4 April 1067 (see Guillot no. 259). Parts I and II were then confirmed by King William I of England in a *vidimus* of 30 March 1073 (see references 1 and 4, above).

No. 5

1020. Angers.
Notice: BISHOP HUBERT dedicates the church of St. Nicholas, built by Count Fulk Nerra within sight of Angers.
  Participant: one: Bishop Hubert.

This information is included in a larger document relating Count Fulk's problems in keeping an abbot at the monastery of St. Nicholas, as well as his gifts to it (see below, Nos. 8, 32, 35).

No. 6

1 September 1022. Angers.
Notice: BISHOP HUBERT consecrates Frederick as abbot of St. Florent, at Angers in the presence of Abbot Evraudus of Marmoutier.
  Participants: three: Hubert, Frederick, Evraudus.

No charter for this act exists, but a once-extant notice for it is inferred from the discussion of Frederick's consecration in the *Historia Sancti Florentii Salmurensis* in *Chroniques des églises d'Anjou*, p. 270. The *Historia* dates this in 1020, but it is correct to 1022 (see *Annales de Saint-Florent* in *Recueil d'annales angevines et vendômoises*, p. 118).
  Reference: Ziezulewicz no. II.

No. 7

25 December 1021–29 December 1022. Vendôme.
Charter: BISHOP HUBERT witnesses the act of Count Fulk Nerra, at the request of his *fidelis* Hildeiardis and of her nephew Gundacrus, for the soul of her son Fulcherius, freeing the *famulus* Raindincus, who had risen from the *familia* of St. Martin, along with his children Richard and Guitberga, and Fulk orders them to chose whomever they would as an *advocatus*.
  Participants: six: Count Fulk, Hildeiardis, Gundacrus, Raindincus, Richard, and Guitberga.
  Witnesses: twenty: Fulk's *fidelis* Hildeiardis, Odo the cleric, Gundacrus, Rannulfus, Bishop Hubert, Otredus, Viscount Radulfus, Lancelinus, Hugh,

Hilgaudus, Ernulfus, Radulfus, Walter, Herveus, Josbertus, Ernulfus, Harduinus, Fulcherius, Guitbertus, Hildeiardis the daughter of Fulcherius.

Manuscripts: A. Original, lost. B. Copy of the eleventh century, Book of the Serfs of Marmoutier, Bibl. de Tours, ms. 1376, p. 35. C. Copy of the eighteenth century, B. n., coll. Baluze, vol. 77, fol. 142 r. D. Copy of the eighteenth century, B. n., D. H. XII², no. 6800, after B.

Edition: *Livre des serfs de Marmoutier*, no. 52.

References: 1. Halphen no. 33. 2. Angot no. 24. 3. Guillot no. 35. 4. Fanning, "Origines familiales de Vulgrin," p. 249.

For the dating, see Guillot no. 35.

No. 8

1020–24 October 1022/23 October 1023. Angers.

I. *Notice:* BISHOP HUBERT consecrates Baudricus, who came from Marmoutier, as abbot of St. Nicholas of Angers.

Participants: two: Bishop Hubert and Baudricus.

II. *Notice:* Not long after he constituted Baudricus as abbot, Count Fulk Nerra gives to St. Nicholas for the sustenance of the monks and the poor, certain of his own properties: above the banks of the Brionneau, his mother's vines and orchard which he himself cleared and leveled, in Pré-d'Alloyau,[1] more than twelve arpents of meadows, returning neither a *census* or *decima*, "ut regale alodium"; the land l'Adézière,[2] free of the *vicaria, fodrum,* and all customs, which Fulk got from Guy the treasurer, who held it from Albericus of Montjean, in exchange for half the church of la Pouèze[3] and two *mansurae* of land; an enclosure of vines between the Maine and the Brionneau and other vines across the Maine, free of the *vinagium;* Fulk fixes the limits of his *bannum* on vines at the torrent of Barre, and forbids his *praepositus* and vicar to enter the monastery's lands unless the abbot should twice refuse to determine a case; at Villenière[4] he gives an assart; the men of the monastery are exempt from serving in the comital army if it is going to build a *castrum* or to pillage; service is to be demanded only in case of war; comital officials are not to seize wagons, cattle, or asses belong to St. Nicholas.

Participant: one: Count Fulk.

Manuscripts and editions: see No. 35 below.

References: 1. Halphen no. 34. 2. Guillot no. 36.

This information is included in the first part of a document relating Count Fulk's establishment of the monastery of St. Nicholas, his difficulties keeping an abbot there, and his gifts to the house (see No. 5 above and Nos. 32, 35 below). It is stated in the document only that Fulk "constituted" Baudricus as abbot, but since Bishop Hubert dedicated the church of St. Nicholas (No. 5 above) and he usually ordained the heads of houses in his diocese (No. 6 above, Nos. 25, 53 below), he probably ordained

Baudricus as well. The ordination would have occurred between the dedication of the church of St. Nicholas in 1020 (No. 5 above) and the writing of the document in 1039 (see No. 35 below).

---

[1] For the identification of Lupellus with Pré-d'Alloyau, see Mailfert, "Fondation de Saint-Nicolas," p. 60 n. 1.

[2] L'Adézière, ferme, commune d'Avrille (Port I, p. 3)

[3] La Pouèze, canton le Lion-d'Angers, arr. Segré (Port III, p. 173).

[4] Villenière, château, commune la Pouèze (Port III, p. 733).

No. 9

13 June 1006–28 October 1024.

Charter: Viscount Hubert (of Vendôme), for his own soul and for the souls of his parents and his son BISHOP HUBERT (of Angers), gives to Marmoutier his alod in the *pagus* of Vendôme in the villa Buziacus (Bezay[1]), which had been left to him by his *parentes.*

Participant: one: Viscount Hubert.

Witnesses: five: Viscount Hubert, Hugh Bospleus, Haimo, Morandus, Robert of Marcilly.

Manuscripts: A. Original, lost. B. Copy of the seventeenth century, B. n., ms. lat. 12878, fol. 88 r. C. Copy of the seventeenth century, B. n., ms. lat. 12880, fol. 213 r.

References: Dom Martène, *Hist. de Marmoutier,* p. 290.

This charter must have been issued after the younger Hubert became bishop of Angers, but before 28 October 1024, the last possible date for the death of Viscount Hubert (see above, chap. 2, n. 24).

---

[1] Bezay, dép. Loire-et-Cher, fief, commune Nourray (*Cart. de la Trinité de Vendôme,* V, p. 266).

No. 10

16 August 1025. Angers.

Charter: On the occasion of the dedication of the cathedral of St. Maurice of Angers, BISHOP HUBERT, who had been aided in the rebuilding by his parents Viscount Hubert of Vendôme and Emma, gives up to the canons, who in their poverty had long withstood the oppression of the counts, certain rights that he had exercised over their lands: in the *curtis* Spiniacus (Epinats[1]), he claimed the customary fifteen *modii* of the *vinagium* and twelve *modii* of the *frumentagium* each year; in the alod Ruiniacum (Reugné[2]), he concedes half the *vicaria* and remits all the *bidannum* and *corvadae* and all customs, retaining only the custom of having *ramatae* (fish traps) made by the *villani* at Vicus (Villevêque[3]), due at the cathedral on the feast of Sts. Peter and Paul; in the *curtis* Morenna (Morannes[4]) and the *curtis* of St. Dionisius (Saint-Denis d'Anjou[5]), half the *vicaria;* he concedes the right formerly exacted by him and his predecessors, that of selling from the *praeposituri* of those *curtes;* in the future, with the consent of the dean and of all the chapter, the canons may freely give, sell, or retain those domains; Bishop Hubert retains only the customary episcopal rights.

Participant: one: Bishop Hubert.

Witnesses: eleven: Bishop Hubert, Guy the treasurer and archdeacon, Burchardus the archdeacon, Joscelin the archdeacon, Bernerius the *levita* and *scholae magister,* Fulcoius the priest, Hubert the abbot of St. Serge, Ansaldus the priest and dean, Giraldus the precentor, Hildinus the priest, Renaud (written by Renaud in the place of Burchardus the archdeacon and chancellor).

Manuscripts: A. Original, lost. B. Copy, cartulary of St. Maurice, fol. 21 r, lost. C. Copy of the seventeenth century, B. n., coll. Baluze, vol. 39, fol. 63 r–v, after B. D. Copy of the eighteenth century, Bibl. d'Angers, ms. 690 (624), fol. 280 r–v, after B. E. Copy of the eighteenth century, B. n., D. H. II¹, nos. 406, 408 (fragments).

Editions: I. Pletteau, *Revue de l'Anjou* 9 (1873), pp. 114–115. II. D'Espinay, ibid. 9 (1873), pp. 230–231, n. 4 (extract). III. D'Espinay, *Notices archéologiques* I, p. 90 (fragment). IV. *Cartulaire noir de la cathédrale d'Angers,* no. 29.

For the dating, see *Cart. noir de la cathédrale,* no. 29.

---

¹ Epinats, commune Cizay, commune Montreuil-Bellay (Port II, p. 109; *Cart. noir de la cathédrale,* p. 509).

² Reugné, commune Villevêque, canton Angers (Port III, p. 246).

³ Villevêque, canton Angers (*Cart. noir de la cathédrale,* p. 513).

⁴ Morannes, canton Durtal, arr. Baugé (Port II, p. 737).

⁵ Saint-Denis d'Anjou, dép. Mayenne, canton Bierné (*Cart. noir de la cathédrale,* p. 499).

No. 11

14 October 1006–1027.

Charter: BISHOP HUBERT witnesses grants made to St. Aubin by Gerorius, for the souls of his father Joscelin of Rennes and his mother Gondrada and his brother Walter, all of whom are buried at the monastery of St. Aubin. These donations are: his church at Chartrené¹ in the *vicaria* of Baugé² with two *mansurae,* the *vicaria,* and all the customs. In return, Abbot Hubert and the monks give Gerorius a fine horse and two tapestries. Count Fulk and his son Geoffrey confirm the gift.

Participants: four are named: Gerorius, Abbot Hubert of St. Aubin, Count Fulk, and his son Geoffrey; and the monks of St. Aubin.

Manuscripts: A. Original, lost. B. Copy of the eleventh century, Arch. Maine-et-Loire, H 100, fol. 74, no. 4. C. Copy of the twelfth century, cartulary of St. Aubin, Bibl. d'Angers, ms. 829 (745), fol. 80 v. D. copy of the eighteenth century, B. n., D. H. II¹, no. 385.

Edition: *St. Aubin*, no. 241.

References: 1. Port, H, p. 19. 2. Halphen no. 38. 3. Guillot no. 38.

For the dating, see Halphen no. 38.

---

[1] Chartrené, canton, arr. Baugé (Port, I, p. 632).
[2] Baugé, chef-lieu, arr., canton Baugé (Port, I, p. 223).

No. 12 (Inauthentic)

25 November 1023–10 April 1028.

Charter: BISHOP HUBERT witnesses the dedication of the church at the *castellum* of Bellême,[1] dedicated to St. Leonard and built by William of Bellême, who recalls that he went to Rome for penance and that he confessed his sins to Pope Leo, who enjoined him to build a church subject only to Rome, as penance. After a delay he built the church of St. Leonard at his *castellum* and wished it to be totally free from all episcopal and lay customs. Now he has invited a number of lay and episcopal authorities to dedicate the church and to authorize its freedom, which they do.

Participants: thirteen: William of Bellême, King Robert II, Count Odo, Archbishop Gelduinus of Sens, Bishop Fulbert of Chartres, Count Richard of Normandy, Archbishop Rodulfus of Rouen, Bishop Richard of Séez, Count Fulk of Anjou, Bishop Hubert of Angers, Archbishop Arnulf of Tours, Count Herbert [Wake-Dog] of Maine, Bishop Avesgaudus of Le Mans.

Witnesses: twelve: all the participants except William of Bellême.

II. *Vidimus:* Because the incursions of the Northmen and negligence caused the seal of the witnesses of William of Bellême's charter to become lost, although the text remained complete, Robert of Bellême takes the charter to King Philip I for his authorization, which Philip gives.

Participants: two: Robert of Bellême and King Philip.

Manuscripts: A. Original, Arch. de l'Orne, H 2151 (Part I only). B. Copy of the end of the eleventh century, Arch. de l'Orne, H 2151 (Parts I and II). C. Copy of the seventeenth century by Gaignières, B. n., cartulary of Marmoutier, ms. lat. 5441[2], p. 289, after A. D. Copy of 1611 in Courtin, *Hist. du Perche*, ms. belonging to Mme de Saint-Hilaire, p. 161, after B. E. Copy of the seventeenth century, B. n., coll. Duchesne, vol. 54, pp. 441–442, after A and B. F. Copy of the eighteenth century, B. n. coll. Moreau, vol. 19, fol. 165, after A. G. Copy of the seventeenth century, B. n., coll. De Camps, vol. 4, fol. 302, after I below.

Editions: I. Bry de la Clergerie, *Histoire des pays et comté du Perche et duché d'Alençon*, pp. 45–47, after E. II. *Cart. de Marmoutier pour le Perche*, no. 2, after B. III. Prou, "Examen de la charte de fondation de Saint-Léonard de Bellême," in *Mélanges Paul Fabre*, p. 232, after A and B. IV. Prou, *Rec. des actes de Philippe Ier*, no. 176, after A and B. V. Fauroux, *Rec. des actes des ducs de Normandie*, no. ⟨56⟩, after B.

References: 1. Bréquigny 1, p. 533. 2. Martène, *Hist. de Marmoutier* I, p. 495. 3. Pfister, *Robert le Pieux* no. 74. 4. Halphen faux no. 6. 5. Lemarignier, *Etude sur les privilèges d'exemption,* pp. 181–192. 6. Prou, *Rec. de Philippe Ier,* pp. ccxix–ccxxxv. 7. Newman no. 134 (faux). 8. Emily Z. Tabuteau, "Transfers of Property in Eleventh-Century Norman Law," pp. 866–872.

Photograph of ms: a. Reference 5, plate II (ms. A).

Prou (reference 6) has demonstrated the inauthenticity of both the charter and the *vidimus.* According to the information in the first part, William of Bellême's charter, the dedication of the church would have been between 25 November 1023 and 10 April 1028, that is, between the elevation of Arnulf to the see of Tours and the death of Fulbert of Chartres.

Prou has also established that the seal of King Philip, put on Part II, was used between 1060 and 7 April 1080 (reference 6, p. ccxxix).

---

[1] Bellême, commune and canton, arr. Mortagne, dép. Orne (Guillot 2: p. 314).

No. 13

13 June 1006–14 July 1028. Angers.
I. *Notice:* BISHOP HUBERT, along with Count Fulk, gives his authorization for Guy, the treasurer of the cathedral of St. Maurice at Angers, to give to St. Aubin the church of St. Martin Vertavensis (de Vertou[1]) in the *vicus* of Legio (le Lion-d'Angers[2]), with a cemetery and everything pertaining to it, the dam of le Lion-d'Angers, and half a mill in Curtisjuncus (Courgeon[3]), his demesne furnace in le Lion-d'Angers (except for the one with two cookhouses where poor men cook their meals), five *mansurae* of land, nineteen arpents of vines, the *pasnagium* of Balgiacus (Baugé), and a market for buying fish, held shortly before the feast of St. Martin.

Participants: nine are named: Guy, his wife Hamelina, his three sons Baldwin, Albericus, and Noah, Count Fulk, Bishop Hubert, and the lords of Craon (first Warinus and then Suhardus), to whose tenement the church and rights pertained; and the monks of St. Aubin.

This notice is the first part of a longer document, the second part is:
II. *Notice:* after Guy became a monk of St. Aubin, his eldest son Baldwin administered the family inheritance and gave new grants to St. Aubin; he then died and the younger son Albericus usurped the grants made by his father and brother. The monks of St. Aubin then purchased Albericus's confirmation of the gifts made by his father, brother, mother, himself, and five other *fideles;* Albericus receives 130 pounds of denarii. This settlement is authorized by Count Geoffrey Martel, Bishop Eusebius, and Robert, lord of Craon, who receives thirty pounds of denarii since the gifts pertained to his tenement.

Participants: four: Albericus, Count Geoffrey, Bishop Eusebius, and Robert.

Witnesses: twenty-nine: Abbot Theodoric of St. Aubin, Odo son of Count Stephen and nephew of Count Tetbaldus, Rainerius de Turre, Guy of Luché, Robert son of Frotgerius, Paulinus son of Geoffrey the *prepositus*, Renaud *grammaticus*, Hamelinus of Corzé, Robert son of Rainildis, Tetbaldus of Noellet; from St. Aubin, John Gravella, Bernerius the *cellararius*, John the *hospitalarius*, Bernerius the *secretarius*, Rannulfus; Albericus's men Lisoius Naso, Joscelin Ferlus, Gosmerus the son of Odo and his brother Geoffrey, Walter son of Hunebaldus; Count Geoffrey Martel, Bishop Eusebius and Count Geoffrey the younger (all three of whom make the sign of the cross), Fulk the nephew of Count Geoffrey (Martel), Babinus son of Judiquel, Albericus, Gestinus son of Ascoith, Geoffrey Rotundellus, Tetbertus the monk and *medicus*.

Manuscripts: A. Original redaction, lost. B. Copy of the twelfth century, cartulary of St. Aubin, Bibl. d'Angers, ms. 829 (745), fol. 51 v–52 r. C. Copy of the eighteenth century, Bibl. d'Angers, ms. 706 (636), p. 78 (lacking the last four witnesses). D. Copy of the eighteenth century, B. n., D. H. II[1], no. 516, after B.

Editions: I. Hiret, *Des antiquitez d'Anjou* (1618), pp. 210–216 (Part I only). II. *St. Aubin*, no. 160.

References: 1. Bertrand de Brouissillon, *Craon* no. 10. 2. Halphen nos. 42 (Part I) and 127 (Part II). 3. Guillot nos. 41 (Part I) and 178 (Part II).

For the dating of Part I, 13 June 1006–14 July 1028, see Halphen no. 42. Part II is dated from the presence of Abbot Theodoric of St. Aubin, who was ordained 14 January 1056 and died 26 December 1059 (*Annales de Saint-Aubin*, pp. 4–5).

---

[1] For the identification of Vertavensis with Vertou, see Guillot, no. 41, p. 44.
[2] Le Lion-d'Angers, petite ville, chef-lieu de canton, arr. Segré (Port II, p. 520).
[3] Courgeon, ferme, commune le Lion-d'Angers (Port I, p. 779).

No. 14

13 June 1006–14 July 1028.

Notice: BISHOP HUBERT gives the mill at Morannes[1] in benefice to the *miles* Ivo. This mill had been built by *servi* of the church of Angers and possessed by BISHOP HUBERT.

Participants: two: Bishop Hubert and Ivo.

This reference is made in a charter of Bishop Eusebius, recording the agreement concerning this mill. After Ivo received the mill, by some means it was given to Ronceray by Countess Hildegardis along with other donations. In Eusebius's time, a controversy arose over the mill. Count Geoffrey Martel mediates the dispute and half the mill is given to the bishop and the nuns obtain part of the episcopal fishpond. In addition, the bishop's men are to have their grain ground at the mill.

Participants: two are named: Bishop Eusebius and Count Geoffrey; and the nuns of Ronceray.

Witnesses: ten: Bishop Eusebius, Joscelin the dean, Berengar the treasurer, Renaud the archdeacon, Abbot Vulgrinus (of St. Serge), Primardus the archpriest, Rudulfus the priest, Andrew the eunuch, Drogo, Ronceray's *stabulus,* and Walter.

Manuscripts: A. Original, lost. B. Copy, white cartulary of Ronceray, fol. 126 r, lost. C. Copy of the thirteenth century, cartulary of Ronceray, Bibl. d'Angers, ms. 847 (760), no. 24 of the fourth roll.
Edition: *Ronceray,* no. 220, after C.
Reference: Guillot no. 160.

This mill was acquired by Countess Hildegardis from Ivo, for on the occasion of the dedication of the convent of Ronceray, she gave it (still paying the *census* to the bishop, which must have been retained by Hubert when he gave the mill to Ivo) to the new house (*Ronceray,* nos. 1 and 3, Nos. 15, 16, and 18 below). Bishop Hubert gave the mill to Ivo after his ordination as bishop, but before the dedication of Ronceray on 14 July 1028 (No. 15 below).

Hildegardis gave the mill to Ronceray on 14 July 1020 (No. 15, Part IV below). Guillot no. 160 has dated Bishop Eusebius's resolution of the dispute as 6 December 1047–31 July 1056 (see also the dating of No. 18 below).

––––––––––

[1] Morannes; see No. 10, note 4.

No. 15

14 July 1028. Angers.
This act is in four parts:
I. *Charter* (down to "ad Morennam"): BISHOP HUBERT dedicates the basilica of Mary (belonging to the convent of Ronceray), which had been restored from total ruin by Count Fulk, Countess Hildegardis, and their son Geoffrey. Four priests are to serve the church, each with his own house, but they share vines, meadows and one-third of the *decima* of the parish of St. Mary; the priests are to serve personally. With the counsel and admonition of BISHOP HUBERT, the oblations received by the priests are to be divided equally between the priests and the nuns of the convent of St. Mary (Ronceray); candles and lights belong solely to the priests; revenues from burials, animals, services of thirty masses, weeks, masses for the dead, private masses, baptisms, confessions, and all other revenues are to be divided equally between the priests and the nuns; gifts to the church or to the nuns belong wholly to the nuns, while those given to the priests belong to them alone. Fulk, Hildegardis, and Geoffrey give one arch on the bridge over the river Maine. After the dedication of the church by BISHOP HUBERT, the following lands are given to the church but are held by the

BISHOP: forty arpents of vines near the church; at Fossae (Fosse) above the Loire, thirty arpents of meadows; two alods, one at Calvun (Chauvon[1]) with one mill, the other at Similiacus (Sémelon[2]); one-fourth of the mill in the Sarthe at Morannes.[3]

Participants: four: Count Fulk, Hildegardis, Geoffrey and Bishop Hubert.

II. *Notice* (down to "ad Campum Sancti Germani"): BISHOP HUBERT dedicates the monastery of St. Mary of Charity (Ronceray) on 14 July 1028 and confirms the gifts made to it; with the treasurer Burchardus, the dean Joscelin, the archpriest Primoldus and many others, HUBERT establishes the borders of the parish of St. Mary, from the gate of Boletus (la Porte-Boulet[4]) to Frigida Fons (Froide-Fontaine[5]), from Spiniatus (Epinard[6]) to Campus Sancti Germani.

Participants: four who are named: Bishop Hubert, Burchardus, Joscelin, and Primoldus.

III. *Charter:* BISHOP HUBERT witnesses gifts made by Count Fulk and Hildegardis to the convent of Ronceray: for their own sins and for the souls of Fulk's parents Geoffrey and Adela, they give two great alods near the *vicus* of Lion (le Lion-d'Angers[7]), that of Quintinus (l'Alleu-Quentin[8]) above the Oudon, and the other of Chauvon[1] above the Mayenne, with one mill; at Fosse, a fiscal villa with the best fishpond of the fishery and thirty arpents of meadows, the *servus* Ermendardus and all his offspring, the *ancillae* Ranois (and her descendants except for her son Giraldus), Gerberga and Fredeburgis; at Angers under the monastery, one tract for a fishery; for the nuns' kitchen, the *servi* Bernard and his brothers Burcardus and Odo.

Participants: two: Fulk and Hildegardis.

Witnesses: seven: Fulk, Hildegardis, Geoffrey their son, Bishop Hubert, the treasurer Burchardus, the dean Joscelin, the archpriest Primoldus.

IV. *Notice:* Countess Hildegardis gives to the church of St. Mary from her own possessions and from her purchases at Morannes[3] (the episcopal seat), one mill paying the *census* to the BISHOP OF ANGERS; at Bria Sarte (Brissarthe[9]), half the mill; in the Mayenne at Carrariae (Charray-sur-Mayenne[10]), half the mill; at Prisciniacus (Précigné[11]), one manse of land; at Travalliacus (Travaillé[12]), one manse paying the *census* to the lord of Juvardeil; at Canciacus (Chanzé[13]), one manse; inside the city of Angers, close to the church of St. Mary, one *area mansionum* to the *census* of the treasurer Burchardus; at Lupellus (Aloyau[14]), ten arpents of meadows; in Angers at various places along the banks of the Maine, many arpents of vines. Rainerius, a *dominicus vassus,* gives two *quartae* of land, the *servus* Adelardus with all his family, at Trodreia when he gives his daughter Lisoia to the convent. Guy the treasurer gives two *mansurae* of arable land at Forgae (les Forges[15]), with the authority of his lord Sigebrannus and his son William. Haduissa gives the mill given to her by her father and her brother Joscelin, with two arpents of land paying the *census* of eight denarii to Basilia and Renaud, without customs, with the confirmation of her *nepotes.* Fromundus and his wife Josberga give three *quartae* of vines and half an arpent of land, paying a *census* of five denarii to Albert and Hugh. This Hugh gives his daughter Ros- [the rest of the name and the nature and location of the land are lacking], with the *vinagium* and *decima.*

Participants: nine: Countess Hildeburgis, Rainerius, Guy, Haduissa, Fromundus, Josberga, Hugh, Sigebrannus, and William.

Manuscripts: A. Original charters, lost. B. Original redaction, lost. C. Copy, white cartulary of Ronceray, fol. 1–2, lost. D. Copy of the thirteenth century, cartulary of Ronceray, Bibl. d'Angers, ms. 844 (760), no. 1 of the first roll. E. Copy of the seventeenth century, B. n., coll. Baluze, vol. 139, pp. 325–328 (Parts I–III only). F. Copy of the eighteenth century, B. n., coll. Baluze, vol. 39, fol. 297 r–298 r (Parts I–III only). G. Copy of the eighteenth century, B. n., D. H. II[1], no. 395, after C.

Editions: I. Hiret, *Des antiquitez d'Anjou* (1605), pp. 100–101 (Parts I and II only). II. Ibid. (1618), pp. 178–186 (Parts I and II only). III. Ste.-Marthe, *Gallia Christiana* 4, pp. 792–793. IV. Tresvaux no. 26 (partial). V. Grandet, *Notre-Dame Angevine,* p. 441–442 (partial). VI. *Ronceray,* no. 1, after D.

References: 1. Bréquigny 1, p. 560. 2. Halphen no. 44. 3. Guillot no. 42.

The dedication of Ronceray is given in the document, 14 July 1028.

Parts I and III seem to be halves of the same charter, with Part II inserted into it, and a separate notice of Hildegardis's and others' donations attached to the principal charter of Ronceray's dedication. For a separate notice of the same act described in Part IV, see *Ronceray,* no. 3, No. 16 below.

---

[1] Chauvon, mill, hamlet, commune le Lion-d'Angers (Port I, p. 657).
[2] Sémelon, ferme, commune Pouancé (Port III, p. 519).
[3] Morannes; see No. 10, note 4.
[4] La Porte-Boulet at Angers (*Ronceray,* p. 401; *Cart. noir de la cathédrale,* p. 391).
[5] Froide-Fontaine, chef-lieu, commune Avrillé (Port II, p. 213).
[6] Epinard, commune Cantenay-Epinard (Port II, p. 108).
[7] Le Lion-d'Angers, petite ville, chef-lieu of canton, arr. Segré (Port II, p. 520).
[8] L'Alleu-Quentin, close to le Lion-d'Angers (*Ronceray,* p. 391).
[9] Brissarthe, canton Châteauneuf-sur-Sarthe, arr. Segré (Port I, p. 513).
[10] Charray-sur-Mayenne, commune Chambellay (Port I, p. 630).
[11] Précigné, commune of canton Sablé, dép. Sarthe (Vallée, p. 748).
[12] Travaillé, ferme, commune Contigné [ferme, commune Juvardeil] (Port III, p. 613).
[13] Chanzé, commune Ste.-Gemmes-sur-Loire (Port I, p. 610).
[14] Aloyau, commune Angers (Port I, p. 15).
[15] Les Forges, ville, commune Savennières (Port II, p. 178).

No. 16

14 July 1028. Angers.
Notice: Countess Hildegardis, for her sins and those of her husband Count Fulk, gives to Ronceray small possessions that she bought in legitimate arrangements from different *fideles:* at Morannes,[1] one mill paying the *census* to the BISHOP OF ANGERS (Hubert); the other donations are

identical to those of No. 15, Part IV, but without the donations made by Haduissa, Fromundus and his wife Josberga, or Hugh.

Participants: five: Countess Hildegardis, Rainerius, Guy, Siebrannus, William.

Manuscripts: A. Original charter, lost. B. Original notice, lost. C. Copy of the thirteenth century, Bibl. d'Angers, ms. 848 (760), no. 58.

Edition: *Ronceray*, no. 3.

The dating is the same as No. 15 above, 14 July 1028.

---

[1] Morannes; see No. 10, note 4.

No. 17

14 July 1028. Angers.

Notice: (1) in a *placitum* of Bishop Eusebius and Count Fulk Réchin settling a dispute concerning the boundary between the parishes of Ronceray and St. Nicholas, it is recalled that BISHOP HUBERT established the borders of the parish of St. Mary when he dedicated Ronceray, *viz.*, from Posterna Boleti (la Porte-Boulet[1]) to Frigidus Fons (Froide-Fontaine[2]), and from Spinatius (Epinard[3]) to Grizilliacus (le Bas-Grésil[4]). (2) Now, however, a dispute has arisen over those boundaries. A young man, Piscis, son of Roger and Lamberga, with his comrades, began the fraternity of St. Nicholas, and when he died, his friends and fellow members of the fraternity attempted to carry his body from the church of St. Mary to that of St. Nicholas for burial. The nuns and men of St. Mary discovered the plan, thwarted it, and carried the body back to St. Mary's, where they buried it within the seven walls. The uproar is taken to a *placitum* held by Bishop Eusebius and Count Fulk (Réchin), the brother of Geoffrey (Barbatus).

The nuns claim that their parish extends all the way to la Port-Boulet, and they produce four witnesses who were present at the dedication ceremonies, Giraldus Calvellus, Andefredus the brother of Aimery the Rich, Fulcoinus Godueth, and Stabilis the vicar, who testifty that BISHOP HUBERT established the borders as abovesaid. Present at the *placitum* and deciding in favor of Ronceray are Bishop Eusebius, Count Fulk, Archdeacon Marbodus, Geoffrey the treasurer, Geoffrey the cantor, Robert the Burgundian, Renaud of Château-Gontier and many others. A ceremony is then held to delimit the boundaries of St. Mary's parish; starting from la Port-Boulet, one man is sent down each bank of the Maine to Port Ligny, pointing out the divisions of the parish.

Participants at the *placitum:* eleven are named above; and the nuns of Ronceray.

Witnesses at the ceremony: fourty-four are named: Bishop Eusebius, Count Fulk Réchin, Geoffrey the treasurer, Geoffrey the cantor, Marbodus the archdeacon, Garnerius, Renaud the archdeacon, Geoffrey, Martin and the rest of the chapter; Durandus Cor Sancto, Eudo Blanchardus, Renaud

Espasterius, Hugh of St. Laud and many other clerics; the laics Bernerius and Giraudus the sons of Andefredus, Garnerius *cellerarius*, Fulbertus *monetarius*, Renaud Burgevinus, Frogerius *pontenarius*, Dagobinus, Engelardus, Giraldus Pilatus, Vitalis tornator, Thebertus the *prepositus*, Renaud Fossardus, Walter Rufus, Renaud the *villanus*, Robert of Châteaubriant, Teobaudus Allobros, Nyldinus Ferronus, Hubert Piterata, Mainerius his brother, Renaud of Orgigné, Fulcoius his brother, Gaius *pistor*, Rohodus *cellerarius*, Christianus of Epinard, Adelelmus the canon, Augerius, Robert, Imberga the *celleraria*, Imberga the daughter of God, Delia the sacristan, Richildis abbess of Ronceray, and a great crowd.

Manuscripts: A. Original redaction, lost. B. Copies of the thirteenth century, cartulary of Ronceray, Bibl. d'Angers, ms. 845 (760), no. 75, ms. 848 (760), nos. 11 and 45.
Edition: *Ronceray*, no. 47.
Reference: Guillot no. 329 (Part 2 only).

Bishop Hubert set the limits of the parish of St. Mary when he dedicated the convent, 14 July 1028 (Part II of No. 15). The settlement of the disputed boundary must have been after the election of Abbess Richildis of Ronceray (*Ronceray*, no. 16, Guillot no. 306), who was a witness to this act. She was elected on 23 June 1073. But Archdeacon Renaud, who also witnessed this settlement, was dead by 31 July 1077 (*Cart. noir de la cathédrale*, no. 49).

Guillot places the resolution of the conflict between 1075 (or 1079) and the death of Bishop Eusebius on 27 August 1081. His *terminus a quo* is based on the succession to the archidiaconate, reasoning that Marbodus succeeded Renaud as archdeacon only at the latter's death, so they both could not be styled archdeacons at the same time, as they are in this act. Guillot cites *Cart. noir de la cathédrale*, no. 49, to support this contention. However, that document does not state that Archdeacon Marbodus succeeded Archdeacon Renaud only after Renaud's death. But it mentions that Marbodus the master of the school received vines and land at Longchamps from the legacy of his *predecessor* Renaud, who was now dead. Since Renaud was both master of the school and archdeacon (*Cart. noir de la cathédrale*, pp. xliv, lvi, and *St. Aubin*, no. 77), he was also Marbodus's predecessor as master of the school. This document in question concerns arrangements made between the canons and the school, so it must refer to Marbodus as the successor to Renaud as *scholasticus*, not as archdeacon. However, Renaud was dead ("bonae memoriae") at the time of the charter, 31 July 1077.

Since it is not known exactly when Marbodus became an archdeacon (although he was in 1076, see No. 64), and it is not known that Marbodus succeeded Renaud as archdeacon, the succession to the archidiaconate will not aid in dating this charter. Such an argument would be helpful only if the document is contemporary with the events described, but this act was clearly drawn up after Bishop Eusebius's death in 1081, for the *placitum* was held "sed vivente Eusebio episcopo." Even if Marbodus and Renaud were never archdeacons at the same time, the redactor of this act could have given them both that title because he knew that they both had been archdeacons.

---

[1] La Porte-Boulet; see No. 15, note 4.
[2] Froide-Fontaine; see No. 15, note 5.
[3] Epinard; see No. 15, note 6.
[4] Le Bas-Grésil, ferme, commune Bouchemaine (Port II, p. 300).

No. 18

14 July 1028. Angers.
Notice: BISHOP HUBERT and Countess Hildegardis give the mill at Morannes[1] to Ronceray.
Participants: two: Bishop Hubert and Hildegardis.
This reference is made in a charter of Ronceray recording the resolution by Bishop Eusebius of a conflict over this mill. An episcopal colibert named Hamelinus claimed the mill, which had once been his father's, by right of inheritance. Joscelin Isnellus, the bishop's *vavassor*, had undertaken to repair an old mill only two stades above this mill. The nuns of Ronceray give up half of their mill to the bishop, while keeping the superior *census* of four solidi, and with the *bannum* the bishop will have men of his land use the nuns' mill and give the nuns half of his fishpond.
Participants: three are named: Bishop Eusebius, Hamelinus, and Joscelin; and the nuns.
Witnesses: eleven: Joscelin the dean, Berengar the treasurer, Abbot Vulgrinus of St. Serge, Renaud the archdeacon, Fulcoius the chaplain, Drogo and Walter *servientes*, Primaldus the archpriest, Radulfus the priest, Stabilis *serviens*, and Andrew the eunuch.

Manuscripts: A. Original, lost. B. Copy, white cartulary of Ronceray, lost. C. Copy of the thirteenth century, cartulary of Ronceray, Bibl. d'Angers, ms. 847 (760), no. 27 of the fourth roll. D. Copy of the eighteenth century, B. n., D. H. II[1], no. 504.
Edition: *Ronceray,* no. 219.

The mill was given to Ronceray on 14 July 1028 (see No. 15, Part IV, and Nos. 14, 16). Bishop Eusebius's decision concerns the same events as *Ronceray,* no. 220 (No. 14 above), and most of the witnesses to this act were also witnesses to it, so these two charters were probably issued at the same time. Guillot no. 160 fixes the date for No. 14 above as 6 December 1047–31 July 1056.

---

[1] Morannes; see No. 10, note 4.

No. 19

28 October 1007–ca. 14 July 1028
Notice: BISHOP HUBERT gives or confirms land at Coëmont[1] with *servi* and *ancillae* to either Aremburgis or her husband Thetuinus Strabo.

This act is inferred from *Ronceray,* no. 391 (No. 20 below), where Bishop Hubert, acting as the head of his family (since his niece Emma, her husband Viscount Radulfus, and their children also participate), gives his authorization for Aremburgis's grant of Coëmont to Ronceray. Hubert would have acted in this role only after the death of his father Viscount Hubert. His father was still alive after Fulbert was ordained bishop of Chartres in September or October of 1006 (Pfister, *De Fulberti Carnotensis Episcopi Vita et Operibus,* pp. 47–48), for Bishop Fulbert wrote a letter to the magnates of the Vendômois, including Viscount Hubert, summoning them to come to him to do their service or else provide a legitimate reason for their holdings (*Letters and Poems of Fulbert of Chartres,* no. 10). It is likely that the letter was sent very soon after Fulbert's ordination, so Viscount Hubert was alive in October 1006. Since he died on an October 28 (see above, chap. 2, n. 24), he could not have died before 28 October 1007, which provides the *terminus a quo* for Bishop Hubert's role here. The *terminus ad quem* is around 14 July 1028, when Aremburgis gave the land to Ronceray as she and her daughter entered that convent (see the dating of No. 20, Part I).

---

[1] Coëmont, ville, commune Vouvray-sur-Loir, dép. Sarthe (Vallée, p. 257).

No. 20

Ca. 14 July 1028. Angers.
This act is in two parts:
I. *Notice* (down to "Tethaldis filius Rainulfi"): BISHOP HUBERT, with his niece Emma, her husband Viscount Radulfus, and their children, give consent for Aremburgis, the widow of Thetuinus Strabo, to give to Ronceray her land at Curia Hamonis (Coëmont[1]), with eight coliberts, which was from BISHOP HUBERT'S benefice. The grant to Ronceray is made on the occasion of the entry into the convent of Aremburgis and her daughter Hildegardis.

Participants: four are named: Aremburgis, Bishop Hubert, Emma, Viscount Radulfus, and their children.
II. *Notice:* after the death of Aremburgis, a claim was made for the coliberts because the mothers were from the *fevum* of Nihard. Abbess Bertarda and the nun Hildegardis, Aremburgis's daughter, requested the *miles* Matthew, husband of Christiana, another daughter of Aremburgis, to ask for the donation of the coliberts from his lord Nihard. This was granted in the presence of Count Geoffrey Martel and of Count Fulk l'Oison of

Vendôme. Matthew then renews the donation of Coëmont and the coliberts, as does his stepson Tethuinus, and the nuns will pray for them and record their deaths in their martyrology.

Participants: eight: Abbess Bertarda, Hildegardis, Nihard, Matthew, Christiana, Tethuinus, Count Geoffrey, Count Fulk.

Witnesses: eighteen: Primardus the archpriest, Radulfus the priest, Algerius the priest, Robert the priest, Robert Malus Mischinus, Joscelin of Saumur, Joscelin Bodel, Euvradus Crispus, Droco de Boscat, Lambert, Joscelin the vicar, Stabilis the vicar of Ronceray, Otgerius de Lation, Walter Treluan, Josbertus, Robert, Warner the cook, Firminus his brother.

Manuscripts: A. Original redaction, lost. B. Copy, white cartulary of Ronceray, fol. 8, lost. C. Copy of the thirteenth century, cartulary of Ronceray, Bibl. d'Angers, ms. 844 (760), no. 38 of the first roll; ms. 846 (760), no. 51 of the third roll. D. Copy of the eighteenth century, B. n., D. H. II[1], no. 454, after B.

Edition: *Ronceray*, no. 391, after C.

References: 1. Dom Piolin, *Hist. Eglise du Mans* III, pp. 173–174 and n. 1. 2. Angot no. 27 (Part I only). 3. Guillot no. 223 (Part II only).

Aremburgis and Hildegardis probably entered Ronceray by July 1028, for nuns by those names appear as witnesses to the election of Abbess Leoburga (*Ronceray*, no. 15), who would have been chosen as first abbess of the convent before or around the dedication day of 14 July 1028 (*Ronceray*, no. 1; see No. 14).

Part II must have occurred after 14 January 1056, by which time Count Geoffrey Martel had recognized Fulk l'Oison as count of Vendôme (Guillot nos. 162 and 223). Guillot's *terminus ad quem* for this act is 22 November 1061, by which time Beliardis had succeeded Bertarda as abbess of Ronceray.

However, the *miles* Matthew of Part II can be identified as Matthew of Montoire, which helps in refining the dating of that section. Matthew of Montoire and his stepson Teduinus appear as witnesses to *Cart. Marmoutier pour le Vendômois*, no. 87, and Matthew of Montoire also gave all the customs that he had in Coëmont to Ronceray (*Ronceray*, no. 393). The lord of Montoire at this time was Nihard, and here in Part II the lord of the *miles* Matthew was Nihard, who had other holdings in close proximity to those of Matthew's mother-in-law Aremburgis (at Gombergean, see *Cart. Trinité de Vendôme* I, nos. 111, 154). It is probable that Nihard, the lord of Matthew here, is Nihard of Montoire, who was dead by 5 December 1059 (*Cart. Trinité de Vendôme* I, no. 128), which is the *terminus ad quem* for Part II. Thus it Count Geoffrey Martel who was present at that grant, not Count Geoffrey the Bearded.

---

[1] Coëmont; see No. 19, note 1.

No. 21

25 December 1028–30 December 1029. Vendôme.
Charter: BISHOP HUBERT witnesses the act of Count Odo II of Blois, who holds things from St. Aignan through the largess of King Robert, freeing the *famulus* Seherius, who is from the *familia* of St. Aignan, so that he might enter holy orders. This is done with the favor of Odo's *fidelis* Renaud of Romorantin and at the request of his *fidelis* Girardus.

   Participants: three: Count Odo, Girardus, Renaud of Romorantin.
   Witnesses: eleven: Geraldus, Count Odo, Ragenardus, Gilduinus, Landricus, Evrardus the abbot of Marmoutier, Salomon, Archbishop Arnulfus of Tours, Bishop Hubert, Hilgaldus, Hugh; written by Fulcherius in the place of the *signator* Vivianus.

   Manuscripts: A. Original, lost. B. Copy of the twelfth century, Book of the serfs of Marmoutier, Bibl. de Tours, ms. 1376, p. 33. C. Copy of the eighteenth century, B. n., coll. Baluze, vol. 77, fol. 149 r–v. D. Copy of the eighteenth century, B. n., D. H. XII^2, no. 6798.
   Editions: I. *Livre des serfs de Marmoutier,* no. 50, after B. II. *Gallia Christiana* 14, Instrumenta, cols. 66–67, after C. III. D'Arbois de Jubainville, *Hist. des ducs et des comtes de Champagne* 1, no. 34, p. 468, after II.
   References: 1. Lex no. 51. 2. Guillot 1: p. 37, n. 183.

The charter is dated "Actum Vindocino castro, anno XL^0 II^0, regnante rege Rotberto." For Robert to have reigned forty-two years, since he died 20 July 1031 (Pfister, *Robert le Pieux,* p. 81), one must use his association on the throne with his father King Hugh Capet in December 987 as the beginning point in this computation. Thus the forty-second year runs from 25 December 1028 to 30 December 1029 (see Guillot no. 35, note).

No. 22

13 May 1007–13 May 1031.
Notice: BISHOP HUBERT, having completed the work begun by Bishop Renaud of dedicating the monastery of St. Maurille, gives donations to it and to the clerics living there: the villa Martiniacus (Martigneau[1]) with ten *mansurae* and the *vinagium;* at Calonna (Chalonnes-sur-Loire[2]), one *borderica* with the *terragium, decima,* and all other customs; in another place eight arpents, which its cleric sold for planting, receiving the *census* and retaining the *decima* and *vinagium;* one mill above Villiacus, sold for the *census;* two arpents of vines in Chalonnes-sur-Loire with every custom; one arpent of meadows in Quailliacus; seven arpents of meadows above the Layon river; fourteen arpents of vines in the same place after his death, but the *decima* during his life; the burials of the church of St. Maurille; in the Loire, one *seclusa;* above Juriacus, one *palagium.*

   Other *fideles* also give donations to St. Maurille: Segenfridus gives the *decima* of one mill while he lives and after his death this mill and half the channel; Gausbertus the deacon gives half the mill above Juriacus; Ingelbaldus de Terra Plana gives six arpents of vines with every custom, four and a half arpents, and two other arpents after his death; BISHOP HUBERT gives his part of the church of St. Peter (the burials, bread, and candles of five feasts, with the remainder to come after the death of the priest); BISHOP HUBERT and Amalbertus give the *decima* of their *seclusa*.

Participants: five: Bishop Hubert, Segenfredus, Gausbertus the deacon, Ingelbaldus de Terra Plana, and Amalbertus.

Manuscripts: A. Original, lost. B. Copy, first cartulary of St. Serge, fol. 14, no. 18, lost. C. Copy of the sixteenth century, Arch. Maine-et-Loire, H 974 (three copies). D. Copy of the seventeenth century, B. n., ms. lat. 5446, fol. 239 v–241 r, no. 18. E. Copy of the eighteenth century, B. n., coll. Moreau, vol. 20, fol. 71 r–74 r, after D. F. Copy of the eighteenth century, B. n., D. H. II[1], no. 412. G. Copy of the nineteenth century by P. Marchegay, Arch. Maine-et-Loire, H 778 bis, vol. I, fol. 165 r–166 r, after C.

References: 1. Port, H, pp. 131–132. 2. Y. Chauvin, "Cartulaire de Saint-Serge," vol. I, no. 18. 3. Hogan no. 31.

The grants were made "in die dedicationis ejusdem basilicae iii Idus Mai," that is, May 13. The first May 13 after Bishop Hubert's consecration was in 1007. The act was completed "rege Roberto," so the *terminus ad quem* is 13 May 1031, since King Robert died 20 July 1031 (see the dating of No. 21).

---

[1] Martigneau, ville, commune Juigné-sur-Loire (Port II, p. 606).
[2] Chalonnes-sur-Loire, petite-ville, chef-lieu of canton, arr. Angers (Port I, p. 577).

No. 23

13 June 1006–20 July 1031.
Charter: King Robert II confirms to St. Serge the grants made to it by BISHOP HUBERT, coming partly from donations from his own possession made for his own soul and for those of his father Hubert and his mother Emma, and partly from restorations repurchased from *pervasores:* the church of St. Samson, which is close to the monastery; the church of St. Michael with the land of Priscinianus (Pressigné[1]); the church of St. Maurice at Esma (St.-Maurille des Ponts-de-Cé[2]); in the *curtis* of Morenna (Morannes[3]) all the land of Prata (la Prée[4]) with the *decima, sepultura, vicaria,* and every custom; in the villa Castra (Chartres[5]) one *hospes,* the *decima* of the villa and the *vicaria* of the land; the *decima* of the *mansilis* called Pina-Rocha (Pineroche[6]); at the old *vicus* the land with coliberts, meadows, and water with fisheries; in the Loire, one *ductile* and one arpent of land on the bank nearby; the villa Campiniacus (Champigné-sur-Sarthe[7]) with all its appurtenances, the land both arable and non-arable, with vines and woods.

It is recalled that Champigné-sur-Sarthe had been granted to someone in a charter by the canons who then inhabited St. Serge, and that it had remained a benefice. BISHOP HUBERT then repurchased the land for St. Serge through Count Fulk's *curtis* and the judgment of nobles, and he restored it to the monastery; BISHOP HUBERT then asked King Robert to confirm his grants to St. Serge.

Participants: two: King Robert II and Bishop Hubert.

Subscriber: one: King Robert.

Manuscripts: A. Original, lost. B. Copy of the eleventh century, first cartulary of St. Serge, fol. 11, no. 17, lost. C. Copy of 1620, Bibl. d'Angers, ms. 838 (754), no. 5, after B. D. Copy of the seventeenth century, B. n., ms. lat. 17030, pp. 35–36, after B. E. Copy of the seventeenth century, B. n., ms. lat. 5446, no. 17, fol. 239 r–v, after B. F. Copy of the eighteenth century, B. n., coll. Moreau, vol. 16, fol. 60 r–62 r, after E. G. Copy of the eighteenth century, B. n., D. H. II[1], no. 351. H. Copy of the nineteenth century by P. Marchegay, Arch. Maine-et-Loire, H 778 bis 1, fol. 11 r–v, after C.

Edition: Pfister, *Robert le Pieux* no. 5, pp. L–LI, after E and G.

References: 1. Pfister no. 41. 2. Newman no. 94.

This confirmation was made between Bishop Hubert's ordination and King Robert's death.

---

[1] Pressigné, ferme, arr. and canton, Angers, commune St.-Sylvain d'Anjou (Newman, p. 118, n. 5).

[2] Les Ponts-de-Cé, chef-lieu of canton, arr. Angers (Port III, p. 150).

[3] Morannes; see No. 10, note 4.

[4] La Prée, disappeared, commune Morannes (Newman, p. 119, n. 8).

[5] Chartres, ferme, commune Morannes, dép. Maine-et-Loire (Newman, p. 119, n. 9; Port I, p. 633).

[6] Pineroche, commune Morannes (Port III, p. 104).

[7] Champigné-sur-Sarthe, canton Châteauneuf, arr. Segré (Port I, p. 589).

No. 24

6 December 1032.

Notice: after the monastery of St. Nicholas was founded by Count Fulk in 1020 and dedicated by BISHOP HUBERT in honor of Sts. Nicholas, Jerome, and Lazarus around 1 December, it is decreed by BISHOP HUBERT, Count Fulk, and the archdeacons of the diocese of Angers that the monks of St. Nicholas, all the *familia*, the poor living there, all the citizens and those living in the suburbs on both sides of the river Maine might be buried in the monastery's cemetery. In addition, those from all *castra* and parishes might be buried there if all their dues are paid to their own churches. Two uterine brothers, Robert and Lambert, carve these decrees on the wall of the church of St. Nicholas.

Participants: five: Count Fulk, Bishop Hubert, and the three archdeacons of Angers.

Manuscripts: A. Original, lost. B. Copy of the cartulary of St. Nicholas, lost. C. Copy of the eighteenth century, B. n., D. H. II¹, no. 413.

Editions: I. Hiret, *Des antiquitez d'Anjou* (1605), pp. 95–96. II. Le Peletier, *Breviculum,* pp. 5–7. III. Hiret, ibid. (1618), p. 170. IV. Le Peletier, *Epitome,* pp. 5–7. V. Modern, by Yvonne Labande-Mailfert, "Cartulaire de Saint-Nicolas d'Angers," appendix I, no. 2, after C, II and IV. VI. Y. Mailfert, "Fondation du Saint-Nicolas d'Angers," p. j. no. 3.

References: 1. Bréquigny 2, p. 5. 2. Guillot no. 50.

The date is given in the document. That three archdeacons of Angers participated in this act is inferred from the emergence of that number of archdeacons of the diocese by 966 (*Cart. noir de la cathédrale,* p. xl, and see above, chap. 4, n. 32).

No. 25

December 1036. Angers.
Charter: BISHOP HUBERT gives his assent, along with the favor of Count Fulk, to the decision of the monks of St. Aubin choosing one of their brothers, Walter, as their new abbot, four months after the death of Abbot Primoldus; noble clerics and laics and distinguished persons of both sexes give their assent as well; the monks who witness the charter give their consent to this legitimate election.

Participants: sixty are named: the fifty-seven monks of St. Aubin listed below as witnesses, Bishop Hubert, Count Fulk, Abbot Walter; and the clerics and laymen who assented to Walter's selection.

Witnesses: fifty-seven monks of St. Aubin: Haimericus, Boso, Robert, Walter, Hildinus, Frotmundus, Letardus, John, Hamo, Mainardus, Segbaldus, Lawrence, Grimoardus, Ermenredus, Haimericus, Hatto, Gelduinus, Barnard, Osbertus, Grento, Clement, Gausbertus, Germundus, Rainerius, Engelardus, Berengar, Genzon, Ulgerius, Perenis, Hubert, Ermenfredus, Isaac, Adraldus, Warinus, Arnulfus, Ascelinus, Renaud, Mafredus, Isaac, Hubert, Durandus, Lanbertus, Daniel, Amfredus, Warinus, Albericus, Waleranus, Ernaldus, Walter, Walfredus, Vitalis, Guy, Andrew, Albert, Richard, Warinus, Engelbodus.

Manuscripts: A. Original, lost. B. Copy of the twelfth century, cartulary of St. Aubin, Bibl. d'Angers, ms. 829 (745), fol. 8 v–9 r. C. Copy of the seventeenth century, B. n., ms. lat. 12658, fol. 62 r–v.

Editions: I. Martène and Durand, *Thesaurus Novus Anecdotorum* 1, cols. 159–161. II. Dachery, *Spicilegium* 6, pp. 436–437. III. *St. Aubin,* no. 27, after B.

References: 1. Bréquigny 2, p. 13. 2. Guillot no. 54.

The charter gives the year of Walter's selection as 1038, but this has been corrected to 1036 by Halphen, *Annales de Saint-Aubin,* p. 4, n. 2 (see also Guillot no. 54).

No. 26

1036.

This act is in three parts:

IA. *Notice* (down to "erat renovatum"): BISHOP HUBERT, at the inter-
cession of Abbot Odo of St.-Maur-des-Fossés, which borders on a cell in
the diocese of Angers at Glannafolium (Glanfeuil[1]), consecrates the monastery of St. Maur at Glanfeuil. That house had been destroyed by the
"pagans," rebuilt by the wealthy man Rorigo, again plundered, and then
renewed by Abbot Odo.

II. *Notice* (down to "prelii abire"): Count Geoffrey Martel, at the request of
his wife Agnes (both of whom are at the consecration), gives to Glanfeuil
all the customs they have in the villa of Cru (Crue[2]), except for his reten-
tion of the right of summoning the men of the villa and the *familia* of St.
Maur to war, although they are actually to be called into battle by the prior
of St. Maur on instructions of Count Geoffrey's legate.

IB. *Notice:* BISHOP HUBERT anathematizes and excommunicates anyone
who should presume to bring a false claim against the monastery.

   Participants: four: Bishop Hubert, Count Geoffrey, Agnes, and Abbot Odo.

   Witnesses: six: Abbot Frederick of St. Florent, Ardennus abbot of St.
Philibert of Tournus, Count Geoffrey's *milites* Hugh Mange-Breton (who
also gave his part of the custom), Geoffrey Fortis of Treive, Aimery Pullus
and Joscelin.

   Manuscripts: A. Original redaction, lost. B. Copy of the twelfth century,
cartulary of St. Maur, Arch. Maine-et-Loire, H 1773, fol. 15 v, no. 33. C.
Copy of the seventeenth or eighteenth century, B. n., coll. Baluze, vol. 139,
p. 107 (without the last three witnesses). D. Copy of the eighteenth century, B. n., D. H. II[1], no. 425, after B.

   Edition: *Cart. Saint-Maur*, no. 33, after B.

   References: 1. Port, H, p. 245. 2. Guillot no. ⟨5⟩. 3. Ziezulewicz no.
XV A.

   It is clear that in the present document, the notice of the gifts of Count
Geoffrey and his wife was inserted into Bishop Hubert's act—after the
notice of the consecration and before the anathematization. Guillot con-
siders this a false act, primarily because at the date given in the document,
1036, Geoffrey Martel was not yet count of Anjou. However, he is not
styled count of Anjou in this act, merely *Gaufridus comes,* and he had been
given the county of Vendôme in 1031 or 1032 and seems to have carried
the comital title by 1 January 1032 (Guillot 1: pp. 44–45). Therefore, it is
insufficient to reject the authenticity of this document on that basis.

   In addition, Geoffrey is clearly named as count in two charters issued
before his father's death (*Cart. Trinité de Vendôme* I, no. 14, with the date
corrected to 1038 in Celier, "Catalogue des actes des évêques du Mans,"
no. 22 and no. 15, of 25 June 1039). He is also called Count Geoffrey in a

charter in which his father Count Fulk Nerra likewise appears, and it is accepted as authentic by Guillot (see No. 27, Guillot no. 57 a).

Guillot also objected to the presence of Count Geoffrey "cum regni sui optimatibus" in this act. But since the present document is an altered form of the original charter, wording could easily have been changed to reflect the usage or conditions at the time of the redaction. Neither of Guillot's objections to the authenticity of this act seems compelling.

---

¹ Glanfeuil, ville, commune Toureil (Port II, p. 428).
² Crue, ville, commune Meigné (Port I, p. 800).

No. 27

20 July 1031–15 November 1037.
Charter: BISHOP HUBERT witnesses gifts to Marmoutier by Rainardus, which are affirmed by Rainardus's lord Landricus of Beaugency. The gifts are: the church of St. Martin of Daumeray,¹ the *census* and the other customs of the *burgus* built around the church, all the *vicaria*, and war if it should be summoned there ("et bellum si ibi fuerit arramitum"), two *meditariae*, all the meadows next to the cemetery there in his demesne, two and a half arpents of demesne vines, all the *census* from the other vines in his demesne, the woods called Castellonium (Châtillon²), except for the third denarius from the *pasnaticum* that his *caballarius* Fulcradus has there; the monks shall have the bees in the woods and jurisdiction over crimes there; the monks have the freedom to cut down and plow the woods.

Participants: two: Rainardus and Landricus.

Witnesses: twenty: Rainardus, his men Fulcradus and Geoffrey, Renaud Farsitus, Ascelinus, Hilgoddus, Landricus of Beaugency and his three sons John, Lancelinus and Herveus, Teodericus Guaillardus, Guarnerius the *prepositus*, Count Odo II of Blois, Count Theobald, Count Stephen, Count Fulk Nerra, Count Geoffrey Martel, Bishop Hubert, Berengar, Joscelin the dean.

Manuscripts: A. Original, Arch. Maine-et-Loire, 40 H 1, no. 1. B. Contemporary or near contemporary copy, Arch. Maine-et-Loire, 40 H 1, no. 1 bis, after A. C. Copy of the seventeenth century, B. n., ms. lat. 12878, fol. 91 r–v, after B. D. Copy of the seventeenth century, B. n., ms. lat. 12880, fol. 25 r–v, after A. E. Copy of the eighteenth century, B. n., coll. Moreau, vol. 21, fol. 222 r–223 v, after B. F. Copy of the eighteenth century, B. n., D. H. II¹, no. 456, after A. G. Copy of the nineteenth century by P. Marchegay, B. n., ms. fr. n. a. 5021, fol. 216 r–v, after A and B.

Edition: Lex, p. j. no. 18, after C.

References: 1. Lex no. 39. 2. Halphen no. 85. 3. Levron, p. 7. 4. Guillot no. 57 a.

Guillot no. 57 a has a lengthy discussion of the paleographical problems of the manuscripts, and has determined the dating.

---

[1] Daumeray, canton Durtal, arr. Baugé (Port II, p. 10).
[2] Châtillon, chef-lieu, commune Daumeray (Port I, p. 644).

No. 28 (Inauthentic)

1037. Angers.

Notice: BISHOP HUBERT witnesses the settlement of disputes concerning Château-Gontier, in contention between St. Aubin and Renaud the lord of Château-Gontier. In 1007, in the fifth indiction (25 September 1006–24 September 1007), Count Fulk Nerra fortified a *castellum* above the Mayenne river, in the *curtis* of Bazouges,[1] which many years before he had exchanged for the *curtis* Hondainville[2] in the Beauvaisis with Abbot Renaud of St. Aubin, which the monks held in permanent possession freely and quietly. After the *castellum* had thus been made into a *castrum*, it was called after one of the count's *villici, castrum Gunterii* (Château-Gontier[3]).

Since the land belonged to St. Aubin, Fulk compensated the monastery with the right to the *census* and sales. The count then began constructing a tower at Château-Gontier, but before the work progressed very far, war interrupted the project and Fulk gave the tower to one of his best *milites*, Renaud Yvonis, who was to continue returning the *census* to St. Aubin. Renaud Yvonis felt that he had too little land, so he sought more in the *curtis.*

At last, after Count Fulk and his son Geoffrey Martel intervened for Renaud, Abbot Walter gives the *miles* one-fourth of the *curtis* of Bazouges, with the condition that the lord of Château-Gontier would hold it in homage from St. Aubin and would guard and defend the other three parts of Bazouges as a "fidelis homo et amicus ecclesie legitime"; in addition, if Château-Gontier should revert to the hands of the count due to lack of heirs, St. Aubin will regain the quarter of Bazouges.

Participants: four are named: Renaud Yvonis, Count Fulk, Geoffrey Martel, Abbot Walter; and the monks of St. Aubin.

Witnesses: thirty-three are named: Bishop Hubert of Angers, Bishop Avesgaudus of Le Mans, Abbot Walter with his monks, Warner the prior, Sicbaldus, John the cantor, Haimericus of Sorges, Otbrannus, Peter, Bernard, "totoque conventu"; the clerics Renaud, Bernard, Joscelin, Marchoardus, Roger, Lisoius, Herbert; the laymen Suhardus of Craon, Tetbaldus of Blaison, Joscelin of Ste. Maur, Joscelin of Rennes, Orrichus de Chatalaunis, Alduinus the *praepositus,* Girardus Calvellus, Haimericus the Rich; from the *familia* of St. Aubin: Giraldus, Walter, Frotmundus, Maurice, Geoffrey, Renaud, "multisque aliis"; Count Fulk and Geoffrey Martel (both of whom make the sign of the cross).

Manuscripts: A. Original redaction, lost. B. Copy of the twelfth century, cartulary of St. Aubin, Bibl. d'Angers, ms. 829 (745), fol. 2 r–v. C. Copy of the seventeenth century, B. n., coll. Baluze, vol. 139, pp. 259–261.

Editions: I. Sirmond, *Notae,* p. 88 (partial). II. Ménage, *Hist. de Sablé* 1, pp. 97–98. III. *St. Aubin,* no. 1, after B.

References: 1. Bertrand de Brouissillon, *Craon* no. 2. 2. Halphen no. 53. 3. Guillot no. ⟨6⟩.

Guillot discusses the inauthenticity of this act.

---

[1] Bazouges, canton de Château-Gontier, dép. Mayenne (*St. Aubin* 3, p. 21).
[2] Hondainville (Undanis villa), dép. Oise (*St. Aubin* 3, p. 198).
[3] Château-Gontier, commune, canton and arr., dép. Mayenne (Guillot 2: p. 316).

No. 29

(1): 13 June 1006–ca. Easter 1039; (2): 1007–ca. Easter 1039.
I. *Notice:* (down to "de tempore Huberti praesulis et Fulconis comitis diximus"): it is recalled that Christiana and her husband Walter Nafragallus were the coliberts of St. Maurice and of BISHOP HUBERT, and that they had a house that had the responsibility of washing the BISHOP'S clothes. (1) Due to poverty, the two coliberts, with BISHOP HUBERT'S consent, sold the laundry house to Achardus Barbatorta and Bernard. (2) When certain of Count Fulk's officials heard of the sale, they understood that the house had left HUBERT'S hands and they entered the house, which had not owed any customs to the count. They seized a box that held the BISHOP'S clothes and carried it back to Fulk's court, keeping in it bread prepared for Easter. BISHOP HUBERT then made a complaint and Count Fulk ordered Michael, the instigator of the action, to carry back the box on his own neck and he forbade any of his agents or their successors to impose any customs on the house or its inhabitants.
Participants: three are named: Count Fulk, Bishop Hubert, and Michael.
II. *Notice:* in the second part of the document, it is further recalled that in the time of Bishop Eusebius, Christianus, with the consent of the bishop, bought the house from Achardus and Bernard and held it under Eusebius free from all customs.
Participants: four: Bishop Eusebius, Christianus, Achardus, and Bernard.

Manuscripts: A. Original redaction, lost. B. Copy, cartulary of St. Maurice, fol. 54 r, lost. C. Copy of the eighteenth century, Grandet, *Index titulorum, cartharum, arrestorum et aliorum quae acta sunt ab episcopis Andegavensibus aut sub eorum episcopatu,* p. 99, after B. D. Copy of the eighteenth century, Bibl. d'Angers, ms. 706 (636), pp. 7–8.

Editions: I. P. Marchegay, "Chartes angevines," *Bibliothèque de l'école des chartes* 36 (1875), no. 3, pp. 387–388. II. *Cart. noir de la cathédrale,* no. 80, after C.

References: 1. Halphen no. 54. 2. Guillot no. 65.

Part (1) occurred after Hubert's ordination, but before Count Fulk's final departure for Jerusalem, by the end of 1039. Part (2) has been dated by

Halphen. The sale of the house under Bishop Eusebius (Part II) can only be dated to the period of his episcopacy, 13 December 1047–27 August 1081.

No. 30

13 June 1006–1039.

BISHOP HUBERT, along with Count Fulk, gives the church of St. Marcel at the *castellum* of Briollay, free of all customs, to Burchardus the treasurer of St. Maurice.

Participants: three: Count Fulk, Bishop Hubert, and Burchardus.

No document for this act exists, but the transfer of the church to Burchardus is inferred from No. 44 below, where he in turn gave it to St. Serge. Bishop Hubert and Count Fulk could have given the church to Burchardus only after Hubert's ordination and before Fulk's last departure from Anjou.

No. 31

1026–1039. Saumur.

Notice: BISHOP HUBERT reestablishes the church rebuilt in Saumur by the monks of St. Florent, and about six monks are placed in the church.

Participant: one is named: Bishop Hubert.

This information is provided as the second event related in a larger document detailing the history of the rights of St. Florent in Saumur. (1) When Count Fulk Nerra took Saumur and burned the monastery of St. Florent there, the monks moved to a nearby church, but they did not abandon their rights in Saumur. (2) BISHOP HUBERT reestablished the rebuilt church, as above. (3) Count Fulk gave Saumur to his son Geoffrey Martel. (4) Meanwhile the monks of St. Florent began to build a new monastery in a nearby *castrum*, in a more secure place. (5) Count Geoffrey Martel inquired as to why they had built there; the monks replied that the new location was safer, not being surrounded by people if fire should break out again. Not satisfied with this excuse, Geoffrey expelled the monks from the church of Saumur and established canons there, giving many of the monks' possessions to the canons as *victualia*. (6) At the time of his death, a penitent Count Geoffrey partially corrected this action and gave orders that other parts also be corrected. (7) The monks then went before Count Geoffrey the Bearded and in a public *placitum* in the presence of Bishop Eusebius of Angers and the leading men of the *patria*, they sought a reformation of the previous wrongs done to them; but only the villa of Meigné,[1] with its church and appurtenances, was restored to them. (8) Then Count Geoffrey the Bearded's brother, Fulk Réchin, was made lord of Saumur. The canons went to him and asked that Meigné be returned to them. This case was presented to Cardinal Stephen, the papal legate with authority to correct Gallican churches, Archbishop Bartholomew of Tours, and other clerics, monks, and noble laymen for judgment.

(9) Now it is decided that everything be returned to St. Florent. However, the judges urge St. Florent to have mercy on the canons and to leave them with their prebends to be held from the monastery, with the canons continuing to serve the church as before. As the canons die, no one else is to receive their prebends, which are to be shared with the remaining canons. When only two canons survive, they are to be made into chaplains. The canons are to receive either one measure of grain and one of wine, or two measures of grain, as St. Florent chooses, each year on the feast of All Saints. The canons and the *famuli* that they feed and clothe are to be buried in the cemetery of the church of Saumur, and anyone else who wanted to be buried there shall be, if the monks receive what the canons were given for that purpose. The canons are to buy the oven whose customs Count Geoffrey gave to the church, and if they do not wish to give their part of the oven to St. Florent when they die, the monks can buy it for thirty-two solidi. All these points are agreed to.

Participants in (9): four are named: Fulk Réchin, Cardinal Stephen, Archbishop Bartholomew, and Abbot Sigo of St. Florent.

Witnesses to (9): twenty-seven: Count Fulk Réchin, Archbishop Bartholomew, Bishop Warechus of Nantes, (Mengisus) the bishop of Vannes, Abbot Sigo of St. Florent, Abbot Rademundus of Dol, Abbot Vitalis of St.-Gildas (-sur-Bois), Abbot Stephen of Beaulieu, Abbot Frotmundus of St.-Amant (-de-Boixe), Bernegarius the *prepositus,* Auramus the monk, Gausbertus the monk, Berengar *grammaticus,* Robert the Burgundian, his brother Guy of Nevers, Guy of Laval, John of Chinon, Joscelin Rotundator, Robert of Moncontour, Durandus the *prepositus* of Saumur, from the men of St. Florent: Fredaldus, Girardus *vitrarius,* Durandus, Judicahelus, Aimery Candoratus, and many others; Wanilo the monk of St. Martin who dictated the charter, Detbertus the monk and *scriptor.*

Manuscripts: A. Original, Arch. Maine-et-Loire, H 1840, no. 9. B. Copy of the eleventh century, black book of St. Florent, B. n., ms. n. a. lat. 1930, fol. 58 r–59 v, after A. C. Copies of the eighteenth century, B. n., D. H. II^2, nos. 702, 709. D. Copy of the nineteenth century by P. Marchegay, Arch. Maine-et-Loire, H 3712, no. 108, after B.

Editions: I. Sainte-Marthe, *Gallia Christiana* 4, pp. 395–396, partial and imperfect. II. Tresvaux no. 18, after I, partial and imperfect.

References: 1. Marchegay, *Livre noir* no. 72, part (9) only. 2. Bertrand de Brouissillon, *La maison de Laval* no. 31, part (9) only. 3. Halphen no. 182, part (9) only. 4. Saché, pp. 13, 483–484. 5. Guillot no. 255, part (9) only.

Fulk's capture of Saumur (1) was in 1026 (*Annales de Vendôme,* pp. 60–61), so Bishop Hubert's reestablishment of the church was after that date, but before Geoffrey Martel received Saumur from his father (3). Halphen placed Geoffrey's gaining of Saumur in 1026, but there is no evidence to support this (see Guillot 1: p. 43 and n. 214). It is not known when Geoffrey received Saumur, but it must have been by 1039, when Fulk left Anjou for the last time. Guillot suggested 1031, but he noted that it was far from certain.

The monks rebuilt their monastery (4) by 15 October 1041, when it was dedicated (No. 40 below). Count Geoffrey's establishment of canons in Saumur (5) was done after he received Saumur but before his death on 14 November 1060. His partial correction of that action (6) was around the time of his death on the date mentioned. The *placitum* of Geoffrey the Bearded (7) was after Geoffrey Martel's death, but before Saumur was taken by Fulk Réchin (25 February 1067, see *Chronicon Sancti Maxentii Pictavensis*, pp. 403–404). The final settlement of the dispute (9) is given in the act, 11 March 1067. See Guillot no. 255 for a discussion of the validity of this notice.

---

[1] Meigné, canton Doué, arr. Saumur (Port II, p. 637).

No. 32

10 April 1028–1039.
Notice: BISHOP HUBERT ordains Renaud as abbot of St. Nicholas of Angers, who was provided by Abbot Albert of Marmoutier.
    Participants: two: Bishop Hubert and Renaud.

Edition: see No. 35.
References: 1. Halphen no. 34. 2. Guillot no. 77.

This information is provided in the second part of a larger document relating Fulk's difficulties in keeping an abbot at St. Nicholas (see Nos. 5, 8, 35). The first abbot Baudricus (No. 8) left St. Nicholas and returned to Marmoutier, dying at the monastery of Tavant. He was then replaced by Renaud. The document does not state that Bishop Hubert ordained him as abbot, but Hubert exercised his usual episcopal functions within the diocese and he was on good terms with Count Fulk.
    Renaud was ordained after 10 April 1028, for Albert, who here is abbot of Marmoutier, was still a monk at that time (see Guillot 1: p. 175 and n. 190), but before Hildinus succeeded Renaud as abbot of St. Nicholas, between December 1036 and 1039 (see No. 35).

No. 33 (Inauthentic)

14 July 1028–1039.
Notice: BISHOP HUBERT witnesses gifts of Count Fulk and Countess Hildegardis in the *curtis* of Petra (la Cour de Pierre[1]) to Ronceray, namely all the *bidanicum* and *vicaria*, and the *curtis* is to be entirely free from all lay power.
    Participants: two: Count Fulk and Hildegardis.
    Witnesses: two are named: Bishop Hubert and Hugh Mansellus; "et pluribus."

Manuscripts: A. Original redaction, lost. B. Copy of the thirteenth century, cartulary of Ronceray, Bibl. d'Angers, ms. 847(760), no. 33 of the fourth roll.

Edition: *Ronceray*, no. 171, after B.

References: 1. Halphen no. 64. 2. Guillot no. ⟨7⟩.

See Guillot for a discussion of this act's inauthenticity.

---

[1] La Cour de Pierre, commune Rochefort (Port I, p. 777).

No. 34

20 July 1031–1039. Angers.

Notice: BISHOP HUBERT, Count Fulk Nerra, and King Henry I make a charter stating that the count has only the custom of the *fodrium* and a *vicaria* of sixty solidi on the land of St. Maurice at the villa of Longus Campus (Longchamps[1]).

Participants: three: Bishop Hubert, Count Fulk, and King Henry.

This information is provided in a notice discussing the resolution of a dispute over the customs at Longchamps between the *prepositus* Giraldus and the canons of the cathedral. Giraldus, supported by the vicars, tried to impose customs on the land of the canons and the villa of Longchamps. But the canons produce the charter of Bishop Hubert, Count Fulk, and King Henry, and Count Fulk the Younger orders Giraldus to demand nothing further from the lands.

Participants: two are named: Count Fulk the Younger and Giraldus; and the canons.

Witnesses: eight are named: the canons Marbodus, Hubert, William of Saumur, Geoffrey Girbaudi, Bernerius; the laymen Clerembaldus, Girorius his brother, Geoffrey of Trèves.

Manuscripts: A. Original redaction, lost. B. Copy, black cartulary of St. Maurice, fol. 38 r, lost. C. Copy of the eighteenth century, Bibl. d'Angers, ms. 689 (624), fol. 309 v. D. Copy of the eighteenth century, B. n., D. H. XVI, no. 124.

Edition: *Cart. noir de la cathédrale*, no. 56.

References: 1. Halphen no. 264. 2. Guillot no. 372. 3. Fanning, "Acts of Henry I Concerning Anjou," pp. 111–112.

For the dating of this act of Bishop Hubert, Count Fulk, and King Henry, see Fanning, "Acts of King Henry I." The references by Halphen and Guillot concern only the act of Fulk the Younger, which is dated in the document, 7 December 1096.

---

[1] Longchamps, communes Saint-Sylvain-d'Anjou and le Plessis-Grammoire, canton and arr. Angers (Guillot 2: p. 331).

No. 35

December 1036–1039.
Notice: BISHOP HUBERT consecrates Hildinus, the prior of St. Aubin who has been provided by Abbot Walter of St. Aubin at the request of Count Fulk, as abbot of St. Nicholas of Angers.

Participants: two: Bishop Hubert and Hildinus.

Manuscripts: A. Original redaction, lost. B. Copy, cartulary of St. Nicholas, fol. 178, lost. C. Copy of the eighteenth century, B. n., D. H. II¹, no. 417, after B.

Editions: I. Hiret, *Des antiquitez d'Anjou* (1605), pp. 94–95 (partial of Nos. 5 and 8 above). II. Sirmond, *Goffridi Abbatis Vindocinensis, Epistolae Opuscula Sermones,* Notae, p. 47 (partial of Nos. 5 and 8 above). III. Le Peletier, *Breviculum,* pp. 5–7. IV. Hiret, ibid. (1618) (partial of Nos. 5 and 8 above), p. 163. V. Le Peletier, *Epitome,* pp. 5–7. VI. Ste.-Marthe, *Gallia Christiana* 4, p. 688 (partial of Nos. 5 and 8 above). VII. Migne, *Patrologia Latina* 155, cols. 481–482, after I. VII. D'Espinay, *Revue de l'Anjou* 12 (1857), p. 124 n. 3 (partial of Nos. 5 and 8 above). IX. Yvonne Labande-Mailfert, "Cartulaire de Saint-Nicolas d'Angers, XIe-XIIème siècles," no. 280, after C, III and V. X. Y. Mailfert, "Fondation du monastère bénédictine de Saint-Nicolas d'Angers," p. j. no. 4.

References: 1. Halphen no. 34. 2. Guillot no. 77.

Abbot Hildinus's ordination is mentioned in the second part of a larger document relating Fulk's efforts to find an abbot for St. Nicholas. The first abbot fled the monastery and returned to Marmoutier, and was replaced by Renaud (Nos. 8, 32). Renaud then left St. Nicholas without permission and became abbot of Geoffrey Martel's newly constructed monastery at Vendôme (Trinité). Fulk then ordered the other monks at St. Nicholas to remain there and he asked Abbot Walter of St. Aubin to provide a new abbot for the house, and Hildinus was named. Fulk then ordered the whole sequence of events (Nos. 5, 8, 32, and 35) to be recorded by Berengar and Renaud before he set out for Jerusalem for the last time.

"For the last time" indicates that the document as it now exists was completed only after Fulk's death in 1040, which may account for the chronological difficulties here. It is stated that Abbot Walter provided Hildinus, who was consecrated 8 July 1033, in the third year of King Henry. But Walter became abbot of St. Aubin only in 1036 (see No. 25). Hildinus could have become abbot of St. Nicholas only after Walter was chosen to head St. Aubin in 1036, but before Fulk set out for Jerusalem in 1039. It is not stated specifically that Hubert consecrated Hildinus, but it is almost certainly so (see No. 32).

No. 36 (Inauthentic)

31 May 1040. Vendôme.
Charter: BISHOP HUBERT witnesses the act of Bishop Theodoric of Chartres for the monastery of Trinité de Vendôme, built by Count Geof-

frey Martel and Countess Agnes and placed by them under papal protection. Theodoric confirms this and exempts Trinité and its possessions from his episcopal jurisdiction and forbids ecclesiastical possessions in the Vendômois that pertain to his diocese to be given to any monastery other than Trinité.

Participant: one: Bishop Theodoric.

Witnesses: sixty-eight: Archbishop Arnulf of Tours, Bishop Isembertus of Poitiers, Bishop Gervais of Le Mans, Bishop Hubert of Angers, Bishop Gerardus of Angoulême, Bishop Amelius of Albi; from Chartres: Arnulf the archdeacon and precentor, George the archdeacon, Sigo the *magister scolarum*, Agivertus the chaplain, Hildegarius the subdean, Hilduinus the youth, Walter the archdeacon; from Tours: Bovo the dean, Vuenilo the archdeacon and treasurer, Robert the *cellerarius*, Walter the sacristan; from St. Martin: Geoffrey the dean, Walter the cantor, Frotgerius the subdean, Albert the *cellerarius*, Odo the subcantor; from Poitiers: Arnulf the dean, William the cantor, Raino the cantor; from Le Mans: Gerardus the cantor, Ingoisus, Isbertus, Ermenulfus *scolasticus*, Manselinus, Renaud the chaplain, William; from ANGERS: Joscelin the dean, Berengar the archdeacon, Burchardus the treasurer, Renaud the archdeacon, Fulcoius the chaplain, John *scolasticus*, Joscelin *puer*, Geoffrey *puer*, Peter the subdeacon; from Angoulême: William the archdeacon, Vivianus the chaplain; from Saintes: Ramnulfus the archdeacon, Acbaldus the archdeacon; the abbots: Hugh of Saint-Sauveur [of Charroux], Frederick of St. Florent, Walter of St. Aubin, Ebrardus of St. Calais, Landricus of Saint-Père [-en-Valée] of Chartres, Durandus of Saint-Gildas [-des-Bois], Salomon of Bonneval, Hugh of Lonlay-l'Abbaye, Fulk of St. John, Ansegisus *peccator*, Peter of Manteuil [-en-Valée], Algerius of Saint-Amant [-de-Boixe], Arnaldus of Saint-Jean-d'Angély, Odo of Saint-Savin [-sur-Gartempe], Azo of Saint-Michel-en-l'Herme, Archembaldus of Saint-Maixent, John of Luçon, Tetbaldus of Quinçay, Ansbertus of Pontlevoy, Teudo of Bourgueil, Odolricus of Saint-Martial [of Limoges], Ermentus of Tuffé, Tetbaldus of Saint-Benôit-sur-Loire.

Manuscripts: A. Original, lost. B. Copy of the seventeenth century, B. n., ms. lat. 12700, fol. 180 and 271 v. C. Extract of the seventeenth century, B. n., ms. lat. 13820, fol. 325 r–v. D. Copy of the seventeenth century, B. n., coll. Baluze, vol. 139, p. 254. E. Copy at Cheltenham, ms. Phillipps, no. 4264, fol. 1. F. Copy of the seventeenth or eighteenth century, B. n., coll. Decamps, vol. 103, p. 194. G. Copy of the eighteenth century, Bibl. d'Orléans, D. Verninac, ms. 394, vol. 3, fol. 227 v.

Editions: I. Abbé Simon, *Hist. de Vendôme* 2, p. 28. II. Migne, *Patrologia Latina* 157, c. 289. III. *Cart. de la Trinité de Vendôme*, no. 39.

References: 1. *Château-du-Loir* no. 14. 2. Meinert, "Die Fälschungen Gottfrieds von Vendôme," pp. 251–257. 3. Ziezulewicz no. (V).

See Meinert on the inauthenticity of this document. However, the witness list of sixty-eight prelates and other ecclesiastical dignitaries presents no problems and is probably from an authentic charter relating to the dedication of the monastery.

No. 37 (Inauthentic)

31 May 1040. Vendôme.

Charter: BISHOP HUBERT witnesses a charter of Archbishop Arnulf of Tours confirming the donations made to the monastery of Trinité de Vendôme by Count Geoffrey Martel and Countess Agnes, who had placed it under papal protection; Geoffrey and Agnes ask Bishop Theodoric and the other bishops present to confirm its possessions within their dioceses, and he affirms Trinité's possessions in the diocese of Chartres.

Participants: four: Archbishop Arnulf, Count Geoffrey and Countess Agnes, and Bishop Theodoric.

Witnesses: 110: all the clerics who witnessed No. 36 above also witness this charter (including Bishop Hubert), with these exceptions: not witnessing here but witnessing No. 36 were Archbishop Arnulf and Joscelin *puer* from Angers; witnessing here but not witnessing No. 36 were Bishop Theodoric of Chartres, Bishop Arnulf of Saintes and the following *barones:* Count Geoffrey of Anjou, Countess Agnes, Count William Alduinus, Viscount Radulfus, Viscount Erfredus, Viscount William, Viscount Herveus of Blois, Haimericus of Rancon, Geoffrey of Preuilly, Isembardus, Tetbaldus of Blaison, Rainardus, Albericus of Montjean, Joscelin of Ste. Maur, Peter of Chemillé, Ingelbaldus, Leo of Amboise, Renaud, Salomon of Lavardin, Nihard of Montoire, Landricus of Beaugency, Odo of Dol, Gislebertus, Helia of Volventum (Vouvent?), Berlaius, Hademarus Malae-Capsae, Hildebertus of Rupis Mahildis, William of Chabocius, Abbot Peter, William of Roches-l'Evêque, Ranaulfus Rabiolus, William of Parthenay, Constantine of Melle, Joscelin Cavana-Granum, Peter Maisnade, Manasses brother of the bishop, Simon of Verruca, Stephen of Mennacum, William brother of Bishop Gervais, Harduinus of Roches-l'Evêque, Albericus of la Ferté-Saint-Aubin, Hubert of Munitio.

Manuscripts: lost.

Editions: I. Labbé and Cossart, *Sacrosancta Concilia* 9, cols. 938–940. II. *Rec. des Historiens de France* 11, p. 506. III. *Cart. de la Trinité de Vendôme,* no. 40.

References: 1. Bréquigny 2, p. 24. 2. *Château-du-Loir* no. 15. 3. Meinert, "Die Fälschungen," pp. 251–257. 4. Guillot no. ⟨10⟩. 5. Ziezulewicz no. (VI).

See the comments on No. 36 above.

No. 38

Ca. 31 May 1040.

Charter: BISHOP HUBERT witnesses grants made to the cathedral of Le Mans by its bishop Gervais, given for his own sins and for those of his uncle Bishop Avesgaudus (of Le Mans) and the rest of his predecessors, of his father Haimo and his mother Hildeburga, and of all *fideles*. The grants are: half the oblations, all the *decimae, census,* and *suburbia* that the treasurers receive, except for the *proferenda* that the archchaplain receives from the bishop for chanting mass. From his own patrimony, Gervais gives the *villula* of Benais, close to Le Mans above the Huisne, with twelve *agripennae* of vines; the church of Parigné-l'Evêque[1] in the territory of les Loudonneaux, receiving half now and half upon the bishop's death; all the customs in the land pertaining to Château-du-Loir that were paid to his father; his father's *aula* in the eastern corner of Château-du-Loir ("aulam patris mei, sitam in ejusdem predio, in orientali scilicet civitatis angulo"), with all its demesne lands within and without the walls, with a grove for constructing workshops, which Gervais used to rebuild the chapel of the Holy Savior. As long as the canons do not waste the oblations, they shall continue to receive them; those who serve in the chapel shall chant the psalm "Levavi oculos meos ad montes [Psalm 120/121]" and pray the proper collect for Gervais and its other benefactors; the canons must personally continue to celebrate masses with collects for Gervais.

The bishop then enumerates the anniversary days of the members of his family for the year roll so that the canons can pray for them: Bishop Avesgaudus, 27 October; Gervais's mother (the sister of Avesgaudus), the same day; his father Haimo, 16 January; Gervais's ordination day, 19 December. Gervais then lists the churches regained by the canons with his help: Saint-Ouen-en-Belin,[2] with the lands in the same parish, Saint Martin at Laigné-en-Belin[3] and the lands of that waste, Mulsanne[4] below the *quinta* (banlieu) of Le Mans, Saint-Aubin, with the lands continuing in the same parish, the villa of Villegermain,[5] Marcé[6] in the *pagus* of Maine, Assé[7] with its power in the same *pagus*, Ste.-Jamme-sur-Sarthe,[8] and the mills in the Sarthe below the *civitas*, which Gervais bought.

Participants: one is named: Gervais.

Witnesses: six are named: Abbot Odilo of Cluny, Archbishop Arnulf of Tours, Bishop Gervais, Bishop Hubert of Angers, Count Geoffrey (Martel) "princeps noster," Geoffrey the dean of St. Martin; "et plures alii."

Manuscripts: A. Original, lost. B. Copy of the thirteenth century, martyrology of the chapter, Bibl. du Mans, ms. 244, fol. 91 r. C. Copy of the thirteenth century, *Liber Albus Capituli,* Bibl. du Mans, ms. 259, fol. 53 v. D. Copy of the seventeenth century by Duchesne, B. n., *Actus Pontificum,* coll. Baluze, vol. 45, fol. 120 r–122 r. E. Copy of the seventeenth century by Gaignières, B. n., ms. lat. 5211/B, p. 80. F. Copy of the seventeenth century, idem., p. 24. G. Copy of the eighteenth century by Gaignières, B. n., ms. lat. 17036, pp. 45–46, after B. H. Copy of the eighteenth century, B. n., ms. lat. 9206, fol. 3 v, after E. I. copy of the eighteenth century, idem., fol. 20 v, after F.

Editions: I. Mabillon, *Vetera Analecta,* pp. 306–307, after D. II. *Chartularium quod dicitur Liber Albus Capituli,* p. 95, no. 177, after C. III. *Actus*

Pontificum Cenomannis, pp. 367–372, after B, C and D. IV. *Château-du-Loir,* no. 17 (extract).

References: 1. *Cartulaire de l'évêché du Mans* no. 9. 2. Halphen no. 84. 3. Celier no. 24. 4. Guillot no. 103.

Both Halphen and Guillot fix the *terminus a quo* of this charter at 21 June 1040, the death of Count Fulk, since Geoffrey Martel is referred to here as "princeps noster." This argument seems overly technical.

It was Geoffrey Martel, not Fulk, who took the initiative in interfering in the county of Maine after the elevation of Gervais to the bishopric of Le Mans (Halphen, *Comté d'Anjou,* pp. 65–71), so it would not be out of place for Gervais to consider Geoffrey as his lord. The reference to Geoffrey here as "count" also can not be used to restrict these events to the period after Fulk's death. As has been seen (above, No. 26), Geoffrey could be named "count" from the time that he received the county of Vendôme. Thus the only sure *terminus a quo* is 19 December 1037, for this charter gives the day of Gervais's episcopal ordination as 19 December, and Bishop Gervais issued one charter as early as 5 November 1038 (*Cart. Trinité de Vendôme* I, no. 14, with the date correction noted in the discussion of No. 26 above). So he was ordained no later than 19 December 1037. The *terminus ad quem* is the death of Bishop Hubert, 2 March 1047.

The most likely date for this charter, however, is around 31 May 1040, the day of the dedication of the monastery of Trinité de Vendôme. That is the only other time that five of the six witnesses named here were all present together, that is everyone named here except for Odilo of Cluny. (Here I accept the authenticity of the witness list of No. 37 above; see Meinert, "Die Fälschungen," pp. 251–257.) The 110 lay and clerical witnesses named in that document may well explain why the scribe of this charter wrote "et plures alii" after the name of Dean Geoffrey.

---

[1] Parigné-l'Evêque, commune of third canton of Le Mans, dép. Sarthe (Vallée, pp. 679, 1034).

[2] Saint-Ouen-en-Belin, commune of canton Ecommoy, dép. Sarthe (Vallée, pp. 847, 873.

[3] Laigné-en-Belin, comm. of cant. Ecommoy, dép. Sarthe (Vallée, pp. 520, 1017).

[4] Mulsanne, comm. of cant. Ecommoy, dép. Sarthe (Vallée, pp. 644, 1030).

[5] Villegermain, mill, commune la Chapelle-Saint-Aubin, dép. Sarthe (Vallée, pp. 957, 1005).

[6] Marcé; for its identification as Marciacum, see Vallée, p. 1023.

[7] Assé; for its identification as Aciacus, see Vallée, p. 969.

[8] Ste.-Jamme-sur-Sarthe, commune of canton Ballon, dép. Sarthe (Vallée, pp. 829, 1047).

No. 39

1040. Angers.

Notice: BISHOP HUBERT witnesses an agreement between Count Geoffrey Martel and Abbot Frederick of St. Florent concerning the comital customs over the parish of St.-Georges-Châtelaison,[1] which belongs to the abbey. In a *generale placitum* held in Angers by Count Geoffrey and his *fideles* to deal with suppressing wicked invasions and evil customs imposed on monastic lands, Abbot Frederick and his monks complain of the evil customs against their abbey in the parish of St.-Georges. Count Geoffrey establishes that no customs will be imposed on the parish beyond those agreed upon by Count Fulk Nerra and Abbot Geraldus, *viz.*, a *bidannum* of eight days with a spade; the *mansoarii* shall return ten denarii from a suckling pig (or lamb); the *bordarii* shall return five denarii; from one arpent of vines, half a *modius* shall be returned; on the day the *vinagium* is returned, one pennyworth of bread and another of meat and one *sectarium* of new wine shall also be returned; the vicars shall not enter except on the cases of blood, rape, fire, and theft, and they shall pay for their own food while in the villa.

Participants: two are named: Abbot Frederick and Count Geoffrey.

Witnesses: sixteen: Bishop Hubert, Albericus of Montjean (who held this *commendisia* from the count), Ebulo of Champchévrier, Wascelinus of Chemillé, Mainerius, Frotmundus, Renaud of Château-Gontier and his two sons Adelardus and Renaud, Peter of Chemillé, Wascelinus of Poitou, Walter Titio, Isembardus of Lude, Mainardus the vicar of Doué, and from the *vicaria* of St.-Georges, Gunterius and Odo Fatot.

Manuscripts: A. Original redaction, Arch. Maine-et-Loire, H 1840, no. 5. B. Copy of the eleventh century, livre noir of St. Florent, B. n., ms. n. a. lat. 1930, fol. 28 v–29 r. C. Copy of the eighteenth century, B. n., D. H. II[1], no. 444. D. Summaries of the eighteenth century, B. n., D. H. XIII[1], nos. 10286, 10315. E. Copy of the nineteenth century by P. Marchegay, Arch. Maine-et-Loire, H 3711, no. 46.

References: 1. Marchegay, *Livre noir,* no. 35. 2. Halphen no. 66. 3. Saché, pp. 12, 478. 4. Guillot no. 80. 5. Ziezulewicz no. XXIII B.

The act is dated in the year 1040. Both Guillot and Halphen date it to after 21 June, when Geoffrey Martel succeeded to the county of Anjou upon his father's death. But Geoffrey was already functioning as count of Anjou from the time of the departure of Fulk for Jerusalem in 1039, so the entire year of 1040 is valid for this act.

---

[1] St.-Georges-Châtelaison, canton Doué, arr. Saumur (Port III, p. 369).

No. 40

15 October 1041. Chardonnet.

Notice: BISHOP HUBERT, along with Archbishop Arnulf of Tours, Bishop Isembertus of Poitiers and Bishop Walter of Nantes, dedicates the new church of the monastery of St. Florent. Abbot Frederick and the monks of St. Florent have completed the rebuilding of their new monastery. Also present are Count Geoffrey Martel, his mother Hildegardis, his wife Agnes, and many nobles, people of both sexes, abbots, monks, and clerics.

Participants: five: Abbot Frederick and bishops Hubert, Arnulf, Isembertus, and Walter.

Witnesses: three are named: Count Geoffrey, Agnes, Hildegardis.

No charter for this act exists, but a once-extant notice is inferred from the passage relating to this information in the *Historia Sancti Florentii Salmurensis* (ed. Marchegay and Mabille, in *Chroniques des églises d'Anjou*, p. 292; it is also printed in Martène and Durand, *Thesaurus Novus Anecdotorum* III, col. 848), which is a twelfth-century compilation based on one or two late eleventh-century redactions (Marchegay and Mabille, p. xxvi).

Reference: Ziezulewicz no. XXVI.

The *Historia* gives the year of the dedication, 1041. The day is learned from the *Annales de Saint-Florent*, p. 118.

No. 41

13 June 1006–12 April 1043.

Notice: BISHOP HUBERT dedicates a church in honor of St. Julian at Baraceius (Baracé[1]), built by Richard of Campania and his wife Juliana, and he authorizes the consecration of three altars for the church. Richard and Juliana commended the church to the priest Dionysius and endowed the church with a priest's house with gardens and vines, in perpetual benefice for the support of a priest. They also gave it more houses and farms located in their lands and all returns pertaining to them, including the small tithe, so that the lands were immune and free of every burden and obedience of dependency to Richard and Juliana.

Participants: three: Richard of Campania, Juliana, and Bishop Hubert.

This information is provided in a charter of an additional grant to the church of Baracé by Geraldus of Lezigné and Hugonia, who asked her husband to follow the example of his predecessors and likewise make grants to the church so that Eusebius, now priest of that church, and his successors might properly discharge their duties. Therefore gifts are made to the church: five *quarteria* of meadows by the ford of Christopher the miller and the lands of Matthew Conpaignon; two *quarteria* of meadows between the meadow of the house and the shelter of Guegestinus and the bed of the river Loir; one *quarterium* of meadow and one *jugurum* of land between the demesnes at Buordiaria and two *jugura* in the plain or patch of land called *Berthe*; six *quarteria* of sandy land and the *conseptum sturnorum* and another *quarterium* in *septum marostarum*; four arpents, or *jugura*, of land at Chemaldiariae and three *quarteria* of vines in *conseptum Blanchardum*. The church is confirmed to be immune and free of every return, gift and service.

Participants: three: Geraldus of Lézigné, Hugonia, and Geraldus [apparently Hugonia's husband, who made these grants].

Witnesses: six are named: Philip, Ogerius, Gavanus les Ulmes, Bartholomew the shield-bearer, Walter de Lezinio, Geraldus (who makes the sign of the cross and places his seal on the document); and many other witnesses.

Both of the above parts, the dedication of the church by Hubert and the subsequent donations by Geraldus, are given in a *vidimus* of John Joubert, archpriest of la Flêche.

Manuscripts: A. Original redaction, lost. B. Vidimus of 1410, lost? C. Copy of the nineteenth century by P. Marchegay, Arch. Maine-et-Loire, H 778 bis I, fol. 115 r–v, after B.

The gifts by Geraldus are dated in the document, 12 April 1043, so Bishop Hubert made his dedication before that date, but after his ordination. The *vidimus* carries the date 5 September 1410.

---

[1] Baracé, arr. Angers, canton Durtal (Lebrun, *Dict. Maine-et-Loire*, p. 50, and Port I, p. 196).

No. 42

1 October 1045. Angers.
Charter: BISHOP HUBERT witnesses Geoffrey Martel's confirmation of the grants made to Ronceray by his father Count Fulk and by other *fideles.* done at the request of his mother Countess Hildegardis and his wife Agnes. Included in these grants are the *bidannum universum* in the entire *burgus* of the monastery, the *fenagium,* the *bannum* of selling the convent's own wine and the *vicaria;* in curtis Petre (la Cour de Pierre[1]), the *vicaria* of minor crimes (from which three pounds are fined), two *fodria,* of which only one was taken there before, the *vaccagium universum* and the *bidannum totum* except for the public summons for building a *castrum* or for battle.

Participants: three: Count Geoffrey, Hildegardis, Agnes.

Witnesses: sixteen: the three participants, in addition to Bishop Hubert, Burchardus the treasurer, Abbess Leburgis, Joscelin the dean, Suhardus of Craon, Primoldus the archpriest and canon of Ronceray, Marcuinus the *levita,* Geoffrey of Preuilly, Bartholomew the *miles,* Berengar the *miles,* Rainerius the *dominicus vassus,* Renaud the son of Ivo, Adelardus his son.

Manuscripts: A. Original, lost. B. Copy of the thirteenth century, cartulary of Ronceray, Bibl. d'Angers, ms. 848 (760), no. 91 of the fifth roll.
Edition: *Ronceray,* no. 5, after B.
References: 1. Halphen no. 72. 2. Guillot no. 89.

The charter is dated 1 October, and Guillot has established the year as 1045. The appearance of Suhardus of Craon among the witnesses of this act is not catalogued by Bertrand de Brouissillon in *La maison de Craon.*

---

[1] La Cour de Pierre, commune Rochefort (Port I, p. 777).

No. 43

21 June 1040–March 1046.

BISHOP HUBERT and count Geoffrey Martel confirm the church of St. Marcel at the *castellum* of Briollay, free of all customs, to Burchardus the treasurer of St. Maurice, just as he held it from Count Fulk and BISHOP HUBERT.

Participants: three: Count Geoffrey, Bishop Hubert, and Burchardus.

No separate document for this act exists, but the confirmation is referred to in No. 44. Since Burchardus held the church from Count Fulk and Bishop Hubert (see No. 30), Count Geoffrey and Bishop Hubert would have confirmed Burchardus's tenure of the church only after Fulk's death, 21 June 1040, but before Burchardus gave it to St. Serge, in March of 1046 (see No. 44).

No. 44

21 June 1040–before March 1046.

Charter: BISHOP HUBERT and Count Geoffrey Martel give their authorization to and witness the gift of Burchardus the treasurer to Abbot Hubert of St. Serge and his monks, consisting of the church of St. Marcel at the *castellum* of Briollay,[1] free of all customs, just as he held it from Count Fulk and Count Geoffrey, and from BISHOP HUBERT—all the land to the right of Briollay all the way to the monastery through the public way; the land of Puteolis; half the mill of Novientus, which he held in common with the *miles* Yvo; half the mill of Bera and six arpents of meadows in the woods; all the meadows in Longa Insula (Longue-Ile); all the *decima* of his fisheries and mills except for the *cenaticum;* his *servi* Oggerius and his sons and daughters; his enclosure of vines at Vitriniacus with the land that the keeper of the enclosure holds and where he remains; all the woods except for the green growing oaks ("quercubus tantum viridibus"), but which the monks may use for building a church and workshops; the *foragium* of 100 pigs; all the arable land from the crossing where the road from the *castellum* and that from Crux meet, all the way to the Loir; Burchardus also authorizes any of his men, whether *miles, servus,* or *colibertus* to make donations to St. Serge.

Participants: four are named: Burchardus, Count Geoffrey, Bishop Hubert, Abbot Hubert; and the monks of St. Serge.

Witnesses: fifteen: Burchardus, his wife Judith, his sons Ingelgerius and Hilarius, Burchardus's brother Ingelgerius, Ivo son of Guy de Cimbriaco, Nihard of Lavardin, Renaud son of Drogo, Hugh, Bishop Hubert, Count Geoffrey, Countess Hildegardis, Countess Agnes, Count William of Poitou, and his brother Guy.

Manuscripts: A. Original, lost. B. Copy, first cartulary of St. Serge, fol. 29–30, no. 51, lost. C. Copy of 1653, Arch. Maine-et-Loire, H 857, no. 1, after A. D. Copy of the seventeenth century, Bibl. d'Angers, ms. 689 (623),

p. 277 (partial). E. Copies of the seventeenth and eighteenth centuries, Arch. Maine-et-Loire, H 778 bis I, fol. 142 r–143 v, after C. F. Extracts of the eighteenth century, B. n., D. H. XIII[1], nos. 9914, 10206; ms. lat. 5446, p. 250; ms. lat. 12658, fol. 88 r–v.

Editions: I. Sainte-Marthe, *Gallia Christiana* 2, p. 125, after A (partial). II. Ménage, *Hist. de Sablé* 1, pp. 157–158 (partial). IV. Modern, by Y. Chauvin, "Cartulaire de St.-Serge," I, no. 51, after C and D.

References: 1. Bréquigny 2: p. 39. 2. Port, H, p. 120. 3. Guillot no. 90.

This charter must fall between 1039, Fulk's final departure from Anjou, and 1 March 1046, by which time Berengar had succeeded Burchardus as treasurer of St. Maurice (see Guillot no. 90).

---

[1] Briollay, chef-lieu of canton, arr. Angers (Port I, p. 503).

No. 45

13 June 1006–1 March 1046.

BISHOP HUBERT gives or confirms the arable land at la Prellé, without the *census*, to Odo the son of Roger.

Participants: two: Bishop Hubert and Odo.

No document for this act exists, but it is referred to in No. 46, when John of Jalesne, who holds the land from Odo, gives it to St. Serge, with Bishop Hubert's authorization. The dating is the same as for No. 46.

No. 46

13 June 1006–1 March 1046.

Notice: BISHOP HUBERT gives his authorization for John of Jalesne, who is becoming a member of the monastery of St. Serge, to give it his arable land at Pratella (la Prellé[1]), without the *census*. John holds the land from Odo the son of Roger and he received ten solidi from Abbot Hubert for consenting to the gift. BISHOP HUBERT also orders Geoffrey, the son of Roger, Odo's brother, to give his authorization for the grant.

Participants: five: John of Jalesne, Odo, Bishop Hubert, Abbot Hubert, Geoffrey.

Manuscripts: A. Original, lost. B. Copy, first cartulary of St. Serge, fol. 17, no. 21, lost. C. Copy of the seventeenth century, B. n., ms. lat. 5446, p. 242, no. 21. D. Copy of the eighteenth century, B. n., coll. Moreau, vol. 20, fol. 79 r–v, after D. E. Copy of the eighteenth century, B. n., D. H. XIII[1], no. 9902 (extract).

The act must fall between Bishop Hubert's ordination and the appointment of Vulgrinus to succeed Abbot Hubert of St. Serge, on 1 March 1046 (see No. 53).

---

[1] La Prellé, mét., canton Aulaines, dép. Sarthe (*Cart. manceau de Marmoutier* II, p. 653).

No. 47

October 1006–1 March 1046.

BISHOP HUBERT gives or confirms his *fevum* at Roche-Foubert in Grand-Launay, consisting of one mill with the customary ban, one house, and arable land, to the priest Leodegarius.

Participants: Bishop Hubert and Leodegarius.

No document for this act exists, but it is inferred from Bishop Hubert's grant of this same land to Marmoutier (see No. 52). Since Hubert's niece Emma and her husband and children gave their agreement to No. 52, this land was probably part of Hubert's family holdings, and he would have given or confirmed it to Leodegarius only after he became head of the family, October 1006 at the earliest (see the dating of No. 9). The grant had to have been made by 1 March 1046, the *terminus ad quem* for Hubert's own gift of the *fevum* to Marmoutier (No. 52).

No. 48

1007–1 March 1046.

Notice: BISHOP Hubert, grieving at the subjection of ecclesiastical things to the rapacity of laymen, made an exchange with Renaud of Château-Gontier and his sons and daughters, removing them from the abbey of St. Maurille in exchange for land in the suburb behind the monastery of St. Aubin, with vines and the *vicaria* that he possessed in his land at Morannes.[1]

Participants: two are named: Bishop Hubert and Renaud of Château-Gontier; and Renaud's sons and daughter.

This information is recalled in a notice of Bishop Eusebius of Angers, where it is stated that he reclaimed the abbey of St. Maurille. Eusebius had placed it under one of his *familiares* who appeared religious. But this rector was not a good one and, due to the bishop's anxiety and the canons' complaints, Eusebius removed the rector, who was paid three pounds by the canons. Bishop Eusebius agrees to keep the abbey under his control and forbids any of his successors to grant it to another.

Participants: one is named: Bishop Eusebius; and the unnamed rector and the canons.

Manuscripts: A. Original, lost. B. Copy, cartulary of St. Maurice, fol. 23 r, lost. C. Copy of the seventeenth century, B. n., coll. Du Chesne, vol. 22, fol. 107 v. D. Copy of the eighteenth century, B. n., D. H. II[1], no. 516, after B. E. Copy of the eighteenth century, Bibl. d'Angers, ms. 706 (636), pp. 6–7.

Editions: I. Ménage, *Hist. de Sablé* 1, pp. 98–99, after B. II. *Cart. noir de la cathédrale*, no. 31, after A–D.

Reference: Bréquigny 2: p. 40.

Renaud was given Château-Gontier by Fulk Nerra after it was constructed in 1007 (*St. Aubin*, no. 1; while the act in its present form is

inauthentic, see No. 28 above, it is not necessary to reject that act's assertion that Fulk built the fortification that came to be called Château-Gontier
in the year 1007), providing the *terminus a quo* for Bishop Hubert's actions,
while the *terminus ad quem* is 1 March 1046, when Bishop Hubert gave St.
Maurille to St. Serge without the authorization of Renaud or any of his
family (No. 53).

Bishop Eusebius's reclamation of the abbey falls within his episcopate, 6
December 1047–27 August 1081.

---

[1] Morannes; see No. 10, note 4.

No. 49

21 June 1040–1 March 1046.
Charter: BISHOP HUBERT witnesses Count Geoffrey Martel's confirmation of the donations made to the monastery of St. Nicholas by his father
Count Fulk; Count Geoffrey also makes additional grants on his own: a
pool below the abbey in the river Brionneau, with all its fish and mills; near
the Ecclesiola de Pruneriis (Pruniers[1]), his demesne Cultura, an assart that
Count Fulk cleared by his own labor.

Participants: three: Count Geoffrey, his wife Agnes, and his mother
Hildegardis.

Witnesses: twenty-two: Count Geoffrey, Bishop Hubert, (Guy) Geoffrey
and William the counts of Poitou, Viscount Joscelin of Brittany, Lancelinus
of Beaugé, Suhardus of Craon, Geoffrey of Preuilly, Albericus of Montjean, Renaud of Château-Gontier with his son Adelardus, Joscelin of Ste.-
Maur, Count Hugh of Maine, Gerald of Faye, Bernard of Chantocé,
Odricus Bibit Vinum, Burchardus the treasurer, Rainerius de Turris, Count
Herbert of Maine, Viscount Radulfus, Renaud son of Drogo, Geoffrey the
dean of Tours.

Manuscripts: A. Original, lost. B. Copy, cartulary of St. Nicholas, lost. C.
Copy of the eighteenth century, B. n., D. H. II[1], no. 445, after B.
Edition: Le Peletier, *Epitome*, pp. 44–45 (witness list lacking).
References: 1. Halphen no. 77. 2. Y. Mailfert, "Cartulaire de Saint-Ni-
colas," appendix I, no. 3. 3. Guillot no. 96.

This act falls between Count Fulk's death and 1 March 1046, by which
time Berengar had replaced Burchardus, who witnessed this act, as treasurer of St. Maurice (see No. 53). The appearance of Suhardus of Craon
among the witnesses is not catalogued by Bertrand de Brouissillon in *La
maison de Craon*.

---

[1] Pruniers, bourg, commune Bouchemaine (Port III, p. 196).

No. 50

21 June 1040–1 March 1046.

Charter: BISHOP HUBERT witnesses Count Geoffrey Martel's gift of the torrent Brionneau to St. Nicholas, and the permission to build mills in the exit of the fishpond, which had been granted in Count Fulk's lifetime, and the land Cultura Comitis, which Fulk had tilled with his own cattle; Count Geoffrey confirms the remainder of Fulk's concessions to St. Nicholas; Count Geoffrey himself gives nine arpents of meadows in Lupellus (Pré d'Alloyau[1]) and twelve arpents in Longue-Ile; and he retains no customs that he has given up.

Participants: two: Count Geoffrey and his mother Hildegardis.

Witnesses: twenty-two: the same as in No. 49.

This charter is included in a larger document consisting of two additional parts. The second part is a notice of Count Fulk Réchin confirming Geoffrey Martel's gifts in Part I above, and adding grants of his own: the vines of Geraldus Calvellus, the *decima* of the *pasnagium* of Monnaie,[2] and he abandons the *rotagium* of Longue-Ile that his *servientes* wished to take away unjustly, for which Abbot Natalis gives him ten pounds of denarii.

Participants: two: Count Fulk Réchin and Abbot Natalis.

Witnesses: twenty-one: Count Fulk, Abbot Natalis; the monks Ingelbaldus, Fulcoius, Stephen, Geoffrey of Nantes; the *miles* Geoffrey the younger of Mayenne, Geoffrey the younger of Châteaubriant, Bartholomew of Angers, Ingelbaldus Eschuis, Paganus the son of Fulbert, Hubert the *monetarius,* in whose house this act was authorized; Hugh the canon of St. Laud, Alan de Meldon, Geoffrey his brother, who received 100 solidi, Briencius Sacegai, who received 100 solidi, Viscount Wadferius, Corbinus de Zalla, Guarinus *parvus,* Renaud Champel, Normannus de Nova Villa.

Count Geoffrey's charter and the notice of Fulk Réchin are confirmed by King Philip I.

Participant: King Philip.

Witnesses: six: Queen B(ertrada), Almaricus son of Berardus, Arnulfus Bulgerius, Geoffrey Ridel, William Conerius, Vivianus the royal fisherman.

Manuscripts: A. Original, lost. B. Copy, cartulary of St. Nicholas, fol. 6, lost. C. Copy of 1701, Arch. Maine-et-Loire, H 397, no. 1, after A. D. Copy of the eighteenth century, B. n., D. H. II², no. 593, after B.

Editions: I. Le Peletier, *Epitome,* pp. 45–46. II. Sainte-Marthe, *Gallia Christiana* 2, pp. 125–126. III. Tresvaux, no. 23 (partial). IV. Prou, *Rec. des actes de Philippe Ier,* no. 157, after C, D, I and II. V. Modern, by Y. Mailfert, "Cartulaire de Saint-Nicolas," nos. II, II bis.

References: 1. Bréquigny 2: p. 23. 2. Bertrand de Brouissillon, *Craon* no. 3 (Part I only). 3. Port, H, p. 69. 4. Halphen no. 78 (Part I only). 5. Latouche no. 24 (Part I only). 6. Guillot nos. 99 (Part I) and 379 (Part II).

For the dating of Geoffrey Martel's charter, see No. 49. Fulk Réchin's confirmation and grants (Part II) fall between 20 June 1079 and 2 July 1093

(Guillot no. 379). King Philip's confirmation (Part III) was on 11 October 1106 (Prou, pp. 391–393, n. a).

---

[1] Pré-d'Alloyau; see Mailfert, "Fondation St.-Nicholas," p. 60, n. 1.
[2] Monnaie, woods, to the southwest of Mouliherne, canton Longué, arr. Saumur, Maine-et-Loire (Guillot 2: p. 333).

No. 51 (Inauthentic)

21 June 1040–1 March 1046.

Charter: BISHOP HUBERT witnesses Count Geoffrey Martel's confirmation of his father's grants to St. Nicholas; this is at the urging of his mother Hildegardis, for the sins of his father Count Fulk, recently dead. He also adds donations of his own: the torrent of Brionneau, the freedom to build mills in the exit of the fishpond, a right that St. Nicholas had possessed in Fulk's lifetime; the land called Cultura comitis, which Fulk had tilled with his own cattle; the *vinagium* of all their vines so long as they or their delegates cultivated them; the *forragium* of all their land. The abbey's men are freed from the authority of comital *prepositi* or *vicarii* unless the abbot or his *prepositus* should be unable to constrain someone or should be negligent after two demands. All the abbey's present and future possessions over which the count has any dominion shall be free from every custom.

Participants: three: Count Geoffrey, Hildegardis, Agnes.

Witnesses: thirty-four: the same as in the first part of No. 50 above (identical to No. 49 above), including Bishop Hubert, except that Geoffrey the dean of Tours is omitted, in addition to the witnesses to the second part of No. 50 above, from Geoffrey the younger of Mayenne through Normannus de Nova Villa (inclusive), except for Bartholomew of Angers and Ingelbaldus Eschuis.

Manuscripts: Original, lost.
Editions: I. Le Peletier, *Breviculum,* pp. 9–10. II. Le Peletier, *Epitome,* pp. 9–11.
References: 1. Halphen no. 76. 2. Latouche no. 23. 3. Guillot no. ⟨11⟩.

This act is clearly inauthentic (see Guillot no. ⟨11⟩). Its provisions are taken from Nos. 49 and 50 above, from other charters of Geoffrey Martel for St. Nicholas (Le Peletier, *Epitome,* pp. 48–49, Guillot no. 203, and Le Peletier, *Breviculum,* pp. 15–16, Guillot no. 184), and the witness list is a combination of those from Geoffrey Martel's charter in No. 50, Part I, above, and Fulk Réchin's confirmation and own donations, No. 50, Part II, above.

No. 52

1 October 1045–1 March 1046.

Notice: BISHOP HUBERT, for the redemption of his own soul and those of his parents Viscount Hubert and Emelina, gives to Marmoutier the *fevum* that the priest Leodegarius holds from him in Curia Alnetensis (Grand-Launay[1]), in the place that is called Ad Rupes Fulberti (Roche-Foubert[2]), which is one mill with the customary ban, one house, and the arable land and whatever else the priest holds from him. Leodegarius agrees to the donation, as do his children, and adds one-fourth of the mill, with Marmoutier to receive all the remaining things after their deaths. Viscount Radulfus and his wife Emelina (Bishop Hubert's niece), their sons Hubert and Radulfus Paganus, and their daughters Hadeburgis[3] and Godehildis agree to the grant. Viscount Radulfus and his sons twice give their authorization for this grant, first at Lude and then when they placed it on the altar of Marmoutier after they had returned from St. Egipdius.

Participants: eight are named: Bishop Hubert, Viscount Radulfus, Emelina, their children Hubert, Radulfus Paganus, Hadeburgis and Godehildis, the priest Leodegarius and his children.

Witnesses: twelve: Bishop Hubert, Berengar the treasurer, Leodegarius the priest, Landricus the cleric, Vulgrinus the monk, Renaud *major,* Viscount Radulfus, his sons Hubert and Radulfus, his men Marcoardus and Renaud, and Robert *major.*

Manuscripts: Original, lost. B. Copy of the eleventh century, Arch. Maine-et-Loire, G 785 no. 2, after A. Copy of the seventeenth century, B. n., ms. lat. 12878, fol. 95 r, after B. D. Copy of the seventeenth century, B. n., ms. lat. 12880, fol. 89 r. E. Extract of the seventeenth century, B. n., ms. lat. 17030, p. 33. F. Extract of the seventeenth or eighteenth century, B. n., ms. lat. 5441[1] fol. 392. G. Copy of the eighteenth century, B. n., D. H. II[1], no. 353, after C. H. Extract of the eighteenth century, B. n., coll. Moreau, vol. 20, fol. 84 r–v, after F.

Edition: Boussard, "Les évêques en Neustrie," p. a. no. 1, pp. 194–195.
References: 1. Mabille no. 353. 2. Port, G, p. 114.

Since Berengar is styled treasurer here, the charter was issued after 1 October 1045, when Burchardus was still the treasurer of St. Maurice (see Guillot no. 91, note). The monk Vulgrinus among the witnesses was almost certainly Hubert's cousin, the future abbot of St. Serge, who was appointed to head that monastery on 1 March 1046 (see No. 53).

---

[1] Grand-Launay, according to Boussard.
[2] Roche-Foubert, according to Boussard.
[3] This is the form given in B, the best manuscript. Boussard has the incorrect form Hildeburgis.

No. 53

1 March 1046.
Charter: BISHOP HUBERT recalls how he labored to restore the monastery of St. Serge, which had fallen into destruction due to the Northmen and other impediments; his predecessor Bishop Renaud began to restore it, placing a small band of monks there under an abbot, but his plans were

incomplete by the time of his death; HUBERT had, from time to time, given small grants to St. Serge. Now, so that the order of the monastic rule might be held there more firmly, HUBERT asks Abbot Albert of Marmoutier to supply an abbot from among his monks, and Vulgrinus has been chosen. BISHOP HUBERT also now gives St. Serge the little cell of St. Maurille at Calonna (Chalonnes-sur-Loire[1]).

Participants: three: Hubert, Albert, and Vulgrinus.

Witnesses: seventeen: Abbot Albert, Abbot Walter of St. Aubin, Berengar the treasurer, Renaud the archdeacon, Joscelin the archdeacon, Gerardus the cantor, Fulcodius the chaplain, Bernaldus the canon, Marcuinus the canon, Hugh the dean, Landricus the canon, John the canon, Hilduinus the *prepositus,* Adelardus the son of Renaud, Raherius of Lué, Count Geoffrey Martel, and Bishop Hubert.

Manuscripts: A. Original, Bibl. d'Angers, ms. 838 (754), no. 1. B. Copy, first cartulary of St. Serge, fol. 15, no. 19, lost. C. Copy of the fourteenth century in the second cartulary of St. Serge, Nantes, Musée Dobrée, ms. 3, no. 301, fol. 131 v (partial). D. Copies of the sixteenth century, Arch. Maine-et-Loire, H 974, nos. 2, 5, probably after B. E. Copy of the sixteenth century, Arch. Maine-et-Loire, H 974, no. 11. F. Copy of the seventeenth century, B. n., ms. lat. 5446, fol. 241 r–v, no. 19, after A. G. Extract of the seventeenth century, B. n., ms. lat. 17030, p. 43, after B. H. Copy of the eighteenth century, Bibl. d'Angers, ms. 706 (636), pp. 163–164. I. Copy of the eighteenth century, B. n., D. H. II[1], no. 412 bis. J. Copy of the eighteenth century, B. n., Coll. Moreau, vol. 21, fol. 195 r–197 v, after F. K. Copy of the nineteenth century by P. Marchegay, Arch. Maine-et-Loire, H 778 bis I, fol. 168 r–v, after A, C, D, E.

Editions: I. Mabillon, *Annales Benedicti* (1701), 4, p. 411 (partial). II. Mabillon, *Annales Benedicti* (1739), 4, p. 378 (partial).

References: 1. Bréquigny 2: p. 12. 2. Port, H, pp. 131–132. 3. BPF, p. 467. 4. Halphen no. 83. 5. Guillot no. 91. 4. Hogan no. 32.

The charter is dated 1 March, and Guillot has argued persuasively for the year of 1046.

---

[1] Chalonnes-sur-Loire; see No. 22, note 2.

No. 54

13 June 1006–20 March 1046. Angers.

Notice: BISHOP HUBERT gives his permission to Girardus the priest to found an oratory and cemetery so that a priest can care for the poor, visit them in sickness, bury them, and celebrate masses for their souls.

Participants: two: Bishop Hubert and Girardus.

Manuscripts: A. Original, lost. B. Copy, black cartulary of St. Maurice, fol. 29 r, lost. C. Resumé of the seventeenth century, Bibl. d'Angers, ms. 689 (623), p. 278.

Edition: *Cart. noir de la cathédrale*, no. 41.

References: 1. Seventeenth-century ms. 689 (623), Bibl d'Angers, pp. 273, 276, 278. 2. Seventeenth-century ms. H 1273, Arch. Maine-et-Loire, fol. 10 v. 3. Eighteenth-century ms. 690 (624), Bibl. d'Angers, fol. 281 r. 4. Eighteenth-century ms., B. n., D. H. II[1], no. 354.

This act falls between Hubert's ordination and the *terminus ad quem* for the dedication of this oratory, named for All Saints (Toussaint), 20 March 1046 (see No. 57 below).

No. 55

13 June 1006–20 March 1046. Angers.
Notice: BISHOP HUBERT responds to the canons' request (No. 54 above) by ordering that meritorious brothers be chosen for the oratory, so that the needs of the poor can be cared for honestly.
Participant: one: Bishop Hubert.

Manuscripts: A. Original, lost. B. Copy, black cartulary of St. Maurice, fol. 30 r, lost. C. Resumé of the seventeenth century, Arch. Maine-et-Loire, H 1273, fol. 14 v.
Edition: *Cart. noir de la cathédrale*, no. 42.
References: 1. Seventeenth- or eighteenth-century ms., Bibl. d'Angers, ms. 689 (623), pp. 276, 278. 2. Eighteenth-century ms., Bibl. d'Angers, ms. 690 (624), fol. 281 r. 3. Eighteenth-century ms., B. n., D. H. II[1], no. 354.

For the dating, see No. 54 above. The second portion of this act in the edition is only a variant form of a portion of *Cart. de la Trinité de Vendôme*, no. 419 (No. 56, Part I, below).

No. 56

13 June 1006–20 March 1046.
Notice: BISHOP HUBERT (who very frequently attended or presided over the meeting of the canons), and the canons of the cathedral grant the request of the co-canon, the priest and precentor Girardus, to build an oratory in honor of all the saints (Toussaint), that a priest be given its title so that he might visit the poor and say masses for all dead Christians, with all alms and other revenues belonging to the canons; brothers of an upright life are chosen to oversee the goods and alms of the oratory.
Participants: two are named: Bishop Hubert and Girardus; and the canons.

This information is mentioned as the first of six parts in a much longer document recording the subsequent history of this oratory of Toussaint and of the resolution of a dispute concerning it. In the second part, it is further recalled that shortly after Part I, Bishop Eusebius of Angers, Girardus, and the canons handed the oratory of Toussaint over to the monks of Trinité de Vendôme.

Participants: two are named: Bishop Eusebius and Girardus; and the canons of St. Maurice and the monks of Trinité de Vendôme.

In the third part, it is stated that the monks of Trinité faithfully maintained the functions of Toussaint and that they built the church of the Holy Trinity (of Evière), near Toussaint. Then Abbot Odricus of Trinité, with certain of his monks, came into the chapter of St. Maurice and voluntarily gave back to Bishop Eusebius and the canons the church of Toussaint.

Participants: two are named: Abbot Odricus, Bishop Eusebius, the monks of Trinité, and the canons of St. Maurice.

In the fourth part, Bishop Renaud III of Angers reviews the history of Toussaint and, wishing to add to it, installs regular canons there to carry on its functions.

Participant: one: Bishop Renaud.

In the fifth part, Abbot Geoffrey of Trinité de Vendôme resists this decision (Part IV), claiming that Toussaint was still of their right, that Abbot Odricus had given it to St. Maurice (Part III) without the chapter's consent. Now, however, Trinité ends its claim, with the reservation that if St. Maurice should ever alienate either the church of Toussaint or its alms, it should be only to the monastery of Trinité. Bishop Renaud III confirms this agreement, along with his canons William and Andrew.

Participants: four are named: Abbot Geoffrey, Bishop Renaud, William, and Andrew.

In the sixth part, eight days after Bishop Renaud's confirmation, Abbot Geoffrey of Trinité de Vendôme and his monks give their confirmation in their chapter.

Participant: one is named: Abbot Geoffrey; and the monks of Trinité.

Witnesses: two: Rualdus and Renaud, two regular canons of Toussaint.

Manuscripts: A. Original, lost. B. Copy of the sixteenth century, Bibl. de Vendôme, ms. 273, fol. 94. C. Copy of the seventeenth century, B. n., coll. Duchesne, vol. 22, fol. 112 r–v. D. Copy of the eighteenth century, B. n., D. H. IV, no. 1277. E. Copy of the eighteenth century, Bibl. d'Angers, ms. 706 (636), pp. 62–64.

Editions: I. Sainte-Marthe, *Gallia Christiana* 4, p. 699. II. *Gallia Christiana* 14, Instrumenta, cols. 153–154. III. *Cart. de la Trinité de Vendôme*, no. 419.

References: 1. Bréquigny 2: p. 452. 2. D'Espinay, *Revue de l'Anjou* 13, (1875), pp. 297–8, n. 2. 3. Thorode, pp. 242–243. 4. Penelope Johnson, *Prayer, Patronage and Power*, pp. 54, 125–126, 162.

The date of Bishop Hubert's action, Part I, is the same as for No. 57 below. Part II, Bishop Eusebius's gift of the oratory to Trinité, was on 6 January 1049 (see *Cart. noir de la cathédrale*, no. 45, *Cart. de la Trinité de Vendôme*, no. 92). Its return to St. Maurice (Part III) was done by the time of the death of Bishop Eusebius (27 August 1081). Part IV, Bishop Renaud III's placing canons in Toussaint, was after his ordination, 12 January 1102, but by the time of Count Fulk Réchin's confirmation of gifts to them in 1103 (see No. 57 below). The document gives the date of Bishop Renaud's

confirmation of Abbot Geoffrey's abandoning his claim to Toussaint (Part
V), 21 September 1108, and states that Abbot Geoffrey's confirmation
(Part VI) was made within eight days after that, 21–29 September 1108.

No. 57

20 March 1040–20 March 1046. Angers.

Notice: BISHOP HUBERT dedicates the church of Toussaint, built by the
precentor Girardus, and Count Geoffrey Martel gives to the church his
customs of the *vicaria, bidampnium, corvada, faragium, chenagium,* and *vinagium* in the lands of Astellinis, Landellis, Peluchardus (Epluchard[1]), and
Baniacus (or Bamarus, Béné[2]).

Participants: two: Bishop Hubert and Count Geoffrey.

This information is given in a charter of Count Fulk Réchin and his son
Fulk the Younger, confirming to the regular canons of the church of Toussaint the donations made by Count Geoffrey in Part I, and adding an
island in Vallée[3] free from all customs, with the *vinagium* and *banagium*
and one *mensura* of land close to Aralazrum (or Stralagium).

Participants: two: Count Fulk Réchin and Count Fulk the Younger.

Witnesses: eleven: Roaldus *prior,* Manerius *magister,* Radulfus, Geoffrey
Guarinus, Geoffrey of Ramefort, Geoffrey, Ursellus, Geoffrey Garnerius,
Andefridus Diabolus, Fulk Réchin, and Fulk the Younger.

Manuscripts: A. Original, lost. B. Copy, cartulary of Toussaint, lost. C.
Copy of the seventeenth century, Arch. Maine-et-Loire, H 1281, no. 4. D.
Copy of the eighteenth century, B. n., D. H. IV, no. 1224, after B.

References: 1. Port, H, p. 173. 2. Halphen nos. 73 (Part I) and 298 (Part
II). 3. Guillot nos. 93 (Part I) and 424 (Part II).

It is recorded here that the dedication took place on 20 March. Since
Geoffrey Martel was functioning as count of Anjou from the time that Fulk
Nerra left Anjou for the last time in 1039, the first possible 20 March for
Part I was in 1040, while the last 20 March of Bishop Hubert's life was in
1046. Part II itself gives the year 1103 for Fulk Réchin's confirmation and
donation.

---

[1] Epluchard, mills, ferme, and chef-lieu, commune Angers, in canton St.-Laud (Port II, p.
114).
[2] Béné, commune Juigné-Béné, canton, arr. Angers (Guillot, 2: p. 314).
[3] Vallée, ferme, commune Bocé (Port III, p. 651).

No. 58

20 March 1040–20 March 1046. Angers.

Notice: When BISHOP HUBERT dedicates the oratory built by Girardus,
Count Geoffrey Martel gives all the customs from two *mansurae* of land,
including the *vicaria, bidannum* and *corvadae,* and the *fodrium* and *vinagium* of seven arpents of vines.

Participant: one: Count Geoffrey.

Manuscripts: A. Original, lost. B. Copy, black cartulary of St. Maurice, fol. 30 v, lost. C. Résumé of the seventeenth century, Bibl. d'Angers, ms. 689 (623), p. 278.

Edition: *Cart. noir de la cathédrale*, no. 43.

References: 1. Seventeenth- or eighteenth-century ms., Bibl. d'Angers, ms. 689 (623), pp. 276, 278. 2. Eighteenth-century ms., Bibl. d'Angers, ms. 690 (624), fol. 281 r, 300 v. 3. Eighteenth-century ms., B. n., D. H. II[1], no. 354. 4. Thorode, p. 244. 5. Halphen no. 74. 6. Guillot no. 93.

This notice appears to have been taken from the same charter as the notice of the first part of No. 57 above, and thus the dating is the same.

No. 59

13 June 1006–2 March 1047.

Notice: BISHOP HUBERT authorizes the gift of Bugno (le Buron or le Bigno[1]) to St. Serge by John of Jalesne, who retains the *census* from the vines for the sustenance of his mother; also authorizing the gift is Odo son of Roger, from whom John holds the land in *beneficium*.

Participants: three: John of Jalesne, Bishop Hubert, and Odo.

Witnesses: three: Bishop Hubert, Odo, and his brother Geoffrey.

Manuscripts: A. Original, lost. B. Copy, first cartulary of St. Serge, no. 22, lost. C. Copy of the sixteenth century, B. n., ms. lat. 5446, p. 243, no. 22. D. Copy of the eighteenth century, B. n., Coll. Moreau, vol. 20, fol. 81 r–v.

This act can be dated only to the episcopate of Hubert, who gives his authorization because Odo himself probably held Bugno from the bishop.

---

[1] Le Buron, ferme, commune Chalonnes-sur-Loire (Port I, p. 343); or le Bigno, ferme, commune Durtal (Port I, p. 344; Durtal, *Cart. Saint-Serge*, p. 175).

No. 60

13 June 1006–2 March 1047.

Notice: BISHOP HUBERT gives to the monastery of St. Serge the altars of the two churches of St. Maurille and St. Peter, reserving the burials and oblations only of the chapel of St. Lawrence.

Participant: one: Bishop Hubert.

This information is provided in a notice of Bishop Eusebius of Angers, recalling Hubert's actions and giving to Abbot Vulgrinus and the monks of St. Serge the two churches of the *vicus* of Chalonnes-sur-Loire[1] (St. Maurille and St. Peter). Eusebius adds what Hubert had reserved and includes the rest of the *decimae* that he and his men hold. Future donations by Eusebius or his successors from these lands cannot be made to another place or person. Eusebius frees all lands and waters that St. Serge has or will have within his diocese from all customs, but if the monastery should alienate them, the customs will return to the bishop. He frees the lands of St. Serge within his diocese from the *synodus, circada,* and *sacrilegium.* In the woods he has or will have, the bishop gives the monks' pigs the right of the *pasnaticum.*

Participants: two are named: Bishop Eusebius and Abbot Vulgrinus.

Witnesses: twenty-four: Bishop Eusebius; from the clerical order, Joscelin the dean, Martin the priest, Hugh the priest, Gerardus the cantor, Radulfus the priest, Odo the priest, Girbaldus the priest and *prepositus* of St. Maurille, Renaud the deacon, Bernard the deacon, Landricus the deacon, Peter the deacon, Ansicerius the deacon, Odolerius the deacon and *servitor* of St. Serge, Aimery the deacon and canon of St. Peter, Emerio the subdeacon, Girardus the subdeacon, Joscelin the subdeacon, Geoffrey the subdeacon, Geoffrey the other deacon, Bernerius the subdeacon; from the monastic order, Abbot Vulgrinus, Hugh the monk, Durandus the *scriptor.*

Manuscripts: A. Original, lost. B. Copy, first cartulary of St. Serge, no. 30, fol. 22, lost. C. Three copies of the sixteenth century, Arch. Maine-et-Loire, H 974. D. Copy of the eighteenth century, B. n., D. H. II[1], no. 508. E. Copy of the nineteenth century by P. Marchegay, Arch. Maine-et-Loire, H 778 bis, I, fol. 174 r–v, after C.

Reference: Port, H, p. 132.

Bishop Hubert's gift can be assigned only to his lifetime. The additional grants by Eusebius were made on 13 September, according to the document, and must fall between 1048 (the first 13 September after his ordination) and 1055 (the last 13 September that Vulgrinus was abbot of St. Serge; see Guillot no. 161, pp. 116–117).

---

[1] Chalonnes-sur-Loire; see No. 22, note 2.

No. 61

13 June 1006–2 March 1047.
Notice: BISHOP HUBERT gives to Marmoutier an oratory in the Angevin *pagus* close to the *castrum* Calumnense (Chalonnes-sur-Loire[1]), named in honor of St. Vincent, which was formerly called Monasterium Aiae.

Participant: one: Bishop Hubert.

This information is recalled in a charter of Bishop Eusebius of Angers, who settles a dispute over the oratory between St. Serge and Marmoutier. After the death of Bishop Hubert, certain monks of St. Serge claimed the oratory, beat up and expelled the monk of Marmoutier serving there, stole the relics of St. Vincent in the altar, and leveled the oratory. Marmoutier protested to Bishop Eusebius and to Abbot Vulgrinus of St. Serge. Both of them pronounce judgments in favor of Marmoutier, confirm its possession of the oratory, restore the relics of St. Vincent to the oratory, and Bishop Eusebius adds to the oratory contiguous land with a *rivulus* called Juncariae (les Jonchères[2]), so that a pond and mill might be built.

Participants: four: Bishop Eusebius, Abbot Vulgrinus, and two monks of Marmoutier.

Witnesses: nineteen: Bishop Eusebius, Fulcodius the chaplain, Albericus the priest, Walter his brother, Marcoardus *nepos* of the cantor Girardus, Haimo the cleric, Rodulfus the Burgundian, Adraldus the bishop's *praepositus,* Bernard the *praepositus,* Tedelinus his son, Girardus of Poitou, Hubert his brother, Hubert *pontinarius,* Amalbertus, Tedgerius, Seinfredus the *miles,* Berno the man of Guy, Aimery of Monasterium Aiae, Lawrence.

Manuscripts: A. Original, lost. B. Two near-contemporary copies, Arch. Maine-et-Loire, 45 H 1, nos. 2 and 3. C. Copy of the seventeenth century, B. n., ms. lat. 12878, fol. 96 r–v, after B, no. 2. D. Copy of the seventeenth century, B. n., ms. lat. 12880, fol. 139 r–v, after B, no. 2. E. Copy of the eighteenth century, B. n., D. H. III, no. 814, after B, no. 2. F. Extract of the eighteenth century, B. n., ms. lat. 5441[1], p. 34. G. Copy of the nineteenth century by P. Marchegay, B. n., ms. Fr. nouv. acq., 5021, ch. 7, no. 59, fol. 151 r–152 v, and no. 60, fol. 154 r–156 r, after B.

Editions: P. Marchegay, "Chartes angevines," *Bibliothèque de l'Ecole des chartes* 36 (1875), no. V A, pp. 389–392, after ms. B, no. 2.

Reference: Levron, p. 8.

It is not known when within his episcopate Bishop Hubert made his gift to Marmoutier. Bishop Eusebius's act was after his ordination, but before Vulgrinus became bishop of Le Mans, 6 December 1047–31 July 1056 (see Nos. 14, 18 above).

---

[1] Chalonnes-sur-Loire; see No. 22, note 2.
[2] Les Jonchères, hamlet, commune Angers (Port II, p. 409).

No. 62

13 June 1006–2 March 1047.
Notice: BISHOP HUBERT gives to St. Maurille *vineolae* that he had bought from many different sources.

Participant: one: Bishop Hubert.

This act is mentioned in a notice of Bishop Eusebius of Angers, who sought those vines from St. Serge. Abbot Vulgrinus and the brothers of St. Maurille agree that Eusebius may have all the vines in his villa, but they retain the *decima* for clothing and they shall regain the vines after the bishop's death.

Participants: two are named: Bishop Eusebius and Abbot Vulgrinus, and the brothers of St. Maurille.

Manuscripts: A. Original, lost. B. Copy, first cartulary of St. Serge, no. 34, lost. C. Copy of the sixteenth century, B. n., ms. lat. 5446, p. 247, no. 34. D. Copy of the sixteenth century, Arch. Maine-et-Loire, H 974, no. 12. E. Extract of the seventeenth century, B. n., ms. lat. 17030, p. 47.

Reference: Port, H, p. 132.

For the dating of both Bishop Hubert's act and the agreement between Bishop Eusebius and Abbot Vulgrinus, see No. 61 above.

No. 63

13 June 1006–2 March 1047.
Notice: BISHOP HUBERT gives the altar of the church of Torreia (Thorée[1]) to the monastery of St. Serge.
Participant: one: Bishop Hubert.

This information is provided in an act of Abbot Vulgrinus of St. Serge, which records a settlement with Hamelinus of Corzé and his family concerning this altar. After Bishop Hubert gave the altar to St. Serge, the *miles* Hamelinus obtained the animal pen (*capsus*) of the church of Thorée from his *seniores* and gave it to his vicar Burchardus in exchange for four pounds of denarii.

Then Hamelinus and Abbot Vulgrinus come to another understanding whereby Hamelinus gives to St. Serge one *mansura* of land (as much as four cattle can work with two *sationes*) in the parish of Thorée and half the altar of the same church, which the abbey is to hold in demesne. In return, Hamelinus, his wife Hildeburgis, and his sons Hubert and Giraldus are to have the perpetual *benefactum* of the brothers, and Hamelinus receives four pounds, forty solidi, and Hamelinus and his heirs are to hold that altar in common with the monastery, and in common they will place a priest there; and the archdeacon's part of the *sinodi* and *circadae* will be returned. Hamelinus and his successors will keep his part of the *vicaria* as long as the vicar lives. When he dies, the priest serving that church will receive the *vicaria* free of any payment due from it. If anyone gives anything to that church, Hamelinus and his successors shall have as much of it as the monastery does.

Participants: five are named: Hamelinus, Hildeburgis, Hubert, Giraldus, Vulgrinus; and the monks of St. Serge.

Witnesses: eleven: Bishop Eusebius, Hugh Normannus, Renaud the deacon, Bernaldus the deacon, Peter the deacon, Geoffrey Festuca, Geoffrey the priest, Hamelinus of Corzé and his sons Hubert and Giraldus, and Guy of Chalonnes the brother of Hamelinus.

Manuscripts: A. Original, lost. B. Copy, first cartulary of St. Serge, fol. 26, no. 40, lost. C. Extract of the sixteenth century, B. n., ms. lat. 5446, pp. 248–249, no. 40. D. Copy of the seventeenth century, Arch. Maine-et-Loire, H 1824, no. 1, after B. E. Copy of the nineteenth century by P. Marchegay, Arch. Maine-et-Loire, H 778 bis, I, fol. 285 r–v, after D.
Reference: Port, H, p. 270.

For the dating of both Bishop Hubert's act and the agreement made by Abbot Vulgrinus with Bishop Eusebius as a witness, see No. 61 above.

---

[1] Thorée, canton Lude, arr. la Flèche, dép. Sarthe (Halphen, *Comté d'Anjou*, p. 423).

No. 64

13 June 1006–2 March 1047.

Notice: under BISHOP HUBERT, just as under Bishop Renaud II, the monastery of St. Aubin has the right to hold the altars of several churches in the diocese of Angers; Bishop Eusebius confirms these rights and establishes the returns due him from those altars: owing him a *sinodus* of twelve denarii and a *circada* of three solidi are Bazouges,[1] Bousse,[2] Signé,[3] and Saint-Rémy-la-Varenne[4]; owing a *sinodus* of six denarii and a *circada* of eighteen denarii are Arthezé,[5] Chartrené,[6] Princé,[7] Trèves,[8] Les Alleuds,[9] and Montreuil[10]; Pruniers[11] owes a *sinodus* of six denarii and no *circada;* owing nothing are Saint-Jean de Château-Gontier,[12] la Pélerine,[13] and les Ponts-de-Cé[14]; owing a *sinodus* of twelve denarii and a *circada* of three solidi are le Lion-d'Angers[15] and Gouis[16]; the half altar of Champigné-sur-Sarthe[17] owes six denarii for the *sinodus* and eighteen denarii for the *circada.*

Participant: one is named: Bishop Eusebius.

Witnesses: seventeen: Renaud the dean, Geoffrey the treasurer, Geoffrey the precentor, Marbodus the archdeacon, Durandus Corpus suum, Geoffrey Martini, Anseherius, Odo, Herbert Bonet, Hildebertus, Halego, Lisoius, Geoffrey and Gedeo the sons of Hardreus, Geoffrey the son of Hubert the *monetarius,* Albericus the bishop's chaplain, and Geoffrey son of Girbaudus.

Manuscripts: A. Original, lost. B. Copy, black cartulary of St. Maurice, fol. 35 r, lost. C. Copy of the twelfth century, cartulary of St. Aubin, Bibl. d'Angers, ms. 829 (745), fol. 6 r–v. D. Copy of the seventeenth century, B. n., ms. lat. 17030, pp. 45–46. E. Two copies of the eighteenth century, Bibl. d'Angers, ms. 690 (624), fol. 321 r–v, 324 r–v, after B. F. Copy of the eighteenth century, B. n., ms. lat. 12658, fol. 137 r–v.

Editions: I. *St. Aubin,* no. 19, after C. II. *Cart. noir de la cathédrale,* no. 50, after C and E.

Reference: Hogan no. 38.

It is not known when during Hubert's episcopacy St. Aubin was given or confirmed these specific rights. Bishop Eusebius's chirograph confirming the rights and establishing the returns was in his thirtieth year, which ran 6 December 1076–5 December 1077.

---

[1] Bazouges, canton de Château-Gontier, dép. Mayenne (*St. Aubin* 3, p. 21).

[2] Bousse, canton Milicorne, dép. Sarthe (*St. Aubin* 3, p. 47).

[3] Signé, former name of Coudray-Marcuard, canton Montreuil-Bellay, arr. Saumur (Port I, p. 766).

[4] Saint-Rémy-la-Varenne, canton les Ponts-de-Cé, arr. Angers (Port III, p. 448).

[5] Arthezé, canton de Malicorne, dép. Sarthe (*Cart. noir de la cathédrale,* p. 383).

[6] Chartrené, canton and arr. Baugé (Port I, p. 632).

[7] Pincé, canton Sablé, dép. Sarthe (*Cart. noir de la cathédrale,* p. 477).

[8] Trèves, bourg, commune Trèves-Cunaud (Port III, p. 627).

[9] Les Alleuds, arr. Angers, canton de Thouracé (Port I, p. 12).

[10] Montreuil, Montreuil-Bellay, chef-lieu de canton, arr. Saumur (Port II, p. 719).

[11] Pruniers, bourg, commune Bouchemaine (Port III, p. 196).

[12] Saint-Jean de Château-Gontier, at Château-Gontier, commune, canton and arr., dép. Mayenne (Guillot 2: p. 316).

[13] La Pélerine, canton Noyant, arr. Baugé (Port III, p. 67).

[14] Les Ponts-de-Cé, chef-lieu de canton, arr. Angers (Port III, p. 150).

[15] Le Lion-d'Angers, petite ville, chef-lieu de canton, arr. Segré (Port II, p. 520).

[16] Gouis, bourg, commune Durtal (Port II, p. 281).

[17] Champigné-sur-Sarthe, canton Châteauneuf, arr. Segré (Port I, p. 589).

No. 65

13 June 1006–2 March 1047.

BISHOP HUBERT gives or confirms half the *curtis* and half the church of St.-Rémy-en-Mauges to his niece Emma.

Participants: two: Hubert and Emma.

No separate document for this act exists, but this transaction is referred to in No. 81, where Emma's husband Viscount Radulfus gives these two holdings to St. Serge, and it is specified that he received them from his wife, who held them from the bishops of Angers. Since Emma was Hubert's niece, it is most likely that he first gave her these holdings.

No. 66

13 June 1006–2 March 1047.

BISHOP HUBERT gives or confirms one *quarterium* of a mill called Novum in Marigné to Germanus of Morannes.

Participants: two: Bishop Hubert and Germanus.

No document for this act exists, but it can be inferred from No. 72, where Germanus gives this *quarterium*, along with other goods, to Marmoutier. The mill is "situm de dominico episcopi Andegavensis Huberti casamento scilicet sancti Mauricii ipso presule annuente," so Bishop Hubert must have given or confirmed its possession to Germanus during his episcopate.

No. 67

October 1006–2 March 1047.

BISHOP HUBERT gives or confirms half the church of Villerable to the *miles* Fulcherius, son of Hersendis and Gradulfus.

Participants: two: Bishop Hubert and Fulcherius.

No document for this act exists, but it can be inferred from No. 71, where Fulcherius sells this half-church to Countess Agnes, and it is stated that he held it from Hubert's benefice, and Hubert gave his authorization for that gift. Since Fulcherius was the son of Hubert's cousin Hersendis, sister to Vulgrinus (see above, chap. 2, n. 41), this half-church appears to be a family holding. Bishop Hubert would have acted in this capacity only after the death of his father Viscount Hubert, October 1006 at the earliest (see No. 19), but before his own death on 2 March 1047.

No. 68

20 July 1031–2 March 1047.
Charter: BISHOP HUBERT requests King Henry I to confirm his grants to Marmoutier, namely the altar of Dalmariacensis (Daumeray[1]) in complete freedom, and this is done.

Participants: three are named: Bishop Hubert, King Henry, Abbot Albert, and the monks of Marmoutier.

Manuscripts: A. Original, lost. B. Copy of the eleventh century, Arch. Maine-et-Loire, 40 H 1, no. 3, after A. C. Copy of the seventeenth or eighteenth century by Dom Martène, B. n., ms. lat. 12878, fol. 92. D. Copy of the seventeenth or eighteenth century, B. n., ms. lat. 12880, fol. 26 r–v. E. Copy of the eighteenth century, B. n., D. H. II[1], no. 472, after B. F. Copy of the eighteenth century, B. n., ms. lat. 5441[2], fol. 440 v. G. Copy of the eighteenth century, B. n., coll. Moreau, vol. 21, fol. 235 r, after B. H. Copy of the nineteenth century by P. Marchegay, B. n., ms. Fr. nouv. acq. 5021, fol. 212 r–v, after B.

Edition: *Recueil des historiens de France* XI, p. 650.
References: 1. Bréquigny 2: p. 38. 2. Mabille no. 473. 3. Soehnée no. 42. 4. Levron, p. 7.

This act was after Henry's accession to the throne, but before Bishop Hubert's death.

---

[1] Daumeray, canton Durtal, arr. Baugé (Port II, p. 10).

No. 69

20 July 1031–2 March 1047.
King Henry confirms the gifts of BISHOP HUBERT to the cathedral of St.-Maurice d'Angers.
Participants: two: King Henry and Bishop Hubert.

Reference: Fanning, "Acts of Henry I of France Concerning Anjou," p. 112.

This act is known only from fragments, the longest of which is in the *Response du chapitre de l'église d'Angers* (Paris, 1626), p. 8; see the discussion in Fanning, "Acts of Henry I," p. 112. For the dating, see No. 68 above.

No. 70

20 July 1031–2 March 1047.
King Henry confirms BISHOP HUBERT'S gifts to St. Serge at Chalonnes-sur-Loire.[1]

Participants: two: King Henry and Bishop Hubert.

Reference: Fanning, "Acts of Henry I of France Concerning Anjou," p. 113.

This act is known only in a fourteenth-century notice added to the second cartulary of St. Serge, Musée Dobrée, Nantes, ms. 3, fol. 131 v; see the discussion in Fanning, "Acts of Henry I," p. 113. For the dating, see No. 68 above.

---

[1] Chalonnes-sur-Loire; see No. 22, note 2.

No. 71

1 January 1032–2 March 1047.

Notice: BISHOP HUBERT gives his authorization for the *miles* Fulcherius to sell half the church at Villerable[1] to Countess Agnes, for twenty denarii; Fulcherius holds the church in *beneficium* from BISHOP HUBERT. Also giving their authorization for this sale are Fulcherius's mother Hersendis and his brothers Peter and Guy.

Participants: seven: Bishop Hubert, Fulcherius, Countess Agnes, Fulcherius's parents Hersendis and Gradulfus, and his brothers Peter and Guy.

This is the first part of a much longer notice. In Part II, Countess Agnes gives the half church of Villerable to the newly built monastery of Trinité de Vendôme.

Participant: one: Countess Agnes.

Witnesses: twenty-eight: Count Geoffrey Martel, Countess Agnes, William, duke of Aquitaine, Viscount Fulk, Hugh Mange-Breton, Geoffrey Fortis, Adhelbertus the Gascon, Geoffrey Cato, Robert the nephew of the countess, Tetbaldus of Montlhéry, Joscelin of la Ferté, Count Guy-Geoffrey, the son of Countess Agnes, Guiscelinus, Odo *secretarius,* Geraldus the abbot of St. Pontius, Herbert Ratorius, Macfridus de Vitroni, Raherius of Lury, Geoffrey the *prepositus,* Hilduinus the *prepositus;* from Vendôme: Joscelin the Bastard, his son Fulcradus, Arnaldus the priest, Alcherus, Robert the *cementarius,* Arduinus the *cementarius,* Constantius, Hubert.

Manuscripts: A. Original, lost. B. Copy of the eleventh century, cartulary of Trinité de Vendôme, B. n., n. a. lat. 1935, fol. 21 r–v, no. 61. C. Extract of the seventeenth century, B. n., ms. lat. 12700, fol. 272. D. Copy of the seventeenth century, B. n., coll. Baluze, vol. 47, fol. 241 r–v. E. Extract of the seventeenth century, B. n., n. a. fr. 7433, fol. 126 v, after B. F. Copy of the eighteenth century, B. n., D. H. II[1], no. 500.

Edition: *Cart. de la Trinité de Vendôme,* no. 69.

References: 1. Halphen no. 87 (Part II). 2. Guillot no. 102.

Countess Agnes could have purchased the half-church only after 1 January 1032, when she became Geoffrey Martel's wife (*Annales de Saint-*

Serge, p. 107), but it was done before Bishop Hubert's death. Her subsequent gift of the church must have been after 31 May 1040, for Villerable does not appear among the possessions of Trinité de Vendôme that are listed in the foundation charter issued on that day (*Cart. Trinité de Vendôme* I, no. 35). There is no evidence that it was in the abbey's possession by the time of Bishop Hubert's death (cp. Guillot no. 102), but it was named in a bull of Pope Clement II of 27 June 1047 (*Cart. Trinité de Vendôme* I, no. 76), which provides the *terminus ad quem* for Agnes's gift.

----

[1] Villerable, comm. of canton Vendôme, dép. Loir-et-Cher (*Cart. de la Trinité de Vendôme* 5, p. 382).

No. 72

Ca. 1032–2 March 1047.

Notice: BISHOP HUBERT agrees to the gift of one *quarterium* of a mill called Novum in Marigniacus (Marigné[1]), which is from the demesne holding of Bishop Hubert, to Marmoutier by Germanus of Morannes; the *quarterium* returns a *census* of three *obola* on the feast of St. Aubin. Other goods are given by Germanus for the purpose of providing for the care of his children, who are commended to Marmoutier, with part of his goods. While he lives, he shall support his children. But when he should die, the boys will remain at Marmoutier until they shall reach a mature and understanding age. If they wish to remain at Marmoutier, they may, but if they should not wish it, they may depart with the goods given by their father. But they may not give, sell, or exchange the goods, which are to return to Marmoutier after the boys' deaths. In addition to the *quarterium* of the mill at Marigné, Germanus gives Marmoutier a mill in the villa Brissarthe[2] and one *quarterium* of land from the *fevum* of Geoffrey Festuca, the son of Archenulfus, who gives his authorization for the gift; the half-mill returns a *census* of six denarii on the feast of St. Aubin and the *quarterium* a *census* of one denarius. Germanus also gives one house in the villa Morannes[3] located in the *areae* of Robert Negrigrunnus, the father of Arnaldus, which Arnaldus himself had sold to Germanus; the house returns a *census* of four denarii, on the feast of St. Aubin. Germanus stipulates that if he should have children by another wife, these gifts shall remain Marmoutier's.

Participants: four: Germanus, Abbot Albert of Marmoutier, Geoffrey Festuca and Bishop Hubert.

Witness: one is named: Germanus's new wife; and his brothers and "multis aliis."

Manuscripts: A. Original, lost. B. Copy of the eleventh century, Arch. Maine-et-Loire, G 785, no. 1, after A. C. Copy of the seventeenth century, B. n., ms. lat. 12878, fol. 95 v.

Reference: Port, G, p. 114.

This act falls between the appointment of Albert as abbot of Marmoutier, ca. 1032, and the death of Bishop Hubert.

---

[1] Marigné, canton Châteauneuf-sur-Sarthe, arr. Segré (Port II, p. 595).
[2] Brissarthe, canton Châteauneuf-sur-Sarthe, arr. Segré (Port I, p. 513).
[3] Morannes; see No. 10, note 4.

No. 73

Ca. 1032–2 March 1047.
Notice: BISHOP HUBERT witnesses the confirmation made by Fulcherius, son of the *miles* Hugh and Adila, of his parents' gifts to Marmoutier, which were benefices, lands, churches, and alods.

Participant: one: Fulcherius.

Witnesses: ten: Fulcherius himself, Bishop Hubert, Radulfus the brother of Otgerius de Viariis, Viscount Radulfus of Vendôme, Hubert the son of Frodo, Herbert Barba, Guarinus the cleric, Algerius the cleric of Morannes, Renaud the son of Burchardus Gena, Hildebertus the cook.

Manuscripts: A. Original, lost. B. Copy of the twelfth century, Vendôme cartulary of Marmoutier, B. n., ms. lat. 5442, fol. 21 r, no. 100.

Edition: *Cart. Marmoutier pour le Vendômois*, no. 100.

The cook Hildebertus who subscribed this act was also a witness to many other acts in the Marmoutier cartularies, and all of those that can be dated with any precision can be assigned to the period of the abbotship of Albert, beginning ca. 1032 (see *Cart. Marmoutier pour le Vendômois*, nos. 65, 98, 117, 125, 16 A). The *terminus ad quem* is Bishop Hubert's death.

No. 74

Ca. 1032–2 March 1047.
Charter: BISHOP HUBERT witnesses gifts made to Marmoutier by Salomon of Lavardin and his wife Adela, with the consent of their daughters Mathilda and Avelina. The gifts are: land above the Loir that they bought from the canons of St. George; a church built there in honor of St. Gelricus the confessor, to which also pertained two ovens and one *mansura* of land in the villa Fargot[1]; in the land of Saint-Genès,[2] land of one and a half *modia* of seed, three arpents of vines, two arpents of meadows above the Breia (la Braye[3]). They also concede to Marmoutier whatever his men, whether *milites, burgenses, servi,* or *ingenui* gave or sold them, both from his *fevum* and outside it. In the lands given by Salomon and his family, the monks are to have all customs and *forifacturae.*

Participants: four are named: Salomon, Adela, Mathilda, and Avelina; and the monks of Marmoutier.

Witnesses: twenty-seven: Bishop Hubert, Salomon, Adela, Mathilda, Avelina, Roger the son-in-law of Salomon and Adela, Fulcherius the Rich, Vulgrinus, Renaud the seneschal, Drogo the son of Francherius, Geoffrey the son of Hilgodus, Hugh Burellus, Raherius of Bouloire, Warinus, Vivianus, William, Winebertus, Roger, Fulbert de Rupe, Waldricus, Ildibertus Vigerius, Arnulfus Prefelinus, Teodericus Claudus; from Marmoutier: Abbot Albert, Walter the monk, Ildebertus the monk, William the monk.

Manuscripts: A. Original, lost. B. Copy of the seventeenth century, B. n., ms. lat. 12878, fol. 111 r–v. C. Copy of the seventeenth century, B. n., ms. lat. 12880, fol. 250 r–v. D. Copy of the seventeenth century, B. n., coll. Duchesne, vol. 22, fol. 303 r–v.

Editions: I. *Marmoutier, cart. blésois*, no. 8. II. *Cart. Marmoutier pour le Vendômois*, no. 11 A.

The *termini* are the abbotship of Albert and the death of Bishop Hubert.

---

[1] Fargot, former fief and château, commune Montoire, dép. Loir-et-Cher (*Cart. Marmoutier pour le Vendômois*, p. 288 n. 1).

[2] Saint-Genès, at Lavardin [commune, canton Montoire, arr. Vendôme, dép. Loir-et-Cher] (Guillot 2: p. 331; and *Cart. Marmoutier pour le Vendômois*, p. 288 n. 2).

[3] Le Braye, stream, dép. Loir-et-Cher (*Marmoutier. cart. blésois*, p. 517).

No. 75

24 August 1044–2 March 1047.

Notice: BISHOP HUBERT witnesses the gift to Marmoutier of the alod of Rigny,[1] made by the *miles* Rainardus, nephew of Girardus of Rigny; the monastery receives half of the customs now and will receive the other half after his death. The gift includes one *carruga* of land in every possession and five arpents of meadows.

Participant: one: Rainardus.

Witnesses: twelve: Bishop Hubert, Herbert the chaplain of Rainardus, Fulbert the son of Walter Bonevenit, Germanus the *serviens* of Rainardus, Otbertus de Camera, Ernulfus the cook, Richard *major*, Renaud *major*, Otbertus *cellararius*, Joscelin *mariscalcus*, Geoffrey the cook, Frotmundus the priest.

Manuscripts: A. Original, lost. B. Copy of the twelfth century, Vendôme cartulary of Marmoutier, B. n., ms. lat. 5442, fol. 30 r, no. 123. C. Copy of the seventeenth century, B. n., ms. lat. 12878, fol. 115 v. D. Extract of the seventeenth century, B. n., ms. fr. nouv. acq. 7433, fol. 99 r.

Edition: *Cart. Marmoutier pour le Vendômois*, no. 123.

The two Otberti who witness this act provide the *terminus a quo*. Before they became the chamberlain and cellarer of Marmoutier, as they are in this act, they seem to have been called Otbertus *senior* and Otbertus *junior*, and the earlier cellarer was Ansegius. These three appear together in sixteen charters of *Livre des serfs de Marmoutier*, and they appear in eleven acts of the same cartulary with Richard *major*, who also is a witness to this act. Never do the Otberti *senior* and *junior* appear in the same acts with the

Otberti who are called chamberlain and cellarer. Thus Otbertus *senior* and Otbertus *junior* seem to have been promoted to the posts of chamberlain and cellarer, as they are designated in this act.

These two Otberti are still called *senior* and *junior* as late as 24 August 1044 (J. Boussard, "L'éviction des tenants de Thibaud de Blois," in *Moyen Age*, 1963, p. 148; Guillot no. 134), so this act must have taken place after that date, but before the death of Bishop Hubert.

---

[1] Rigny, near St.-Amand, dép. Loir-et-Cher (*Cart. Marmoutier pour le Vendômois*, p. 206).

No. 76

24 August 1044–2 March 1047.

Notice: BISHOP HUBERT witnesses the settlement of differences between the canons of St. John and St. Licinius of Angers (Saint-Lézin, or Saint-Jean-Baptiste d'Angers), and Eudo of Blaison at a *placitum* of Count Geoffrey Martel. Earlier Count Geoffrey Greymantle had given the office of *prepositus,* half the *decima,* and six of eighteen prebends to Cadilo of Blaison. After Cadilo's death, his son Tetbaldus infringed on the remaining rights of the canons, but then promised to act properly towards them, which he failed to do. This continued under his son Tetbaldus, and the canons gave him another three prebends, but the abuse persisted under him and his son Eudo after his death. Now, at the complaint of the canons, Count Geoffrey Martel reconciles Eudo and the canons.

Participants: two are named: Count Geoffrey and Eudo; and the canons of St. Jean and St. Lézin.

Witnesses: fourteen are named: Count Geoffrey, Bishop Hubert, Count H(ugh) of Maine and Viscount R(adulfus) of Le Mans, G(eoffrey) the dean of St. Martin, Odricus of Champtoceaux, Albericus of Montjean, Adelardus son of Renaud (probably of Château-Gontier), Salomon of Lavardin, Hugh son of Geldinus, John of Chinon, Alo of Loudun, Arduinus of Maillé, Joscelin of Ste.-Maur; and "C alii nobiles viri quos taedium est nominare."

Manuscripts: A. Original, lost. B. Copy of an old register in parchment containing the life of St. Lézin, lost. C. Copy of the eighteenth century, B. n., D. H. II², no. 594, after B. D. Copy of the eighteenth century, Bibl. d'Angers, ms. 690 (624), fol. 312 r–v.

Edition: Ledru, *Hist. maison de Maillé* 2: no. 4, p. 5.

References: 1. Halphen no. 88. 2. Guillot no. 104.

For the dating, see Guillot no. 104.

No. 77

1 March 1046–2 March 1047.

Charter: BISHOP HUBERT, belatedly taking care for the salvation of his soul, having been brought to this point by bodily infirmities, extends a little charity towards the monastery of St. Serge, which both he and his predecessor Bishop Renaud raised up to the rule of monks, and gives to Abbot Vulgrinus and the monks the *vicariae* and all the customs that he holds in their lands; he also abandons the customs over the little cell of St. Maurille (at Chalonnes-sur-Loire[1]), but should they alienate it, the customs shall return to him.

Participants: two are named: Bishop Hubert, Abbot Vulgrinus, and the monks of St. Serge.

Witnesses: twenty-three: Bishop Hubert, Renaud *grammaticus*, Gerardus the cantor, Landricus the canon, Guy the son of Gradulfus, Albericus the *nepos* of the bishop, Hubert Borellus, Segebrandus son of Ogerius, Eudo son of Otbrannus, Algerius the seneschal, Hubert the butler, Frederick the seneschal, Mainardus the *marischalcus*, Gehardus, Manselinus the canon, Tescelinus son of Bernard, Ingelbaldus the *prepositus*, Rannulfus the *miles*, Peter the canon, Raimbaldus the chamberlain, Isenardus the chamberlain, Warinus the chamberlain, Lambert the cook.

Manuscripts: A. Original, lost. B. Copy, first cartulary of St. Serge, no. 20, lost. C. Copy of the sixteenth century, Arch. Maine-et-Loire, H 974, no. 7 (partial). D. Copy of the seventeenth century, B. n., ms. lat. 5446, fol. 241 v, no. 20. E. Extract of the seventeenth century, B. n., ms. lat. 17030, p. 33. F. Copy of the eighteenth century, Bibl. d'Angers, ms. 706 (636), pp. 161–162. G. Copy of the eighteenth century, B. n., coll. Moreau, vol. 20, fol. 76 r–78r, after F. H. Copy of the eighteenth century, B. n., D. H. II[1], no. 494. I. Copy of the nineteenth century by P. Marchegay, Arch. Maine-et-Loire, H 778 bis I, fol. 170 r–v, after C.

References: 1. Fourteenth-century insertion in the second cartulary of St. Serge, Musée Dobrée, Nantes, ms. 3, fol. 131 v. 2. Seventeenth-century references, Bibl. d'Angers, ms. 689 (623), p. 280. 3. Thorode, *Notice de la ville d'Angers*, p. 233. 4. Marchegay, Arch. Maine-et-Loire, H 778 bis II, fol. 301 v. 5. Port, H, p. 132. 6. Durville, p. 207. 7. Hogan no. 33.

This charter must fall between 1 March 1046, when Vulgrinus was installed as abbot of St. Serge (see No. 53), and 2 March 1047, the death of Bishop Hubert.

Durville (reference no. 6) mistakes reference no. 1 for an allusion to a confirmation of a charter of Bishop Renaud made by Bishop Hubert.

---

[1] Chalonnes-sur-Loire; see No. 22, note 2.

No. 78

1 March 1046–2 March 1047.
Charter: BISHOP HUBERT, having little to give to the monastery of St. Serge, concedes that whatever is given to it or to the cell at Calomna (Chalonnes-sur-Loire[1]), whether lands, houses, vines, or waters, may be done freely, and whatever custom or revenue of any kind pertaining to

those grants and belonging to the episcopal right will be held by St. Serge as long as the monks do not alienate such revenues or customs; in case of such an alienation, made for any reason, the customs shall revert to the episcopal right.

Participant: one: Bishop Hubert.

Witnesses: eleven are named: Bishop Hubert, Abbot Vulgrinus of St. Serge, Ingelbaldus the *prepositus*, the monk Andrew, Algerius the seneschal, Renaud *grammaticus*, Warinus the chamberlain, Gerardus the cantor, Jovinus *venator*, Hubert Borellus, Eudo son of Otbrannus, Gebardus; "et cetera."

Manuscripts: A. Original, lost. B. Copy, first cartulary of St. Serge, lost. C. Copy of the sixteenth century, Arch. Maine-et-Loire, H 974, no. 1. D. Copy of the nineteenth century by P. Marchegay, Arch. Maine-et-Loire, H 778 bis I, fol. 172 r–v, after C.

Reference: Port, H, p. 132.

For the dating, see No. 77.

---

[1] Chalonnes-sur-Loire; see No. 22, note 2.

No. 79

Ca. 2 March 1047.

Notice: BISHOP HUBERT, at the time of his death, gives to Marmoutier and Abbot Albert two small pieces of land, one at Palesus above the river Layon, between the land of Hubert de Porta and the *juratum* of Joscelin the son of the *prepositus;* the other is at Radiolaria next to the land of the cleric Geoffrey; this land is at Calumna (Chalonnes-sur-Loire[1]) and is free of the *census* and every other custom. Ingelbaldus the *prepositus* and Ingelbertus *major* manage the transaction for Bishop Hubert, and the gift is received by Abbot Vulgrinus of St. Serge and Inisianus *medicus*.

Participants: six: Bishop Hubert, Abbot Albert, Ingelbaldus and Ingelbertus, Abbot Vulgrinus, and Inisianus.

Witnesses: eight: Renaud the seneschal, Hubert the butler, Bernard the *prepositus*, Peter *venator*, Algerius the seneschal, Guy the son of Gradulfus, Walter the man of St. Martin, Stephen Bella Barba the man of St. Martin.

Manuscripts: A. Original, lost. B. Copy of the eleventh century, Arch. Maine-et-Loire, 45 H 1, no. 1. C. Copy of the seventeenth century, B. n., ms. lat. 12878, fol. 100 r. D. Copy of the eighteenth century, B. n., D. H. II[1], no. 496 (partial). E. Copy of the nineteenth century by P. Marchegay, B. n., ms. Fr. nouv. acq. 5021, fol. 150 r, no. 58.

References: 1. Mabille no. 496. 2. Levron, p. 8.

The grant was made very near Hubert's death, "vita decessurus," on 2 March 1047.

---

[1] Chalonnes-sur-Loire; see No. 22, note 2.

No. 80

Ca. 2 March 1047.
Notice: BISHOP HUBERT, at the time of his death, returns to St. Serge (where he ordered his body to be buried) a canonical prebend of the cathedral of St. Maurice, which BISHOP HUBERT had given to the monks before but later had be taken from the monastery.

Participant: one: Bishop Hubert.

This information is included in the notice of the confirmation of this grant by Count Geoffrey Martel ("in cuius provisione vel substitutione pontificis ecclesia remanebat") and by the future bishop (Eusebius Bruno). The confirmation was after Hubert's death, but before 6 December 1047, the ordination of Bishop Eusebius.

Manuscripts: A. Near contemporary redaction, Bibl. d'Angers, ms. 5–6 (3), fol. 277 v. B. Copy, first cartulary of St. Serge, fol. 45, lost. C. Three copies of the seventeenth century, B. n., ms. lat. 12696, fol. 289 r–v, 290 r–v, 306 r–v. D. Copy of the seventeenth century, B. n., ms. lat. 12878, fol. 199 r. E. Copy of the nineteenth century by P. Marchegay, Arch. Maine-et-Loire, H 778 bis I, fol. 45 r, after A.

Edition: Martène and Durand, *Thesaurus Novus Anecdotorum* I, cols. 168–169.

References: 1. Bréquigny 2: p. 40. 2. BPF, p. 192.

This confirmation by Count Geoffrey Martel and Bishop Eusebius does not appear in Guillot's catalogue.

No. 81

3 March 1047.
BISHOP HUBERT was buried in the monastery of St. Serge on 3 March 1047, with Bishop Gervais of Le Mans, Abbot Frederick of St. Florent, Abbot Vulgrinus of St. Serge, and a large crowd of abbots, monks, clerics, and other people present.

This information is included in the first part of a notice recalling that Viscountess Emma of Le Mans, the niece of Bishop Hubert, died on 12 September 1058 and was also buried in the monastery of St. Serge, as were her parents Stephen and Adeberga.[1]

In the second part of the notice, for the funeral rites of Emma, her husband Viscount Radulfus of Le Mans, with the authority of Bishop Eusebius of Angers, gives to St. Serge half the *curtis* of St. Remigius in the *pagus* Metallicus (Saint-Rémy-en-Mauges[2]). This grant is actually a return because long before Bishop Renaud of Angers had left St. Serge the remainder of his alods in the region Metallica (the Mauges) and in the *pagus* of Poitou, but Count Fulk Nerra had taken them away by violence when he built the *castellum* of Mons Rebellis (Montrevault[3]) and gave everything to his *milites* in *beneficium*. Viscount Radulfus received Saint-Rémy-en-Mauges through his wife, who held it from the bishops of Angers, and he gave it to St. Serge so that the *milites* there might retain their lands *beneficialiter* from the monastery and would have the freedom to return the lands to St. Serge.

Radulfus also gives St. Serge half the land that the *villanus* works both inside and outside of the forest, and half the chapel next to the forest, and in the suburb of Montrevault he gives the *suburbanus* Hilgodus with all his custom and his successors, and he gives two arpents of vines next to Angers and one *mansio* in Angers's suburb.

Participants: two: Viscount Radulfus and Bishop Eusebius.

Witnesses: sixteen: Abbot Teodericus of St. Aubin, Viscount Radulfus, Adalardus of Château-Gontier, Tescelinus of Montrevault, Girardus the seneschal, Sewinus *nepos* of Marcoardus, Radulfus Grandis, Radulfus Patraster, Bishop Eusebius, Landricus the archdeacon, Mansellus the chaplain, Renaud the seneschal, Algerius of Morannes, Girardus Manens, Adam des Vaux, Warinus the vicar.

Manuscripts: A. Original, Arch. Maine-et-Loire, H 1242. B. Copy in the first cartulary of St. Serge, no. 67, after A, lost. C. Copy of the twelfth century, second cartulary of St. Serge, Nantes, Musée Dobrée, ms. 3, fol. 137 r–v, no. 314. D. Copy of the seventeenth century for Gaignières, B. n., ms. lat. 5446, p. 254, no. 67, after B. E. Extract of the seventeenth century, B. n., ms. lat. 17030, p. 41. F. Copy of the eighteenth century, B. n., D. H. II², no. 582, after C. G. Copy of the eighteenth century, Bibl. d'Angers, ms. 706 (636), pp. 8–10. H. Copy of the nineteenth century by P. Marchegay, B. n., ms. Fr. nouv. acq. 5021, no. 67, after B. I. Copy of the nineteenth century by P. Marchegay, Arch. Maine-et-Loire, H 778 bis II, fol. 314 r–v, after C.

Editions: I. Martène and Durand, *Thesaurus Novus Anecdotorum* I, cols. 184–186. II. Robert Latouche, "Les premiers vicomtes du Maine," pp. 87–8, after A. III. J. Boussard, "Les évêques en Neustrie," p. a. no. 2, pp. 195–196, after A, C, D, and E.

References: 1. Bréquigny 2: p. 67. 2. Port, H, p. 167. 3. Angot nos. 35, 36. 4. Durville no. 314, p. 142. 5. Hogan no. 34.

Viscount Radulfus's grants were made as alms for his wife's funeral, and she died 12 September 1058. The grants would have been made shortly afterwards.

---

[1] Boussard (edition no. III) incorrectly gives her name as Adalberga, but manuscript A has this form.

[2] Saint-Rémy-en Mauges, canton Montrevault, arr. Cholet (Port III, p. 447).

[3] Montrevault, chef-lieu of canton, arr. Cholet (Port II, p. 727).

INDEX OF CUSTOMS IN DOCUMENTS IN PART II

(The numbers refer to the entries in Part II)

INDEX OF ECCLESIASTICAL RIGHTS

INDEX OF ECCLESIASTICAL ESTABLISHMENTS IN DOCUMENTS IN PART II

(The numbers refer to the entries in Part II)

Saint-Aubin, Angers: 2, 11, 13, 25, 28, 48, 64.
Saint-Florent, Saumur: 6, 31, 39, 40.
Saint-Jean-Baptiste, Angers: 76.
Saint-Lézin, Angers: 2, 76.
Saint-Maur-sur-Loire, Glanfeuil: 25.
Saint-Maur-des-Fossés, dép. Seine: 25.
Saint-Maurille, Chalonnes-sur-Loire: 22, 48, 53, 60, 62, 77.
Saint-Nicolas, Angers: 5, 8, 17, 24, 32, 35, 49, 50, 51.
Saint-Pierre, Couture: 3, 4.
Saint-Serge, Angers: 23, 44, 46, 53, 59, 60, 61, 62, 63, 70, 77, 78, 80, 81.
Trinité de Vendôme: 1, 36, 37, 56, 71.
Oratory of Toussaint, Angers: 54, 56, 57, 58.

INDEX OF PERSONAL NAMES IN DOCUMENTS IN PART II

(The numbers refer to the entry numbers in Part II):

Arnaldus: abbot of St.-Jean-d'Angély, 36, 37; bishop of Le Mans, 4.III; priest, 71.II.

Arnulfus: archbishop of Tours, 12, 21, 36, 37, 38, 40; archdeacon and precentor of Chartres, 36, 37; Bulgerius, 50.III; dean of Poitiers, 36, 37; monk of St. Aubin, 25; prefelinus, 74.

Ascelinus: 27; monk of St. Aubin, 25.

Auramus: monk, 31 (9).

Avelina: daughter of Salomon of Lavardin, 74.

Avesgaudus: bishop of Le Mans, 3, 4, 12, 28, 38.

Azo: abbot of St.-Michel-en-l'Herme, 36, 37.

Babinus: son of Judiquel, 13.II.

Baldwin: son of the treasurer Guy, 13.

Barnard: monk of St. Aubin, 25.

Bartholomew: of Angers, 50.II; archbishop of Tours, 31 (8–9); *miles*, 42; the shield-bearer, 41.

Basilia: 15.

Baudricus: abbot of St. Nicholas of Angers, 8.

Berengar: 27; archdeacon, 36, 37; *grammaticus*, 31 (9); *miles*, 42; monk of St. Aubin, 25; treasurer, 14.II, 18, 52, 53.

Berengisius: 2.IV.

Berlaius: 37.

Bernaldus: canon, 53; deacon, 63.II.

Bernard: 29; of Chantocé, 49, 50, 51; cleric, 28; deacon, 60.II; monk of St. Aubin, 28; *prepositus*, 79; *praepositus*, father of Tedelinus, 61.II; *servus*, 15.

Bernegarius: *prepositus*, 31 (9).

Bernerius: canon of St. Maurice, 34.II; *cellararius* of St. Aubin, 13.II; *levita* and school master, 10; *secretarius* of St. Aubin, 13.II; subdeacon, 60.II.

Berno: man of Guy, 61.II.

Bertarda: abbess of Ronceray: 20.I.

Bertrada: queen, wife of Philip I, 50.II.

Boso: monk of St. Aubin, 2.IV, 25.

Bovo: dean of Tours, 36, 37.

Breverius: monk, 4.

Briencius: Sacegai, 50.II, 51.

Burchardus, Burcardus: archdeacon, 10; *servus*, 15; son of Geoffrey of Sablé, 4; treasurer, 15, 16, 30, 36, 37, 42, 43, 44, 49, 50, 51; vicar, 63.II.

Cadilo: of Blaison, 76.

Christiana: daughter of Aremburgis, 20.II; wife of Walter Nafragallus, 29.

Christianus: 29.II; of Epinard, 17.

Christopher: miller, 41.

Clement: monk of St. Aubin, 25.

Clerembaldus: 34.II.

Constantine: of Melle, 37.

Constantius: 71.II.

Corbinus: de Zalla, 50.II, 51.

Dagobinus: 17.

Daniel: monk of St. Aubin, 25.

Delia: sacristan of Ronceray, 17.

Detbertus: monk and scribe, 31 (9).

Dionysius: priest, 41.

Drogo, Droco: de Boscat, 20.II; *serviens*, 18; son of Francherius, 74; son of Geoffrey of Sablé, 3, 4; *stabulus* of Ronceray, 14.II.

Durandus: abbot of St.-Gildas-des-Bois, 36, 37; Corpus Suum, 64; Cor Sancto, 17; monk of St. Aubin, 25; monk of St. Florent, 31 (9); monk of St. Serge, scribe, 60, II; *prepositus* of Saumur, 31 (9).

Ebo: canon of St. Laud, 4.II.

Ebrardus: abbot of St. Calais, 36, 37.

Ebulo: of Champchévrier, 39.

Emerio: subdeacon, 60.II.

Emma, Emelina: mother of Bishop Hubert, 10, 23, 52; niece of Bishop Hubert, 20, 52, 65, 81.II.

Engelardus: 17; monk of St. Aubin, 25.

Engelbodus: monk of St. Aubin, 25.

Erbaldus: bishop, 4.II.

Erfredus: viscount, 37.
Ermendardus: *servus*, 15.
Ermenfredus: monk of St. Aubin, 25.
Ermenredus: monk of St. Aubin, 25.
Ermentus: abbot of Tuffé, 36, 37.
Ermenulfus: *scolasticus* of Le Mans, 36, 37.
Ernaldus: monk of St. Aubin, 25.
Ernulfus: 7.
Eudo: of Blaison, father of Tetbaldus, 76; of Blaison, son of Tetbaldus, 76; Blanchardus, 17; son of Otbrannus, 77, 78.
Eusebius: bishop of Angers, 13.II, 14.II, 17 (1), 20.II, 31 (7), 48.II, 56.II, 60.II, 61.II, 62.II, 64, 80.II, 81.II; priest, 41.
Euvradus: Crispus, 20.II.
Evraudus, Evrardus: abbot of Marmoutier, 6, 21.
Firminus: brother of Warner the cook, 20.II.
Fredaldus: of St. Florent, 31 (9).
Fredeburgis: *ancilla*, 15.
Frederick: abbot of St. Florent, 6, 26, 36, 37, 39, 40, 81; monk, 4; seneschal, 77.
Frogerius, Frotgerius: *pontenarius*, 17; prior, 4; subdean of St. Martin, 36, 37.
Fromundus, Frotmundus: 15, 39; abbot of St.-Amand-de-Boixe, 31 (9); *famulus* of St. Aubin, 28; monk of St. Aubin, 2.IV, 25; priest, 75.
Frotgerius, see Frogerius.
Frotmundus, see Fromundus.
Fulbert: bishop of Chartres, 12; *monetarius*, 17; de Rupe, 74; son of Walter Bonevenit, 75.
Fulcherius: the Rich, 74; scribe, 21; son of Hersendis and Gradulfus, 67, 71 (*miles*); son of Hildeiardis, 7; son of Hugh and Adila, 73.
Fulcradus: *caballarius*, 27; son of Joscelin the Bastard, 71.II.
Fulcoinus: Godueth, 17.
Fulcoius, Fulcodius: brother of Renaud of Orgigné, 17; chaplain, 18, 36, 37, 53, 61.II; monk of St. Nicholas, 50.I; priest, 10.
Fulk: abbot of St. John, 36, 37; chaplain, 4.II; de Boeria, 4.II; Nerra, count of Anjou, 1, 2.III, 5, 7, 8, 11, 12, 13, 15, 16, 23, 24, 25, 27, 28, 29, 30, 31, 33, 34, 35, 39, 42, 43, 44, 49, 50, 51, 81.II; l'Oison, count of Vendôme, 20.II; Réchin, count of Anjou, 4.II, 13.II, 17 (1), 31 (8–9), 50.II, 57; viscount, 71.II; the Young, count of Anjou, 34.II, 57.
Gaius: *pistor*, 17.
Garnerius (see also Guarnerius, Warner): 17; *cellerarius*, 17; monk, 3.
Gaudebertus: cleric, 4.III.
Gausbertus: deacon, 22; monk, 31 (9); monk of St. Aubin, 25.
Gauterius (see also Walter): *miles*, 3.II.
Gavanus: of les Ulmes, 41.
Gebardus: 78.
Gedeo: son of Hardreus, 64.
Gehardus: 77.
Gelduinus, Gilduinus: 21; archbishop of Sens, 12; monk of St. Aubin, 25.
Genzon: monk of St. Aubin.
Geoffrey: 17, 57.II; abbot of Trinité de Vendôme, 56.V, 56.VI; the Bearded, count of Anjou, 4.II, 31 (7–9); brother of Alan de Meldon, 50.II, 51; brother of Odo, 59; cantor, 17; Cato, 71.II; cleric, 79; cook of Marmoutier, 75; count of Poitou (see also Guy-Geoffrey), 50, 51; Crassis, 4.II; deacon, 60.II; dean of St. Martin, 36, 37, 38, 49, 50, 76; *famulus* of St. Aubin, 28; Festuca, 63.II, 72 (son of Archenulfus); Fortis (see also Geoffrey of Treive), 26 (of Treive), 71.II; Garnerius, 57.II; Girbaudi, canon of St. Maurice, 34.II; Greymantle, count of Anjou, 2.II, 76; Guarinus, 57.II; *juvenis*, brother of Malramnus, 1; man of Rainardus, 27; Martel, count of Anjou, 1, 11. 13, 13.II, 14.II, 15, 20.II, 26, 27, 28, 31, 36, 37, 38, 39, 40, 42, 43, 44, 49, 50, 51, 53, 57, 58, 71.II, 76, 80.II; Martini, 64; of Nantes, monk of St. Nicholas, 50.II; de Pliaco, 4.II; of Preuilly, 37, 42, 49, 50, 51; precentor 64; *prepositus*, 71.II; priest, 63.II; *puer*, 36, 37; of Ramefort, 57.II; Ridel, 50.III; Rotundellus, 13.II; of Sablé, 3, 4; son of Girbaudus, 64; son of Hardreus, 64; son of Hilgodus, 74; son of Hubert *monetarius*, 64; son of Liziardus, 3.II, 4, 4.III; son of Odo, 13.II; son of Roger, 46; subdeacon, 60.II; treasurer, 64; of Treive (see also Geoffrey Fortis), 34.II; the Younger, count of Anjou, 13.II; the younger, of Châteaubriant, 50.II, 51; the younger, of Mayenne, *miles*, 50.II, 51.
George: archdeacon of Chartres, 36, 37.

Liziardus: son of Geoffrey of Sablé, 4.
Macfridus: de Vitroni, 71.II.
Mafredus: monk of St. Aubin, 25.
Mainardus: *marischalcus*, 77; monk of St. Aubin, 2.IV, 25; vicar of Doué, 39.
Mainerius: 17, 39; *magister*, 57.II.
Manasses: brother of the bishop, 37.
Manselinus: canon, 77; cleric of Le Mans, 36, 37.
Mansellus: chaplain, 81.II.
Marbodus: archdeacon, 17, 64; canon of St. Maurice, 34.II.
Marchoardus, Marcoardus: cleric, 28; man of Viscount Radulfus, 52; *nepos* of the cantor Girardus, 61.II.
Marcuinus: canon, 53; *levita*, 42.
Martin: 17; priest, 60.II; son of Ingellundus the cleric, 4.II.
Mathilda: daughter of Salomon of Lavardin and Adila, 74.
Matthew: Conpaignon, 41; of Montoire, 20.II.
Maurice: *famulus* of St. Aubin, 28.
Mengisus: bishop of Vannes, 31 (9).
Michael: official of Count Fulk Nerra, 29.
Morandus: 9.
Natalis: abbot of St. Nicholas, 50.II.
Nefingus: bishop of Angers, 2.II.
Nihard: of Lavardin, 44; of Montoire, 20.II, 37.
Noah: son of the treasurer Guy, 13.
Normannus: de Nova Villa, 50.III, 51.
Nyldinus: Ferronus, 17.
Odilo: abbot of Cluny, 38.
Odo: 64; abbot of St.-Maur-des-Fossés, 26; abbot of St.-Savin-sur-Gartempe, 36, 37; brother of Viscount Radulfus, 3, 4; cleric, 7; count (II, of Blois), 12, 21, 27; of Dol, 37; Fatot, 39; priest, 60.II; *secretarius*, 71.II; *servus*, 15; son of Roger, 45, 46, 59; son of Count Stephen of Blois, 13.II; subcantor of St. Martin, 36, 37.
Odolerius: deacon and *servitor* of St. Serge, 60.II.
Odolricus: abbot of St. Martial of Limoges, 36, 37.
Odricus (see also Orricus, Otricus): abbot of la Trinité de Vendôme, 56.II, 56.V; Bibit Vinum, 49, 50, 51; of Champtoceaux, 76.
Orricus (see also Odricus, Otricus): de Chatalaunis, 28; *praepositus*, 3.II.
Oggerius, Ogerius (see also Otgerius): 41; *servus*, 44.
Osbertus: monk of St. Aubin, 25.
Otbertus: de Camera, of Marmoutier, 75; *cellararius*, of Marmoutier, 75.
Otbrannus: monk of St. Aubin, 28.
Otgerius (see also Oggerius): de Lation, 20.II.
Otredus: 7.
Otricus (see also Odricus, Orricus): *prepositus*, 4.III.
Paganus: son of Fulbert, 50.II, 51.
Patrick: 3, 3.II, 4, 4.III.
Paulinus: son of the *prepositus* Geoffrey, 13.II.
Perenis: monk of St. Aubin, 25.
Peter: abbot, 37; abbot of Manteuil-en-Valée, 36, 37; canon, 77; of Chemillé, 37, 39; deacon, 60.II, 63.II; Maisnade, 37; monk of St. Aubin, 28; subdeacon of Angers, 36, 37; *venator*, 79.
Philip: 41; king of France (I): 12.II, 50.III.
Piscis: 17.
Primaldus, Primardus, Primoldus: 25; abbot of St. Aubin, 2.IV; archpriest, archpriest of Ronceray, canon of Ronceray, 14.II, 15, 18, 20.II, 42; monk, 3.
Rademundus: abbot of Dol, 31 (9).
Radulfus, Rodulfus, Rudulfus: 7, 57.II, 81.II; archbishop of Rouen, 12; brother of Otgerius de Viariis, 73; the Burgundian, 61.II; Grandis, 81.II; Paganus, son of Viscount Radulfus and Emma, 52; Patraster, 81.II; priest, 14.II, 18, 20.II, 60.II; viscount, 3, 4, 7, 20, 37, 49, 50, 51, 52, 73, 76.
Ragenardus: 21.
Raherius: of Bouloire, 74; of Lué, 53; of Lury, 71.II.
Raimbaldus: chamberlain, 77.
Rainandus: Crasselus, 3, 4.

Tescelinus: of Montrevault, 81.II; son of Bernard, 77.
Tetbaldus: abbot of Quinçay, 36, 37; abbot of St.-Benoît-sur-Loire, 36, 37; of Blaison, 28, 37, 76 (Tetbaldus, son of Eudo, and Tetbaldus, son of Tetbaldus); of Montlhéry, 71.II; of Noellet, 13.II.
Tetbertus: monk and *medicus*, 13.II.
Tethuinus, see Thetuinus.
Teudo: abbot of Bourgueil, 36, 37.
Thebertus: *prepositus*, 17.
Theobaldus, Teobaudus, Theobald: Allobros, 17; count, 27; the Old, abbot of St. Lézin, 2.II.
Theodoric, Theodericus, Teodericus: abbot of St. Aubin, 13.II, 81.II; bishop of Chartres, 36, 37; Claudus, 74; Guaillardus, 27.
Thetuinus, Tethuinus: 20.II; Strabo, 19, 20.
Ulgerius: monk of St. Aubin, 25.
Ursellus: 57.II.
Vitalis: abbot of St.-Gildas-sur-Bois, 31 (9); monk of St. Aubin, 25; tornator, 17.
Vivianus: 74; chaplain of Angoulême, 36, 37; royal fisherman, 50.III; signator, 21.
Vuenilo (see also Wanilo): archdeacon and treasurer of Tours, 36, 37.
Vulgrinus: 74; abbot of St. Serge, 14.II, 18, 53, 60.II, 61.II, 62.II, 77; monk, 52, 78, 81.
Wadferius: viscount, 50.II, 51.
Waldricus: 74.
Waleranus: monk of St. Aubin, 25.
Walfredus: monk of St. Aubin, 25.
Walter (see also Gauterius): 7, 14.II; abbot of St. Aubin, 25, 28, 36, 37, 53; archdeacon of Chartres, 36, 37; bishop of Nantes, 40; brother of Albericus the priest, 61.II; brother of Gerorius, 11; *famulus* of St. Aubin, 28; de Lezinio, 41; man of St. Martin, 79; monk of Marmoutier, 74; monk of St. Aubin, 2.IV, 25 (two by that name); *miles*, 4.III; Nafragallus, 29; Rufus, 17; sacristan of Tours, 36, 37; *serviens*, 18; son of Hunebaldus, 13.II; Titio, 39; Treluan, 20.II.
Wanilo (see also Vuenilo): monk of St. Martin, 31 (9).
Warechus: bishop of Nantes, 31 (9).
Warinus (see also Guarinus): 74; chamberlain, 77, 78; of Craon, 13; monk of St. Aubin, 25 (three by that name); vicar, 81.II.
Warner (see also Garnerius, Guarnerius): cook, 20.II; prior of St. Aubin, 28.
Wascelinus: of Chemillé, 39; of Poitou, 39.
William: 56.V, 74; Alduinus (William Aigret), count of Poitou, 37, 49, 50, 51, 71.II; archdeacon of Angoulême, 36, 37; of Bellême, 12; brother of Bishop Gervais, 37; canon of Saumur, 34.II; cantor of Poitiers, 36, 37; Chabocius, 37; cleric of Le Mans, 36, 37; Conerius, 50.III; king of England (I), 3.II, 4; monk, 4, 4.III; monk of Marmoutier, 74; of Parthenay, 37; of Roches-l'Evêque, 37; son of Constantine, 4.II; son of Sigebrannus, 15, 16; Three Lances, 3, 4; viscount, 37.
Winebertus: 74.
Yvo, see Ivo.

INDEX OF PLACE NAMES IN PART II DOCUMENTS

(The numbers refer to entry numbers in Part II.)

l'Abbaye Bousse: 3, 4.
l'Adézière: 8.
les Alleuds: 64.
l'Alleu-Quentin: 15.
Aloyau: 15, 16.
Angers: 5, 6, 8, 10, 13, 15, 16, 17, 18, 20, 25, 28, 34, 39, 42, 54, 55, 57, 58, 81.II.
Aralazrum: 57.II.
Arthezé: 64.
Assé: 38.
Astellinis: 57.
Bamarus: 57.
Baniacus: 57.
Baracé: 41.
Barre (torrent): 8.

Correspondence to Other Catalogues

Guillot—Here	Halphen—Here	Angot—Here
No. 35—No. 7	No. 33—No. 7	No. 18—No. 3
36—5, 8	34—5, 32, 35	19—4
38—11	36—8	21—3
41—13	38—11	22—4
42—15	42—13	24—7
45—2	44—15	27—20
50—24	53—28	35—81
54—25	54—29	36—81
57 a—27	64—33	
65—29	66—39	Craon—Here
77—32, 35	72—42	No. 2—No. 28
80—39	73—57	3—50
89—42	74—58	10—13
90—44	76—51	
91—53	77—49	Hogan—Here
92—57	78—50	No. 30—No. 2
93—58	83—53	31—22
96—49	84—38	32—53
99—50	85—27	33—77
102—71	87—71	34—81
103—38	88—76	38—64
104—76	127—13	
160—14	182—31	Latouche—Here
178—13	204—4	No. 17—No. 4
196—1	264—34	23—51
223—20	298—57	24—50
255—31	faux 6—12	
259—4		Levron—Here
329—17	Ziezulewicz—Here	p. 7—No. 27
372—34		p. 7—68
379—50	No. II—No. 6	p. 8—61
424—47	XV A—26	p. 8—79
⟨5⟩—26	XXIII B—39	
⟨6⟩—28	XXVI—40	Lex—Here
⟨7⟩—33	(V)—36	No. 39—No. 7
⟨10⟩—37	(VI)—37	51—21
⟨11⟩—51	Fauroux—Here	
	No. ⟨56⟩—No. 12	Newman—Here
		No. 94—No. 23
		134 faux—12
		Pfister—Here
		No. 41—No. 23
		74—12
		Soehnée—Here
		No. 42—No. 68

BIBLIOGRAPHY

I. Manuscripts

Angers, France. Archives départementales de Maine-et-Loire. Mss. G 785, H 100, H 397, H 778 bis, vols. 1, 2, H 857, H 974, H 1242, H 1273, H 1281, H 1773, H 1824, H 1840, H 2071, H 3712, H 3713, H 3714, H 3715, 40 H 1, 45 H 1.

Angers, France. Bibliothèque municipale d'Angers. Mss. 5–6 (30), 689 (623), 690 (624), 706 (636), 707 (637), 829 (745), 838 (754), 844 (760), 845 (760), 846 (760), 847 (760), 848 (760), 849 (761), 850 (762).

Nantes, France. Musée départementale Dobrée. Ms. 3.

Paris, France. Bibliothèque nationale. Mss. fr. n. a. 5021, 7433. Mss. lat. 5211/B, 5441, vol. 1–4, 5442, 9206, 12568, 12658, 12696, 12700, 12878, 12880, 13820, 17030, 17036. Mss. n. a. lat. 1930, 1935. Collection Baluze, vols. 39, 45, 47, 77, 139. Collection Decamps, vols. 4, 10. Collection Duchesne, vols. 22, 54. Collection Moreau, vols. 16, 19, 20, 21. Collection Touraine-Anjou (Dom Housseau), vols. I, II, parts 1, 2, III, IV, XII, Part 2, XIII, Part 1, XVI.

II. Printed Sources

Actus Pontificum Cenomannis in Urbe Degentium. Ed. G. Busson and A. Ledru. Archives historiques du Maine, vol. 2. Le Mans, 1902.

Annales de Saint-Aubin, in *Recueil d'annales angevines et vendômoises.* Ed. Louis Halphen. Paris, 1903.

Annales de Saint-Serge, in *Recueil d'annales angevines et vendômoises.* Ed. Louis Halphen. Paris, 1903.

Annales de Vendôme, in *Recueil d'annales angevines et vendômoises.* Ed. Louis Halphen. Paris, 1903.

Annales dites de Renaud, in *Recueil d'annales angevines et vendômoises.* Ed. Louis Halphen. Paris, 1903.

Cartulaire de l'abbaye cardinale de la Trinité de Vendôme. Vols. 1, 2. Ed. Ch. Métais. Vendôme, 1892–94.

Cartulaire de l'abbaye de Noyers. Ed. C. Chevalier. Mémoires de la Société archéologique de Touraine, vol. 22. Tours, 1872.

Cartulaire de l'abbaye du Ronceray d'Angers. Ed. Paul Marchegay. Archives d'Anjou, vol. 3. Paris, 1900.

Cartulaire de l'abbaye de Saint-Aubin d'Angers. Vols. 1–3. Ed. Bertrand de Broussillon. Documents historiques sur l'Anjou, vols. 1–3. Paris, 1903.

Cartulaire de l'abbaye de Saint-Père de Chartres. Vols. 1–2. Ed. Guérard. Paris, 1840.

Cartulaire des abbayes de Saint-Pierre de la Couture et de Saint-Pierre de Solesmes. Ed. Benedictines of Solesmes. Le Mans, 1881.

Cartulaire de Château-du-Loir. Ed. Eugène Valée. Archives historiques du Maine, vol. 6. Le Mans, 1905.

Cartulaire de l'Evêché du Mans (936–1790). Ed. Bertrand de Broussillon. Archives historiques du Maine, vol. 1. Le Mans, 1900.

Cartulaire manceau de Marmoutier. Vols. 1, 2. Ed. E. Laurain. Laval, 1945.

Cartulaire de Marmoutier pour le Dunois. Ed. Emile Mabille. Châteaudun, 1874.

Cartulaire de Marmoutier pour le Perche. Ed. Barret. Documents sur la Province du Perche, Third Series, vol. 2. Mortagne, 1894.

Cartulaire de Marmoutier pour le Vendômois. Ed. Trémault. Vendôme, 1893.

Cartulaire noir de la cathédrale d'Angers. Ed. Ch. Urseau. Documents historiques de l'Anjou, vol. 5. Angers, 1908.

Cartulaire de Notre-Dame de Chartres. Ed. E. de Lepinois and Lucien Merlet. Chartres, 1862.

Cartulaire du prieuré de Saint-Hippolyte de Vivoin et ses annexes. Ed. L.-J. Denis. Paris, 1894.

Cartulaire de Saint-Maur-sur-Loire, in *Archives d'Anjou,* vol. 1. Ed. Paul Marchegay. Angers, 1843.

178

Cartulaire de Saint-Victeur au Mans. Ed. Paul de Farcy. Paris, 1895.

Cartulaire de Saint-Vincent du Mans. Ed. S. Menjot d'Elbenne. Le Mans, 1888–1913.

Chartes de Saint-Julien de Tours (1002–1227). Ed. L.-J. Denis. Archives historiques du Maine, vol. 12. Le Mans, 1912.

Chartes vendômoises. Ed. Ch. Métais. Vendôme, 1905.

Chartularium Insignis Ecclesiae Cenomanensis Quod Dicitur Liber Albus Capituli. Institut des provinces de France, Second Series, vol. 2. Le Mans, 1869.

Chronicon Sancti Maxentii Pictavensis, in *Chroniques des églises d'Anjou.* Ed. Paul Marchegay and Emile Mabille. Paris, 1869.

Chronicon Sancti Sergii Andegavensis, in *Chroniques des églises d'Anjou.* Ed. Paul Marchegay and Emile Mabille. Paris, 1869.

Chroniques des comtes d'Anjou. Ed. Louis Halphen and René Poupardin. Paris, 1913.

Chroniques des églises d'Anjou. Ed. Paul Marchegay and Emile Mabille. Paris, 1869.

Chronique de Nantes (570 environ–1049). Ed. René Merlet. Collection de textes pour servir à l'étude et à l'enseignement de l'histoire, fasc. 19. Paris, 1869.

The Ecclesiastical History of England and Normandy by Ordericus Vitalis. Vols. 2, 3. Ed. and tr. Thomas Forestor. London, 1853.

The Ecclesiastical History of Orderic Vitalis. Vols. 2–4. Ed. and tr. Marjorie Chibnall. Oxford, 1969–73.

Gesta Ambaziensium Dominorum, in *Chroniques des comtes d'Anjou.* Ed. Louis Halphen and René Poupardin. Paris, 1913.

Guillaume de Jumièges, Gesta Normannorum Ducum. Ed. Jean Marx. Société de l'histoire de Normandie, vol. 48. Rouen and Paris, 1914.

Historia Sancti Florentii, in *Chroniques des églises d'Anjou.* Ed. Paul Marchegay and Emile Mabille. Paris, 1869.

Imperial Lives and Letters. Ed. Theodor Mommsen and Karl F. Morrison. New York, 1962.

The Letters and Poems of Fulbert of Chartres. Ed. and tr. Frederick Behrends. Oxford, 1976.

Liber Miraculorum Sancte Fidis. Ed. A. Bouillet. Collection de textes pour servir à l'étude et à l'enseignement de l'histoire, fasc. 21. Paris, 1897.

Livre des serfs de Marmoutier. Ed. André Salmon. Publications de la Société archéologique de Touraine, vol. 16. Tours, 1864.

Marmoutier, Cartulaire blésois. Ed. Ch. Métais. Blois, 1891.

L'obituaire de la cathédrale d'Angers. Ed. Ch. Urseau. Angers, 1930.

Patrologiae Cursus Completus. Series Latina. Vols. 139, 141, 155. Ed. J.-P. Migne. Paris, 1880.

Les quatre âges de l'homme, traité moral de Philippe de Navarre. Ed. Marcel de Fréville. Société des anciens textes français, vol. 26. Paris, 1888.

Recueil des actes de Charles II, le Chauve. Ed. Georges Tessier. Paris, 1952.

Recueil des actes des ducs de Normandie (911–1066). Ed. Marie Fauroux. Caen, 1961.

Recueil des actes de Philippe Ier, Roi de France (1059–1108). Ed. M. Prou. Paris, 1908.

Recueil d'annales angevines et vendômoises. Ed. Louis Halphen. Paris, 1903.

Recueil des chartes de l'abbaye de Cluny. Vol. 1. Ed. Auguste Bernard and Alexandre Bruel. Paris, 1876.

Recueil des chartes de l'abbaye de Saint-Benoît-sur-Loire. Documents publiés par la Société historique et archéologique du Gâtinais, vol. 5. Paris, 1900–1907.

Recueil des historiens des Gaules et de la France. Vols. 9–10. New Edition by Léopold Delisle. Paris, 1874.

Sacrosancta Concilia. Vol. 9. Ed. Philippe Labbé and Gabr. Cossart. Paris, 1671.

Spicilegium. Ed. Luc Dachery. Paris, 1714.

Thesaurus Novus Anecdotorum. Vols. 1, 3. Ed. Edmond Martène and Ursind Durand. Paris, 1717.

Vetera Analecta. New edition by Jean Mabillon. Paris, 1723.

Vie de Bouchard le Vénérable, Comte de Vendôme, de Corbeil, de Melun et de Paris (Xe et XIe siècles) par Eudes de Saint-Maur. Ed. Charles Bourel de la Roncière. Collection de textes pour servir à l'étude et à l'enseignement de l'histoire, fasc. 13. Paris, 1892.

III. SECONDARY LITERATURE

Amann, Emile and Dumas, Auguste. *L'église au pouvoir des laïques (888–1057).* Vol. 7 of *Histoire de l'église depuis les origines jusqu'à nos jours.* Ed. Augustin Fliche and Victor Martin. Paris, 1948.

Amann, Emile. "Papes impériaux et papes romain." *L'église au pouvoir des laïques (888–1057).*

Vol. 7 of *Histoire de l'église depuis les origines jusqu'à nos jours*. Ed. Augustin Fliche and Victor Martin. Paris, 1948.

Angot, A. *Dictionnaire historique, topographique et biographique de la Mayenne*. 4 vols. Mayenne, 1962.

——. "Les vicomtes du Maine." *Bulletin de la Commission historique et archéologique de la Mayenne* 30 (1914), pp. 180–232, 321–342.

d'Arbois de Jubainville, H. *Histoire des ducs et des comtes de Champagne depuis le VIe siècle jusqu'à la fin du XIe*. Vol. 1. Paris, 1859.

Bachrach, Bernard S. "The Angevin Strategy of Castle Building in the Reign of Fulk Nerra, 987–1040." *American Historical Review* 88 (1983), pp. 533–560.

——. "The Cost of Castle Building: The Case of the Tower at Langeais, 992–994." *The Medieval Castle: Romance and Reality*. Ed. Kathryn Reyerson and Faye Powe. Dubuque, Iowa, 1984, pp. 47–62.

——. "Early Medieval Fortifications in the 'West' of France: A Revised Technical Vocabulary." *Technology and Culture* 16 (1975), pp. 531–569.

——. "Enforcement of the *Forma Fidelitatis*: The Techniques Used by Fulk Nerra, Count of the Angevins (987–1040)." *Speculum* 59 (1984), pp. 769–819.

——. "The Family of Viscount Fulcoius of Angers: Some Methodological Observations at the Nexus of Prosopography and Diplomatics." *Medieval Prosopography* 4:1 (1983), pp. 1–8.

——. "Fortifications and Military Tactics: Fulk Nerra's Strongholds circa 1000." *Technology and Culture* 20 (1979), pp. 531–549.

——. "Fulk Nerra and His Accession as Count of Anjou." *Saints and Heroes, Studies in Medieval Culture in Honour of Charles W. Jones*. Ed. Margot H. King and Wesley Stevens. Collegeville, Minn., 1979, pp. 331–342.

——. "Geoffrey Greymantle, Count of the Angevins, 960–987: A Study in French Politics." *Studies in Medieval and Renaissance History* 17 (1985), pp. 3–67.

——. "Henry II and the Angevin Tradition of Family Hostility." *Albion* 16 (1984), pp. 111–130.

——. "The Idea of the Angevin Empire." *Albion* 10 (1978), pp. 293–299.

——. "The Pilgrimages of Fulk Nerra, Count of the Angevins, 987–1040." *Religion, Culture, and Society in the Early Middle Ages. Studies in Honor of Richard E. Sullivan*. Ed. Thomas F. X. Noble and John J. Contreni. Kalamazoo, Mich., 1987, pp. 205–217.

——. "Pope Sergius IV and the Foundation of the Monastery of Beaulieu-lès-Loches." *Revue bénédictine* 95 (1985), pp. 240–265.

——. "Robert of Blois, Abbot of Saint-Florent de Saumur and Saint-Mesmin de Micy (985–1011): A Study in Small Power Politics." *Revue bénédictine* 88 (1978), pp. 123–146.

——. "A Study in Feudal Politics: Relations Between Fulk Nerra and William the Great, 995–1030." *Viator* 7 (1976), pp. 111–121.

——. "Toward a Reappraisal of William the Great, Duke of Aquitaine." *Journal of Medieval History* 5 (1979), pp. 11–21.

Bates, David. *Normandy Before 1066*. London and New York, 1982.

Beech, George. "Prosopography." *Medieval Studies: an Introduction*. Ed. James M. Powell. Syracuse, N.Y., 1976, pp. 156–171.

Bensen, Robert L. *The Bishop-Elect: a Study in Medieval Ecclesiastical Office*. Princeton, N.J., 1968.

Besse, J.-M. *Province ecclésiastique de Tours*. Vol. 8 of *Abbayes et prieurés de l'ancienne France*. Ed. Dom Beaunier. *Archives de la France monastique*, vol. 19. Paris, 1920.

Behrends, Frederick. "Kingship and Feudalism according to Fulbert of Chartres." *Mediaeval Studies* 25 (1963), pp. 93–99.

Bienvenu, Jean-Marc. "Les caractères originaux de la réforme grégorienne dans le diocèse d'Angers." *Bulletin philologiques et historiques du Comité des travaux historiques et scientifiques* 2 (1968), pp. 141–157.

——. "Les conflits de sépulture en Anjou aux XIe et XIIe siècles." *Bulletin philologique et historique du Comité des travaux historiques et scientifiques* 2 (1966), pp. 673–685.

——. "Des origines à l'an mil." *Angers. Histoire des diocèses de France*, vol. 13. Ed. François Lebrun. Paris, 1981, pp. 9–18.

——. "Pauvreté, misères et charité en Anjou aux XIe et XIIe siècles." *Moyen Age* 72 (1966), pp. 389–424; 73 (1967), pp. 5–34.

——. "Renouveau de l'Eglise angevin (an mil-1148). *Angers. Histoire des diocèses de France*, vol. 13. Ed. François Lebrun. Angers, 1981, pp. 19–42.

Bloch, Marc. *Feudal Society*. 2 vols. Tr. L. A. Manyon. Chicago, 1970.

Bouchard, Constance Brittain. *Spirituality and Administration: The Role of the Bishop in Twelfth-Century Auxerre.* Cambridge, Mass., 1979.

Bouillet, A., and Servières, L. *Sainte Foy, vierge & martyre.* Rodez, 1900.

Jacques Boussard. "Les destinées de la Neustrie du IXe au XIe siècle." *Cahiers de civilisation médiévale* 11 (1968), pp. 15–28.

——. "Le droit de *vicaria* à la lumière de quelques documents angevins et tourangeaux." *Etudes de civilisation médiévale (IXe–XIIe siècles). Mélanges offerts à Edmond-René Labande.* Poitiers, 1974, pp. 39–54.

——. "Les évêques en Neustrie avant la réforme grégorienne (950–1050 environ)." *Journal des savants,* 1970, pp. 61–196.

——. "L'éviction des tenants de Thibaut de Blois par Geoffroy Martel, comte d'Anjou, en 1044." *Moyen Age* 69 (1963), pp. 141–149.

——. "L'origine des comtés de Tours, Blois et Chartres." *Actes du 103e Congrès national des Sociétés savantes* (1979), pp. 85–112.

——. "L'origine des familles seigneuriales dans la région de la Loire moyenne." *Cahiers de civilisation médiévale* 5 (1962), pp. 303–322.

——. "La seigneurie de Bellême aux Xe et XIe siècles." *Mélanges d'histoire du moyen âge dediés à la mémoire de Louis Halphen.* Paris, 1951, pp. 43–54.

——. "La vie en Anjou aux XIe et XIIe siècles." *Moyen Age* 56 (1950), pp. 29–68.

Boyle, Leonard E. "Diplomatics." *Medieval Studies: an Introduction.* Ed. James M. Powell. Syracuse, N.Y., 1976.

de Bréquigny, M. *Table chronologique des diplômes, chartes, titres et actes imprimés, concernant l'histoire de France.* Vols. 1, 2. Paris, 1769–1775.

Brown, Elizabeth A. R. "The Tyranny of a Construct: Feudalism and Historians of Medieval Europe." *American Historical Review* 79 (1974), pp. 1063–1088.

Bry, Gilles, Sieur de la Clergerie. *Histoire des Pays et Comté du Perche et duché d'Alençon.* Paris, 1620.

de Broussillon, Bertrand. *La maison de Craon, 1050–1480.* Vol. 1. Paris, 1893.

——. *La maison de Laval, 1020–1605.* Vol. 1, *Les Lavals, 1020–1264.* Paris, 1895.

Bullough, D. A. "Early Medieval Social Groupings: the Terminology of Kinship." *Past and Present* 45 (1969), pp. 3–18.

——. "Europae Pater: Charlemagne and his achievement in the light of recent scholarship." *English Historical Review* 84 (1970), pp. 59–105.

Bulst, Neithard. "Zum Gegenstand und zur Methode von Prosopographie." *Medieval Lives and the Historian: Studies in Medieval Prosopography.* Ed. Neithard Bulst and Jean-Philippe Genet. Kalamazoo, Mich., 1986, pp. 1–16.

Bur, Michel. *La formation du comté de Champagne, v. 950–v. 1150.* Nancy, 1977.

Calendini, P. "Bernard Ier, scholastique d'Angers." *Dictionnaire d'histoire et de géographie ecclésiastiques.* Vol. 8. Ed. Alfred Baudrillart, A. de Meyer, and Et. Van Cauwenbergh. Paris, 1935, cols. 578–580.

Callahan, Daniel F. "Adémar de Chabannes et la paix de Dieu." *Annales du Midi* 89 (1977), pp. 21–43.

Candé, J.-B. "Les seigneurs du Lude au temps de la féodalité." *Revue historique et archéologique du Maine* 25 (1889), pp. 328–348.

Cappuyns, M. "Bérenger de Tours." *Dictionnaire d'histoire et de géographie ecclésiastiques.* Vol. 8. Ed. Alfred Baudrillart, A. de Meyer, and Et. Van Cauwenbergh. Paris, 1935, cols. 385–407.

——. "Eusèbe Bruno." *Dictionnaire d'histoire et de géographie ecclésiastiques.* Vol. 15. Ed. R. Aubert and E. Van Cauwenbergh. Paris, 1963, cols. 1435–1436.

Carré de Busserolle, J.-X. *Dictionnaire géographique, historique, et biographique d'Indre-et-Loire et de l'ancienne province de Touraine.* 6 vols. Mémoires de la Société archéologique de Touraine, vols. 27–32. Tours, 1878–1884.

Cartier, E. "Charte de 908 concernant un accommodement devant Thibaut, vicomte de Tours." *Mémoires de la Société royale des antiquaires de France* 15 (1840), pp. 436–451.

Catalogue général des manuscrits des bibliothèques publiques de France. Départments. Vol. 31. Paris, 1898.

Celier, Léonce. "Catalogue des actes des évêques du Mans jusqu'à la fin du XIIIe siècle." *Revue historique et archéologique du Maine* 62 (1908), pp. 32–63; 63 (1909), pp. 144–185.

Chantelou, Dom Claude. *Cartulaire tourangeau et sceaux des abbés.* Ed. Paul Nobilleau. Tours, 1879.

Chédeville, André. *Chartres et ses campagnes, XIe–XIIIe siècles.* Publications de l'Université de Haute-Bretagne, vol. 1. Paris, 1973.

Clerval, A. "Albert." *Dictionnaire d'histoire et de géographie ecclésiastiques.* Vol. 1. Ed. Alfred Baudrillart, Albert Vogt, and Urbain Rouziés. Paris, 1912, cols. 1432–1435.

——. "Les écoles de Chartres au moyen-âge du Ve au XVIe siècle." *Mémoires de la Société archéologique d'Eure-et-Loir* 11 (1895).

Coolidge, Robert T. "Adalbero, Bishop of Laon." *Studies in Medieval and Renaissance History* 2 (1965), pp. 1–114.

Cowdry, E. E. J. *The Cluniacs and the Gregorian Reform.* Oxford, 1970.

——. "The Peace and Truce of God in the Eleventh Century." *Past and Present* 46 (1970), pp. 42–67.

Davis, H. W. C., and Whitwell, R. J., eds. *Regesta Willelmi Conquestoris et Willelmi Rufi, 1066–1100.* Vol. 1 in *Regesta Regum Anglo-Normannorum, 1066–1154.* Oxford, 1913.

Delaville le Roulx, J. *Notice sur les chartes originales relatives à la Touraine antérieures à l'an mil.* Tours, 1879.

Depoin, J. "Les premiers anneaux de la maison de Bellême." *Bulletin historique et philologique du Comité des travaux historiques et scientifiques* (1909), pp. 147–167.

——. "Recherches sur la chronologie des vicomtes du Maine." *Bulletin historique et philologique du Comité des travaux historiques et scientifiques* (1909), pp. 125–167.

Devailly, Guy. *Le Berry du Xe siècle au milieu du XIIIe, Etude politique, religieuse, sociale et économique.* Ecole pratique des hautes études, VIe section: Sciences économiques et sociales, Civilisations et Sociétés, vol. 19. Paris-Le Haye, 1973.

Dhondt, Jan. *Etudes sur la naissance des principautés territoriales en France (IXe-Xe siècle).* Bruges, 1948.

——. "Henri Ier, l'Empire et l'Anjou (1043–1056)." *Revue belge de philologie et d'histoire* 25 (1946–47), pp. 87–109.

——. "Sept femmes et un trio de rois (Robert le Pieux, Henri Ier et Philippe Ier)." *Contributions à l'histoire économique et sociale* 3 (1965), pp. 38–70.

——. "Une crise du pouvoir capétien (1032–1034)." *Miscellanea in memoriam Jan Frederick Niermeyer.* Groningen, 1967, pp. 137–148.

Dillay, Madeleine. "Le régime de l'église privée du XIe au XIIIe siècle dans l'Anjou, le Maine, la Touraine." *Revue historique de droit français et étranger,* 4th Series, 4 (1925), pp. 253–294.

Douglas, David C. "The Norman Episcopate Before the Norman Conquest." *Cambridge Historical Journal* 13 (1957), pp. 101–115.

——. *William the Conqueror. The Norman Impact upon England.* Berkeley, 1967.

Duby, Georges. *The Early Growth of the European Economy. Warriors and Peasants from the Seventh to the Twelfth Century.* Tr. Howard B. Clarke. Ithaca, N.Y., 1974.

——. "Etudes dans la France du Nord-Ouest au XII siècle: les 'Jeunes' dans la société aristocratique." *Annales, Economies, Sociétés, Civilisations* 19 (1964), pp. 835–846.

——. *The Knight, the Lady and the Priest. The Making of Modern Marriage in Medieval France.* Tr. Barbara Bray. New York and Toronto, 1981.

——. *Rural Economy and Country Life in the Medieval West.* Tr. Cynthia Postan. Columbia, S.C., 1968.

——. *La société aux XIe et XIIe siècles dans la région mâconnaise.* Bibliothèque générale de l'Ecole pratique des hautes études, VIe section. Paris, 1971.

——. *The Three Orders. Feudal Society Imagined.* Tr. Arthur Goldhammer. Chicago, 1980.

Dumas, Auguste. "La réforme monastique." *L'église au pouvoir des laïques (888–1057).* Vol. 7 of *Histoire de l'église depuis les origines jusqu'à nos jours.* Ed. Augustin Fliche and Victor Martin. Paris, 1948.

——. "Les vices du clergé et les aspirations à une réforme de l'église seculière." *L'église au pouvoir des laïques (888–1057).* Vol. 7 in *Histoire de l'église depuis les origines jusqu'à nos jours.* Ed. Augustin Fliche and Victor Martin. Paris, 1948.

Dunbabin, Jean. *France in the Making (843–1180).* Oxford, 1985.

Durville, A. *Le cartulaire de Saint-Serge d'Angers.* Nantes, 1903.

Fanning, Steven. "Charters of Henry I of France Concerning Anjou." *Speculum* 60 (1985), pp. 111–114.

——. "Family and Episcopal Election, 900–1050, and the Case of Hubert, Bishop of Angers (1006–1047)." *Medieval Prosopography* 7:1 (1986), pp. 39–56.

——. "From *Miles* to *Episcopus:* The Influence of the Family on the Career of Vulgrinus of Vendôme (ca. 1000–1065)." *Medieval Prosopography* 4:1 (1983), pp. 9–30.

——. "La lutte entre Hubert de Vendôme, Evêque d'Angers, et l'Archevêque de Tours in 1016: Un épisode dans l'histoire de l'Eglise des principautés territoriales." *Bulletin de la Société archéologique, scientifique et littéraire du Vendômois.* Année 1980, pp. 31–33.

——. "Les origines familiales de Vulgrin, Abbé de Saint-Serge d'Angers (1046–1056), et évêque du Mans (1056–1065), petit-fils du vicomte Fulcrade de Vendôme." *La Province du Maine* 82 (1980), pp. 243–255.

de Farcy, Louis. "Les fouilles de la cathédrale d'Angers." *Bulletin monumental* 66 (1902), pp. 488–498.

de Farcy, Paul. "Construction de la cathédrale d'Angers." *Congrès archéologique de France* 38 (1871), pp. 250–257.

Favre, Edouard. *Eudes Comte de Paris et Roi de France (882–898)*. Paris, 1893.

Fleckenstein, Josef. "Fulrad von Saint-Denis und der fränkische Ausgriff in den süddeutschen Raum." *Studien und Vorarbeiten zur Geschichte des grossfränkischen und frühdeutschen Adels. Forschungen zur Oberrheinischen Landesgeschichte*. Ed. Gerd Tellenbach. Freiburg, 1957, pp. 9–39.

Fletcher, R. A. *The Episcopate in the Kingdom of León in the Twelfth Century*. Oxford, 1978.

Forsyth, George H. Jr. *The Church of St. Martin at Angers*. Princeton, N.J., 1953.

Fossier, Robert. *La terre et les hommes en Picardie jusqu'à la fin du XIIIe siècle*. Vol. 1. Paris, 1968.

Freedman, Paul H. *The Diocese of Vic: Tradition and Regeneration in Medieval Catalonia*. New Brunswick, N.J., 1983.

Gallia Christiana in Provincias Ecclesiasticas Distributa. Vols. 8, 14. Paris, 1744, 1853.

Ganshof, F.-L. "The Church and the royal power in the Frankish Monarchy under Pippin III and Charlemagne." Tr. Janet Sondheimer. *The Carolingians and the Frankish Monarchy, Studies in Carolingian History*. Ithaca, N.Y., 1971, pp. 205–239.

Gasnault, Pierre. "Les actes privés de l'abbaye de Saint-Martin de Tours du VIIIe au XIIe siècles." *Bibliothèque de l'Ecole des chartes* 112 (1954), pp. 24–66.

Genicot, L. "La noblesse au Moyen Age dans l'ancienne 'Francie'." *Annales, Economies, Sociétés, Civilisations* 17 (1962), pp. 1–22.

Gerault. *Notice historique sur Evron*. 2nd Edition. Laval, 1840.

Giry, Arthur. "Etude critique de quelques documents angevins de l'époque carolingienne." *Mémoires de l'Institut national de France. Académie des inscriptions et belles-lettres* 36. 1 (1901), pp. 179–248.

——. *Manuel de diplomatique*. Paris, 1894.

Godard-Faultrier. "Histoire inédite de l'abbaye de Saint-Serge au diocèse d'Angers." *Revue des Sociétés savantes* 5th series, 2 (1870), pp. 372–397.

Grandet, Joseph. *Notre-Dame angevine*. Ed. Albert Lemarchand. Angers, 1884.

de Grandmaison, Ch. "Fragments de chartes du Xe siècle provenant de Saint-Julien de Tours." *Bibliothèque de l'Ecole des chartes* 41 (1885), pp. 373–429; 42 (1886), pp. 226–273.

Guilloreau, Léon. "L'abbaye d'Etival-en-Charnie et ses abbesses (1109–1790)." *Revue historique et archéologique du Maine* 52 (1902), pp. 121–160.

Guillot, Olivier. *Le comte d'Anjou et son entourage au XIe siècle*. 2 vols. Paris, 1972.

Halphen, Louis. *Charlemagne et l'empire carolingien*. Paris, 1947.

——. "Les chartes de fondation de la Trinité de Vendôme et de l'Evière d'Angers." *Moyen Age* 17 (1904), pp. 401–411.

——. *Le comté d'Anjou au XIe siècle*. Paris, 1906.

——. "Etude critique sur les chartes de fondation et les principaux privilèges pontificaux de la Trinité de Vendôme." *Moyen Age* 14 (1901), pp. 69–112.

——. "La lettre d'Eude II de Blois au Roi Robert." *Revue historique* 97 (1908), pp. 287–296.

Herlihy, David. "The Generation in Medieval History." *Viator* 5 (1974), pp. 347–364.

Hill, Boyd J. *The Medieval Monarchy in Action: the German Empire from Henry I to Henry IV*. New York, 1972.

Hiret, Jean. *Des antiquitez d'Anjou*. Angers, 1605.

——. *Des antiquitez d'Anjou*. Angers, 1618.

Hogan, Richard. "The *Rainaldi* of Angers: 'New Men' or Descendants of Carolingian *Nobiles?*" *Medieval Prosopography* 2:1 (1981), pp. 35–62.

Hucher, E. "Monuments funéraires et sigillographiques des vicomtes de Beaumont au Maine." *Revue historique et archéologique du Maine* 11 (1882), pp. 319–329.

Imbart de la Tour, P. *Les élections épiscopales dans l'église de France du IXe au XIIe siècle (Etude sur la décadence du principe électif) (814–1150)*. Paris, 1891.

Isidore of Seville, *Isidori Hispalensis episcopi Etymologiarum sive originum*. Ed. W. M. Lindsay. Oxford, 1911.

Jenal, Georg. *Erzbischof Anno II. von Köln (1056–75) und sein politisches Werken*. 2 vols. Stuttgart, 1974.

Johnson, Edgar Nathaniel. *The Secular Activities of the German Episcopate, 919–1024.* University Studies 30–31. Lincoln, Nebr., 1930–33.

Johnson, Penelope D. *Prayer, Patronage and Power: the Abbey of la Trinité, Vendôme, 1032–1187.* New York and London, 1981.

Kempf, Friedrich. "The Church and the Western Kingdoms from 900 to 1046." *The Church in the Age of Feudalism.* Tr. Anselm Biggs. Vol. 3 of *Handbook of Church History.* Ed. Hubert Jedin and John Dolan. New York, 1969.

——. "The Gregorian Reform." *The Church in the Age of Feudalism.* Tr. Anselm Biggs. Vol. 3 of *Handbook of Church History.* Ed. Hubert Jedin and John Dolan. New York, 1969.

Kienast, Walther. *Studien über die französischen Volksstämme des Frühmittelalters.* Stuttgart, 1968.

Knowles, David. "Jean Mabillon." *The Historian and Character and Other Essays.* Cambridge, 1963.

Kraus, Henry. *Gold Was the Mortar: the Economics of Cathedral Building.* London, Henley and Boston, 1979.

Kurth, Godefroid. *Notger de Liège et la civilisation au Xe siècle.* Paris, 1905.

Latouche, Robert. *The Birth of the Western Economy.* Tr. E. M. Wilkinson. London, 1967.

——. *Histoire du comté du Maine pendant le Xe et le XIe siècle.* Paris, 1910.

——. "Les premiers vicomtes du Maine." *Revue historique et archéologique du Maine* 65 (1909), pp. 80–88.

——. "Un vicomte du Maine imaginaire au XIe siècle: Roscelin." *Revue historique et archéologique du Maine* 66 (1909), pp. 94–95.

Lebrun, François. *Paroisses et communes de France. Dictionnaire d'histoire administrative et démographique. Maine-et-Loire.* Paris, 1974.

Leclercq, Henri. "Levita." *Dictionnaire d'archéologie chrétienne et de liturgie.* Vol. 8. Ed. Fernand Cabrol and Henri Leclercq. Paris, 1929, col. 2993.

Ledru, Ambroise and Denis, L.-J. *La maison de Maillé.* Vol. 2. Paris, 1905.

Lemarignier, Jean-François. "La dislocation du 'pagus' et le problème des 'consuetudines' (Xe–XIe siècle)." *Mélanges d'histoire du moyen âge dediés à la mémoire de Louis Halphen.* Paris, 1951, pp. 401–410.

——. "Le domaine de Villeberfol et le patrimoine de Marmoutier (XIe siècle)." *Etudes d'histoire du droit privé offertes à Pierre Petot.* Paris, 1959, pp. 347–362.

——. "Encadrement religieux des campagnes et conjoncture politique dans les régions du royaume de France situées au nord de la Loire, de Charles le Chauve aux derniers carolingiens (840–987)." *Christianizzazione ed organizzazione ecclesiastica delle campagne nell'alto medioevo: espansione e resistenze.* Settimane di studio del Centro Italiano di Studi sull'Alto Medioevo 28. Spoleto, 1982, pp. 765–811.

——. *Etude sur les privilèges d'exemption et de juridiction ecclésiastique des abbayes normandes depuis les origines jusqu'en 1140.* Archives de la France monastique, vol. 24. Paris, 1937.

——. "Les institutions ecclésiastiques en France de la fin du Xe au milieu du XIIe siècle." Book 1 of *Institutions ecclésiastiques.* Ed. J.-F. Lemarignier, Jean Gaudemet and Guillaume Mollat. Vol. 3 of *Histoire des institutions françaises au moyen âge.* Ed. Ferdinand Lot and Robert Fawtier. Paris, 1962.

——. "Political and Monastic Structures in France at the End of the Tenth and the Beginning of the Eleventh Century." Tr. Frederick L. Cheyette. *Lordship and Community in Medieval Europe.* Ed. Frederick L. Cheyette. New York, 1968, pp. 100–127.

Le Peletier, Laurent. *Breviculum Fundationis et Series Abbatum Sancti Nicolai Andegavensis.* Angers, 1616.

——. *Rerum Scitu Dignissimarum a Prima fundatione Monasterii S. Nicolai Andegavensis ad hunc usque diem, Epitome, Nec non eiusdem Monasterii Abbatum series.* Angers, 1635.

Lesne, Emile. *Les écoles de la fin du VIIIe siècle à la fin du XIIe.* Vol. 5 of *Histoire de la propriété ecclésiastique en France.* Lille, 1940.

Levron, Jacques. *Répertoire numérique des Archives départementales de Maine-et-Loire antérieures à 1790. Archives ecclésiastiques, Série H (fin).* Angers, 1954.

Leyser, K. "The German Aristocracy from the Ninth to the Early Twelfth Century." *Past and Present* 41 (1968), pp. 25–53.

——. "Maternal Kin in Early Medieval Germany: a Reply." *Past and Present* 49 (1970), pp. 126–138.

Lex, Léonce. "Eudes comte de Blois, de Tours, de Chartres, de Troyes et de Meaux (995–1037), et Thibaud, son frère (995–1004)." *Mémoires de la Société de l'Aube* (1891), pp. 191–383.

Lynch, Joseph H. *Simoniacal Entry into Religious Life from 1000 to 1260: a Social, Economic and Legal Study.* Columbus, Ohio, 1976.

Liron. *Bibliothèque d'Anjou.* Nantes, 1897.

Longnon, Auguste. *Atlas historique de la France depuis César jusqu'à nos jours. Texte explicatif des planches,* Part I. Paris, 1907.

——. *Pouilles de la province de Tours.* Vol. 3 of Recueil des historiens de France—Pouilles. Paris, 1903.

Lot, Ferdinand. *Etudes sur le règne de Hughes Capet et la fin du XIe siècle.* Paris, 1903.

Mabille, Emile. *Catalogue analytique des diplômes, chartes, et actes relatifs à l'histoire de Touraine contenus dans la collection de Dom Housseau. Mémoires de la Société archéologique de Touraine* 14 (1863).

——. *Chroniques des comtes d'Anjou. Introduction.* Paris, 1856–77.

——. "Les invasions normandes dans la Loire et les pérégrinations du corps de Saint Martin." *Bibliothèque de l'Ecole des chartes,* 6th series, 5 (1869).

Mabillon, Jean. *Annales Ordinis Sancti Benedicti.* vol. 4. Paris, 1707.

——. *Annales Ordinis Sancti Benedicti.* Vol. 4. Paris, 1739.

MacKinney, L. C. *Bishop Fulbert and Education at the School of Chartres.* Notre Dame, Ind., 1957.

Mailfert, Yvonne. "Fondation du monastère bénédictine de Saint-Nicolas d'Angers." *Bibliothèque de l'Ecole des chartes* 92 (1931), pp. 43–61.

Maitre, Léon. *Les écoles épiscopales et monastiques en Occident avant les universités (768–1180).* Vol. 26 of Archives de la France monastique. Paris, 1924.

Marchegay, Paul. "Chartes angevines des onzième et douzième siècles." *Bibliothèque de l'Ecole des chartes* 36 (1875).

——. "Chartes mancelles de l'abbaye de Saint-Florent près Saumur, 848–1200." *Revue historique et archéologique du Maine* 3 (1878).

——. "Le livre noir de Saint-Florent de Saumur." *Archives d'Anjou.* Vol. 1. Ed. Paul Marchegay. Angers, 1843.

Martène, Edmond. *Histoire de l'abbaye de Marmoutier.* Ed. C. Chevalier. *Mémoires de la Société archéologique de Touraine.* Vol. 24.

Martindale, Jane. "The French Aristocracy in the Early Middle Ages: a Reappraisal." *Past and Present* 75 (1977), pp. 5–45.

McKitterick, Rosamund. *The Frankish Church and the Carolingian Reforms, 789–895.* London, 1977.

Meinert, Hermann. "Die Fälschungen Gottfrieds von Vendôme." *Archiv für Urkundenforschungen* 10 (1928), pp. 232–325.

Ménage. *Histoire de Sablé.* 1st Part. Paris, 1683.

Menjot d'Elbenne, S. "Les sires de Braitel au Maine du XIe au XIIIe siècle." *Revue historique et archéologique du Maine* 1 (1876), pp. 192–239.

Merlet, René and Clerval, A. *Un manuscrit chartrain du XIe siècle.* Chartres, 1893.

Métais, Ch. "De l'authenticité des chartes de fondation et bulles de l'abbaye de la Trinité de Vendôme." *Moyen Age* 17 (1904), pp. 1–44.

Mitterauer, Michael. *Karolingische Markgrafen im Südosten.* Vol. 123 of *Archiv für österreichische Geschichte.* Vienna, 1963.

de Montclos, Jean. *Lanfranc et Bérenger, la controverse eucharistique du XI siècle.* Université catholique de Louvain. Spicilegium Sacrum Lovaniense. Etudes et documents, fasc. 37. Leuven, 1971.

de Moreau, E. *La formation de l'église médiévale en Belgique du premier quart du VIIIe au premier quart du XIIe siècle.* Vol. 2 of *Histoire de l'église en Belgique des origines aux débuts du XIIIe siècle.* Brussels, 1940.

Morel, Abbé. *Dictionnaire raisonné de diplomatique chrétienne.* Ed. Abbé Migne. *Encyclopédie théologique,* vol. 47. Paris, 1846.

Morrison, Karl Frederick. *The Two Kingdoms: Ecclesiology in Carolingian Political Thought.* Princeton, N.J., 1969.

Mussat, André. *Le style gothique de l'Ouest de la France (XIIe-XIIIe siècles).* Paris, 1963.

Newman, William Mendel. *Catalogue des actes de Robert II, Roi de France.* Paris, 1937.

de Pétigny, J. *Histoire archéologique du Vendômois.* 2nd Edition. Vendôme and Blois, 1882.

Pfister, Christian. *De Fulberti Carnotensis Episcopi Vita et Operibus.* Nancy, 1885.

——. *Etudes sur le règne de Robert le Pieux (996–1031).* Paris, 1885.

Piolin, Paul. *Histoire de l'église du Mans.* Vol. 3. Paris, 1856.

Port, Célestin. *Dictionnaire historique, géographique et biographique de Maine-et-Loire.* 3 Vols. Paris, 1878.

———. *Inventaire-sommaire des Archives départementales antérieure à 1790. Maine-et-Loire. Archives ecclésiastiques. Série G. Clergé séculier.* Angers, 1880.

———. *Inventaire-sommaire des Archives départementales antérieure à 1790. Maine-et-Loire. Archives ecclésiastiques. Série H. Clergé régulier.* Vol. 1. Angers, 1898.

Prinz, Friedrich. *Klerus und Krieg im früheren Mittelalter: Untersuchungen zur Rolle der Kirche beim Aufbau der Königsherrschaft.* Vol. 2 in Monographien zur Geschichte des Mittelalters. Stuttgart, 1971.

Ramackers, Johannes. "Papsturkunden in Frankreich." *Abhandlungen der Akademie des Wissenschaften in Göttingen.* Philologisch-Historische Klasse. Dritte Folge, no. 35. 1956.

Rangeard, Pierre. *Histoire de l'université d Angers.* Vol. 1. Ed. Albert Lemarchand. Angers, 1872.

Rashdall, Hastings. *The Universities of Europe in the Middle Ages.* 2 Vols. New edition by F. M. Powicke and A. B. Emden. Oxford, 1936.

Response du chapitre de l'Eglise d'Angers. Paris, 1626.

Riché, Pierre. "Conséquences des invasions Normandes sur la culture monastique dans l'occident franc." Settimane di studio del Centro Italiano di Studi sull'Alto Medioevo 16 (Spoleto, 1969), pp. 705–721.

Robin, Gérard. "Le problème de la vie commune au Chapître de la cathédrale Saint-Maurice d'Angers du XIe et XIIe siècle." *Cahiers de civilisation médiévale* 13 (1970), pp. 305–322.

Round, J. Horace, ed. *Calendar of Documents Preserved in France, Illustrative of the History of Great Britain and Ireland.* Vol. 1, A. D. 918–1206. London, 1899.

Saché, Marc. *Inventaire-sommaire des Archives départementales antérieures à 1790. Maine-et-Loire. Archives ecclésiastiques. Série H.* Vol. 2. Abbaye de Saint-Florent de Saumur. Angers, 1926.

Sainte-Marthe, Scevola and Louis. *Gallia Christiana.* Vols. 2, 4. Paris, 1656.

de Saint-Venant, R. "Commentaires sur deux chartes vendômoises du XIe siècle." *Bulletin de la Société archéologique, scientifique et littéraire du Vendômois* 64 (1906), pp. 146–164.

———. *Dictionnaire topographique, historique, biographique, généalogique et héraldique du Vendômois et de l'arrondissement de Vendôme.* 4 Vols. Mayenne, 1969.

Schmid, Karl. "Königtum, Adel und Klöster zwischen Bodensee und Schwarzwald." *Studien und Vorarbeiten zur Geschichte des grossfränkischen und frühdeutschen Adels. Forschungen zur Oberrheinischen Landesgeschichte.* Ed. Gerd Tellenbach. Freiburg, 1957, pp. 225–334.

Sirmond, Isaac. *Goffridi Abbatis Vindocinensis S. Priscae Cardinalis Epistolae, Opuscula, Sermones.* Paris, 1610.

Simon. *Histoire de Vendôme et de ses environs.* 3 Vols. Vendôme, 1834–35.

Soehnée, Frédéric. *Catalogue des actes d'Henri Ier, Roi de France.* Fasc. 161, Bibliothèque de l'Ecole des hautes études. Sciences historiques et philologiques. Paris, 1907.

Stutz, U. *Die Eigenkirche als Element des mittelalterlich-germanischen Kirchenrechts.* 1895.

Tellenbach, Gerd. *Church, State, and Christian Society at the Time of the Investiture Contest.* Tr. R. F. Bennet. *Studies in Mediaeval History,* Vol. 3. Ed. G. Barraclough. Oxford, 1959.

———. "Der Grossfränkische Adel und die Regierung Italiens in der Blütezeit des Karolingerreiches." *Studien und Vorarbeiten zur Geschichte des grossfränkischen und frühdeutschen Adels. Forschungen zur Oberrheinischen Landesgeschichte.* Ed. Gerd Tellenbach. Freiburg, 1957, pp. 40–70.

———. "Zur Bedeutung der Personenforschung für die Erkenntnis des früheren Mittelalters." *Freiburger Universitätsreden.* 1957.

———. *Königtum und Stämme in der Werdezeit des deutschen Reiches.* Weimar, 1939.

Thorode. *Notice de la ville d'Angers.* Ed. Emile Longin. Angers, 1897.

Tresvaux du Fraval, François Marie. *Histoire de l'église et du diocèse d'Angers.* 2 Vols. Paris, 1859.

Ullmann, Walter. *The Growth of Papal Government in the Middle Ages.* London, 1970.

———. *A Short History of the Papacy in the Middle Ages.* London, 1972.

Urseau, Ch. *La cathédrale d'Angers.* Paris, 1930.

———. "La cathédrale d'Angers, a-t-elle été incendiée en 1032?" *Bulletin monumentale* 86 (1927), pp. 103–111.

Uzureau, F. "Angers." *Dictionnaire d'histoire et de géographie ecclésiastiques.* Vol. 3. Ed. Alfred Baudrillart, R. Aigrain, P. Richard, and U. Rouziés. Paris, 1924, cols. 85–113.

Vallée, Eugène. *Dictionnaire topographique du département de la Sarthe.* Reviewed and edited by Robert Latouche. Paris, 1950.

Van de Kieft, C. "Une église privée de l'abbaye de la Trinité de Vendôme au XIe siècle." *Moyen Age* 69 (1963), pp. 157–168.

Vezin, Jean. *Les 'scriptoria' d'Angers au XIe siècle.* Fasc. 322 of Bibliothèque de l'Ecole des hautes études. IVe section. Sciences historiques et philologiques. Paris, 1974.

Verdon, Jean. "Les moniales dans la France de l'Ouest aux XIe et XIIe siècles, Etude d'histoire sociale." *Cahiers de civilisation médiévale* 19 (1976), pp. 247–264.

de Vregille, Bernard. "Aldebald the Scribe of Cluny and the Bible of Abbot William of Dijon." Tr. Frideswide Sandleman and Maria Boulding. *Cluniac Monasticism in the Central Middle Ages.* Ed. Noreen Hunt. Hamden, Conn., 1971, pp. 85–97.

Wallace-Hadrill, J. M. *The Frankish Church.* Oxford, 1983.

——. *The Long-Haired Kings and Other Studies in Frankish History.* London, 1962.

Ware, R. Dean. "Medieval Chronology: Theory and Practice." *Medieval Studies: an Introduction.* Ed. James M. Powell. Syracuse, N.Y., 1976.

Weber, N. A. *A History of Simony in the Christian Church From the Beginning to the Death of Charlemagne (814).* Baltimore, 1909.

Werner, Karl Ferdinand. "Bedeutende Adelsfamilien im Reich Karls des Grossen." *Karl der Grosse—Lebenswerk und Nachleben.* Vol. 1, *Persönlichkeit und Geschichte.* Ed. Helmut Beumann. Düsseldorf, 1965, pp. 83–142.

——. "Untersuchungen zur Frühzeit des französischen Fürstentums (9.–10. Jahrhundert)." *Die Welt als Geschichte* 18 (1958), pp. 256–289; 19 (1959), pp. 146–193; 20 (1960), pp. 87–119.

——. "Zur Arbeitsweise des Regino von Prüm." *Die Welt als Geschichte* 19 (1959), pp. 96–116.

White, G. H. "The First House of Bellême." *Transactions of the Royal Historical Society,* 4th Series, 20 (1940), pp. 67–99.

——. "The Lords of Bellême and Alençon." *Notes and Queries* 152 (1927), pp. 399–401, 417–419, 435–438; 156 (1929), pp. 165–168.

Whitney, J. P. *Hildebrandine Essays.* Cambridge, 1932.

Wollasch, J. "Königtum, Adel und Kloster im Berry während des 10en Jahrhunderts." *Neue Forschungen über Cluny und die Cluniacenser.* Ed. Gerd Tellenbach. Freiburg, 1959, pp. 17–165.

Ziezulewicz, William. "Etude d'un faux monastique à une période réforme: une charte de Charles le Chauve pour Saint-Florent-de-Saumur (8 juin 848)." *Cahiers de civilisation médiévale* 28 (1985), pp. 201–211.

——. "From Serf to Abbot: the Role of the 'Familia' in the Career of Frederick of Tours." *American Benedictine Review* 36 (1985), pp. 278–291.

——. "A Monastic Forgery in an Age of Reform, a Bull of Pope John XVIII for Saint-Florent-de-Saumur (April 1004)." *Archivum Historicae Pontificae* 23 (1985), pp. 7–42.

——. "'Restored' Churches in the Fisc of St. Florent-de-Saumur (1021–1118)." *Revue bénédictine* 96 (1986), pp. 106–117.

Zimmerman, Harald. *Papstregesten 911–1024.* Vienna-Cologne-Graz, 1969.

IV. Unpublished Theses and Dissertations

Chauvin, Yves. "Cartulaire de l'abbaye Saint-Serge et Saint-Bach d'Angers." Faculté des Lettres de Caen, 1969.

Hogan, Richard. "The Angevin Church in the First Feudal Age: A Study of the Career, Family and Politics of Bishop Rainald II (973–1005)." Ph. D. thesis. University of Minnesota, 1978.

Labande-Mailfert, Yvonne. "Cartulaire de Saint-Nicolas d'Angers, XIe–XIIIèmes siècles (Resitution)." Ecole nationale des Chartes, Paris, 1931.

Tabuteau, Emily Zack. "Transfers of Property in Eleventh-Century Norman Law." Unpublished Ph. D. thesis. Harvard University, 1975.

Ziezulewicz, William. "The Monastery of Saint-Florent-de-Saumur During the Abbacy of Frederick of Tours (1021–1055)." Ph.D. thesis. University of Minnesota, 1981.

188

GENERAL THEOLOGICAL SEMINARY
NEW YORK

DUE